Mermaid Boys 3

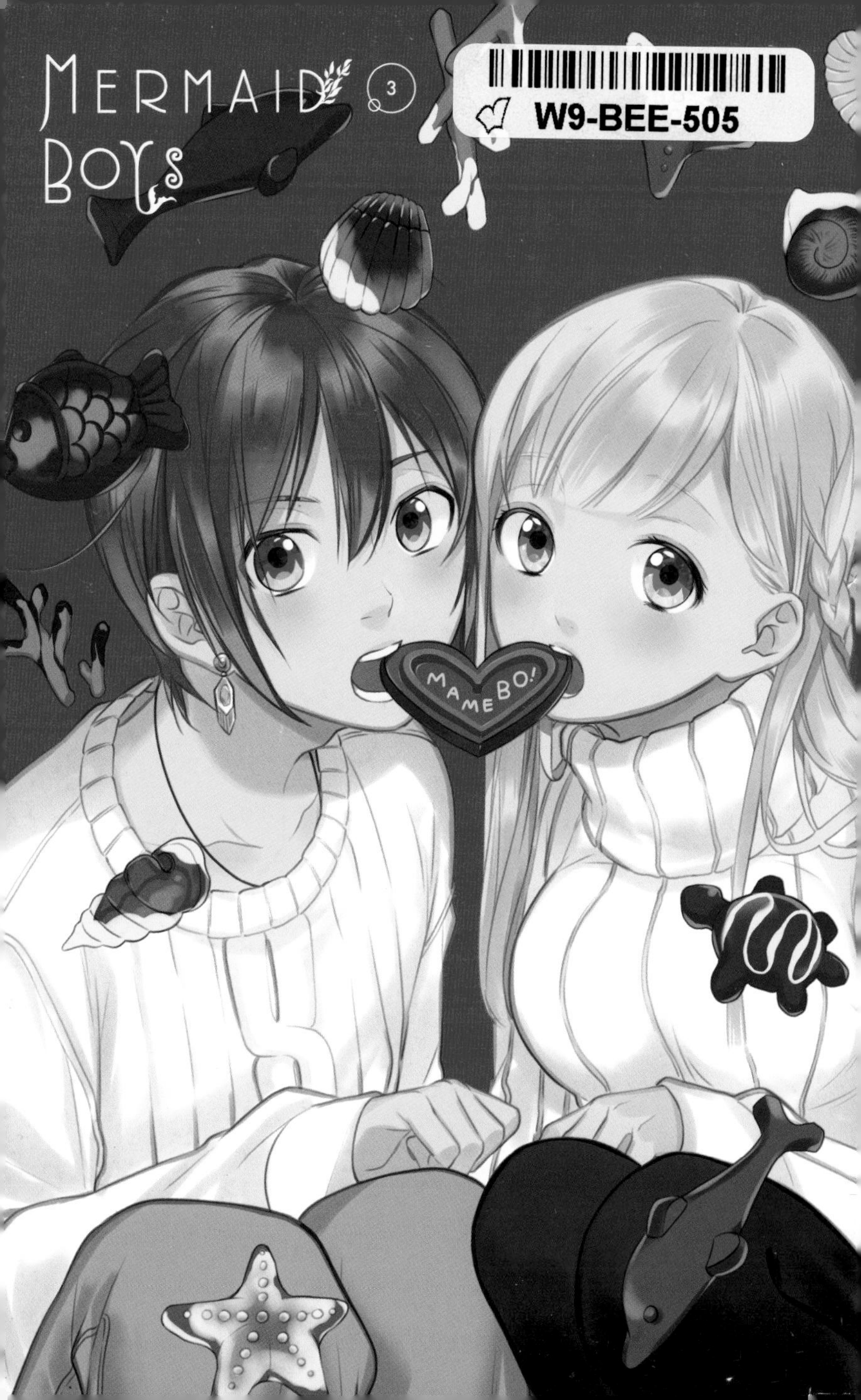
MAMEBO!

MERMAID BOYS

3

contents

STAGE 10

Priceless Love

007

STAGE 11

Confession

029

Bonus Story

065

STAGE 12

Summer Break!! ①

083

STAGE 13

Summer Break!! ②

107

STAGE 14

Summer Break!! ③

127

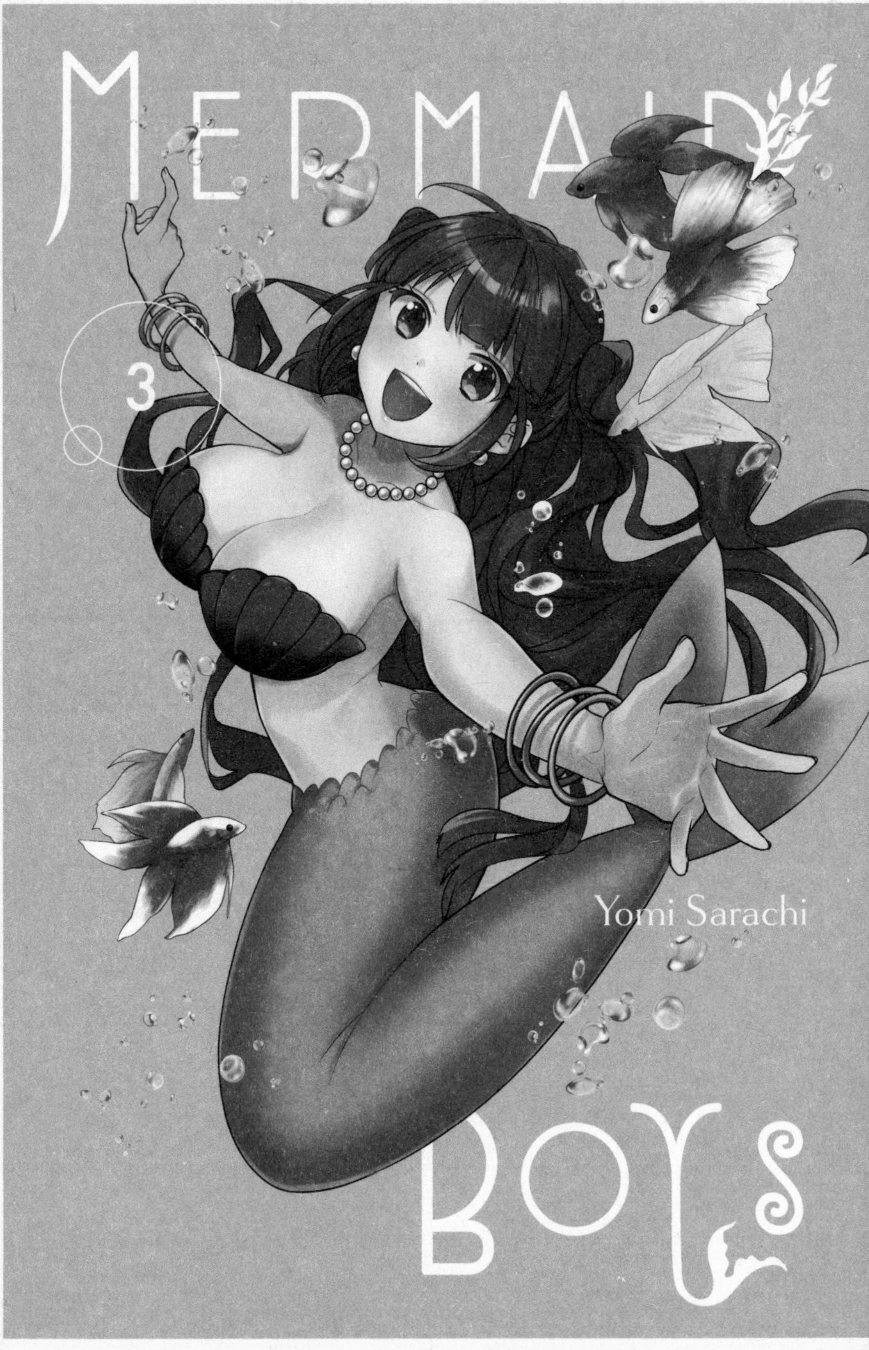
MERMAID
3
Yomi Saracti
BOYS

MERMAID BOYS

CHARACTERS & STORY

A merman prince falls in love with a human girl—

BEFORE

AFTER

CHARACTER PROFILE
○2
–

Nami Sakuragai

The high school girl Naru fell in love with. She's a hard worker who has inherited the inn her father left her. She's got beautiful legs.

CHARACTER PROFILE
○1
–

Naru

Prince of a merfolk kingdom, he falls in love with Nami and becomes human, thanks to magic! He's very curious and a bit full of himself.

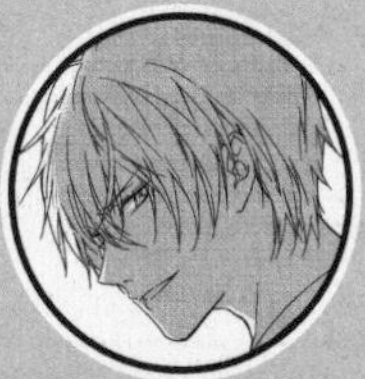

CHARACTER PROFILE 03

—

Arashi

Nami's childhood friend. He likes Nami.

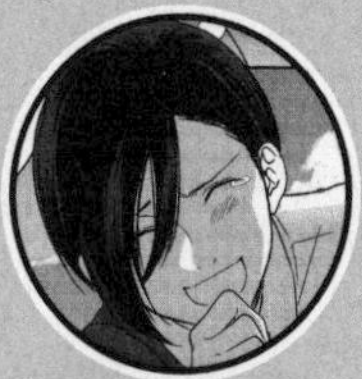

CHARACTER PROFILE 04

—

Ryou

Nami's other childhood friend. He gave up his sense of taste to become human.

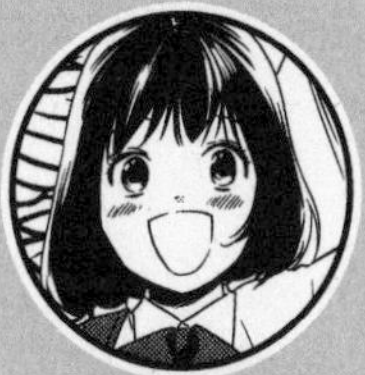

CHARACTER PROFILE 05

—

Natsuko

Nami's classmate. She's a hard-core romanticist.

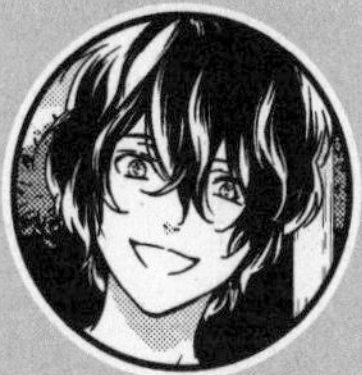

CHARACTER PROFILE 06

—

Hikaru

The property manager who lives with Nami. He's like an older brother to her.

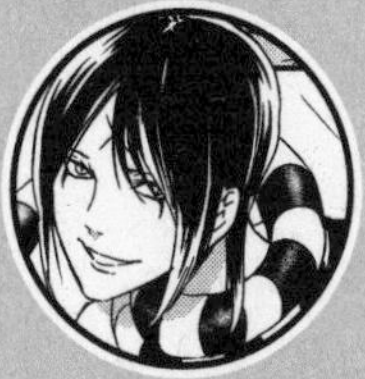

CHARACTER PROFILE 07

—

Mellow

The sorcerer who turned Naru human. What's the scheme he seems to be plotting...?

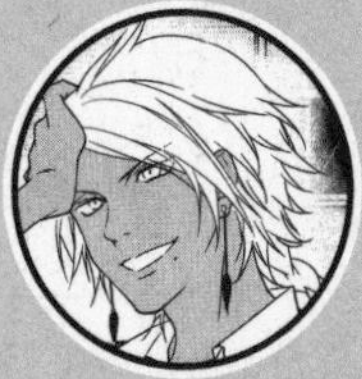

CHARACTER PROFILE 08

—

Loa

A merman who has transferred to Nami's school. Why does he seem to be working for Mellow...?

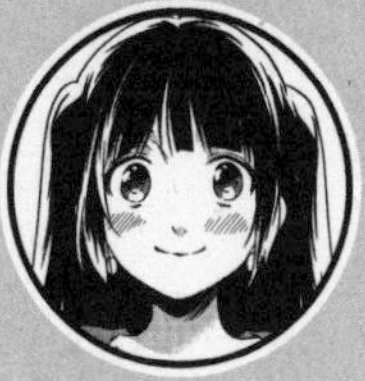

CHARACTER PROFILE 09

—

Moana

Self-proclaimed fiancée of Naru. She gave up her "massive boobs" to become human.

STORY

Naru is prince of a merkingdom. He falls in love at first sight with Nami, a human girl, and asks the sorcerer Mellow to turn him human so that he can meet her. In exchange, he has to give up his good looks and make a connection with her within one year, or else he'll turn into sea foam!

Meanwhile, a handsome merman named Loa suddenly transfers to their school and starts aggressively coming on to Nami! But when Naru declares, "It's because I like her that I don't want to disappear!" he remembers once more how much he cares about Nami.

Just when that matter is settled, this time Naru's mermaid fiancée Moana shows up, having been turned human too! What will Naru do now that he's found out she has to form a connection with him or else turn into sea foam...!?

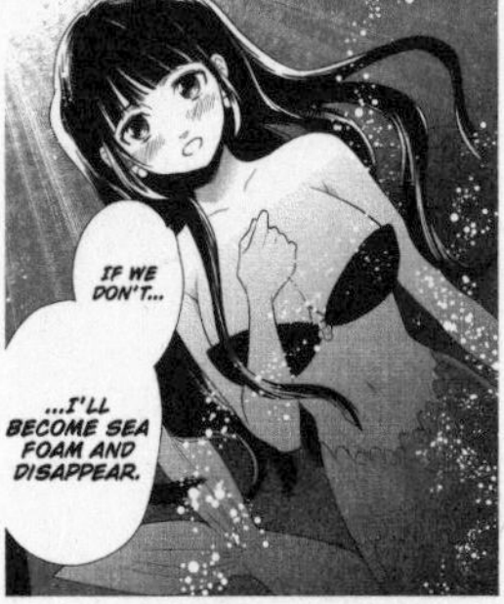
IF WE DON'T...
...I'LL BECOME SEA FOAM AND DISAPPEAR.

MERMAID BOYS

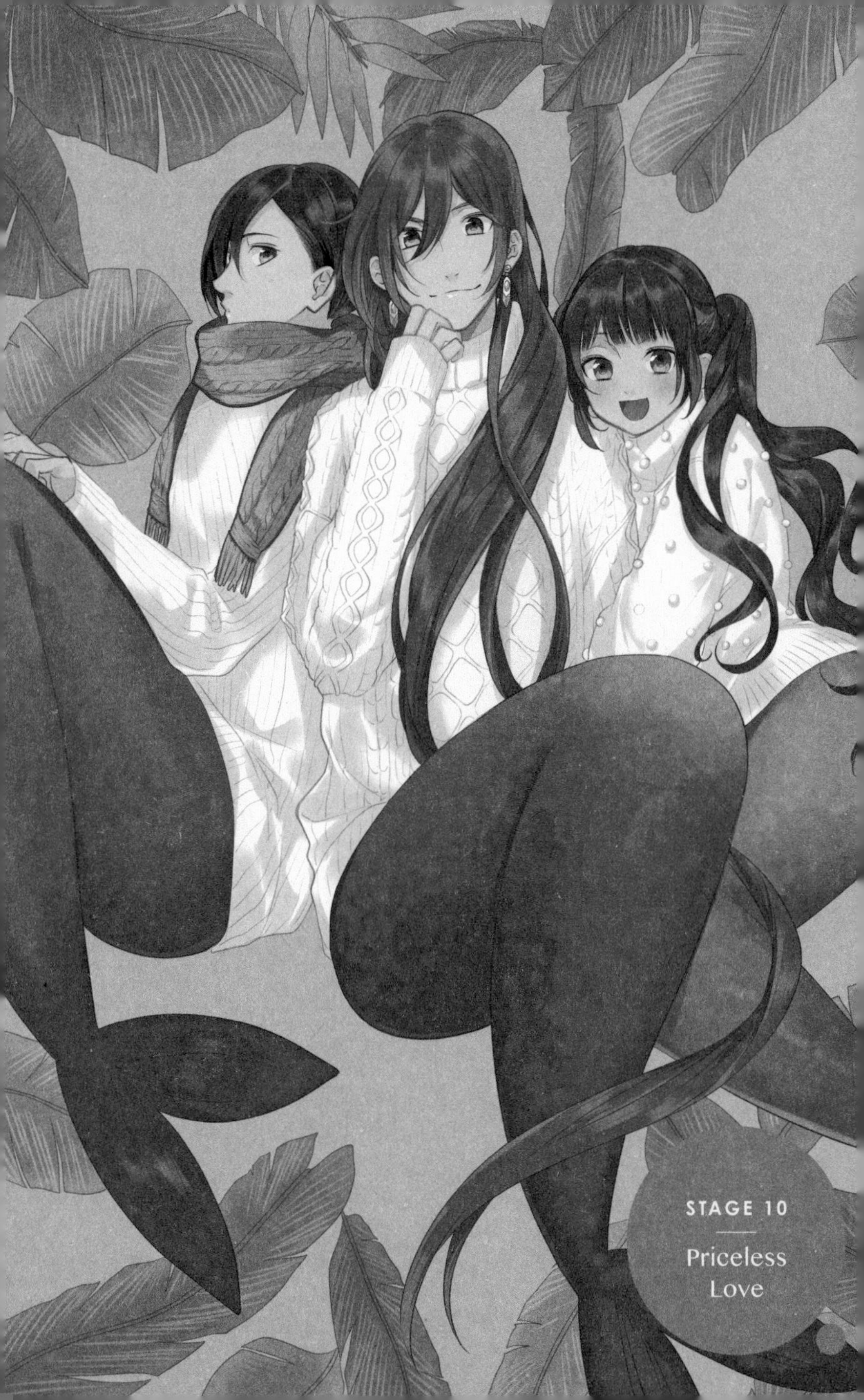
STAGE 10
Priceless Love

MERMAID BOYS

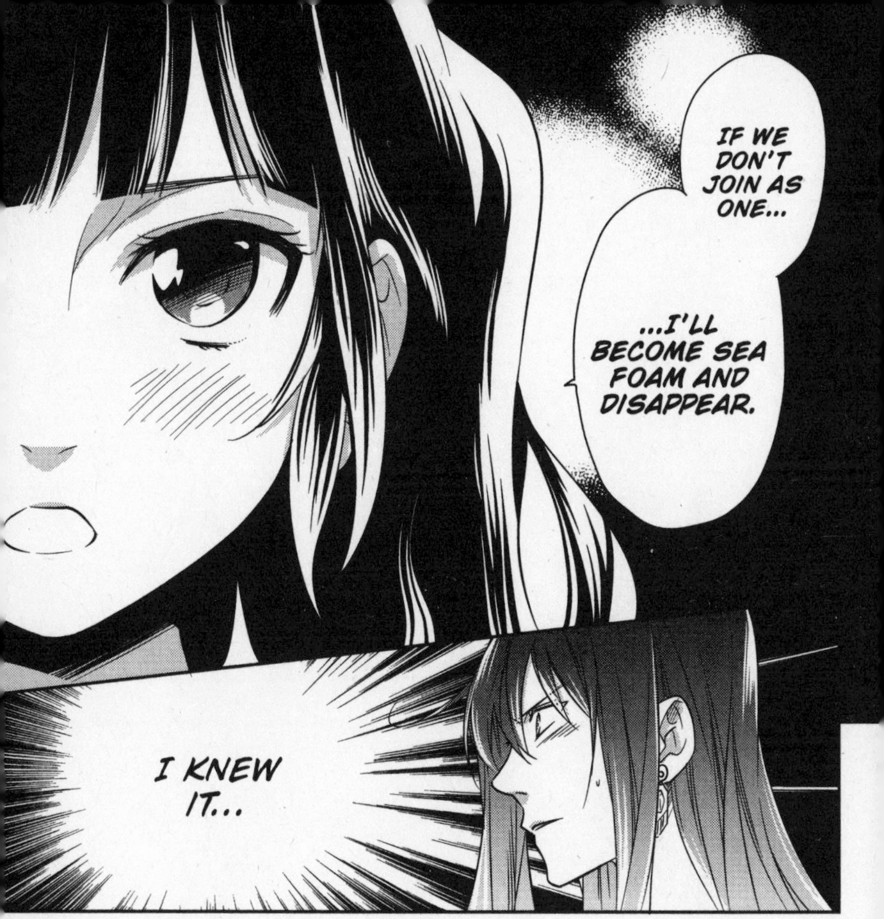
IF WE DON'T JOIN AS ONE...
...I'LL BECOME SEA FOAM AND DISAPPEAR.
I KNEW IT...

MERMAID BOYS

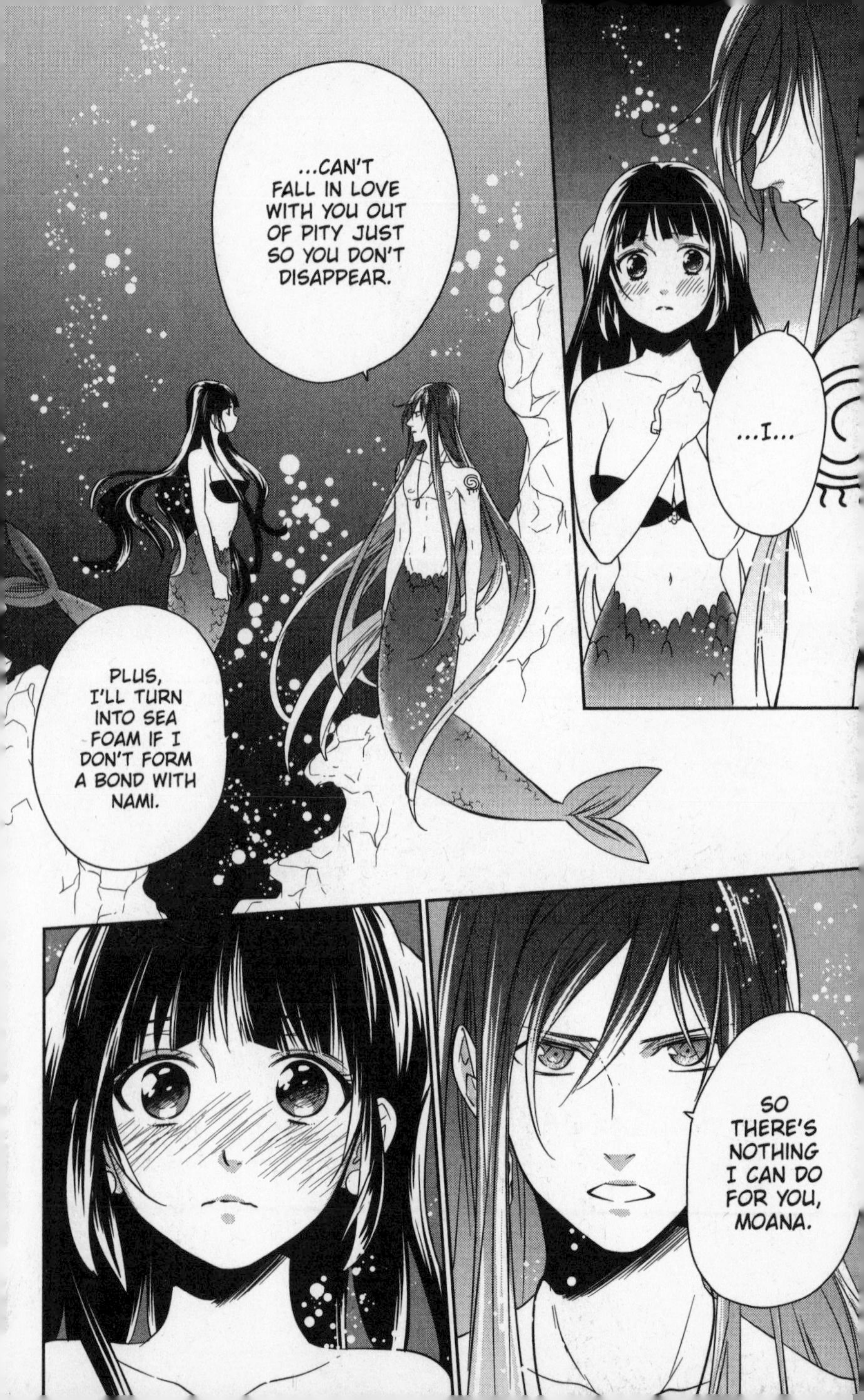
...I...
...CAN'T FALL IN LOVE WITH YOU OUT OF PITY JUST SO YOU DON'T DISAPPEAR.
PLUS, I'LL TURN INTO SEA FOAM IF I DON'T FORM A BOND WITH NAMI.
SO THERE'S NOTHING I CAN DO FOR YOU, MOANA.

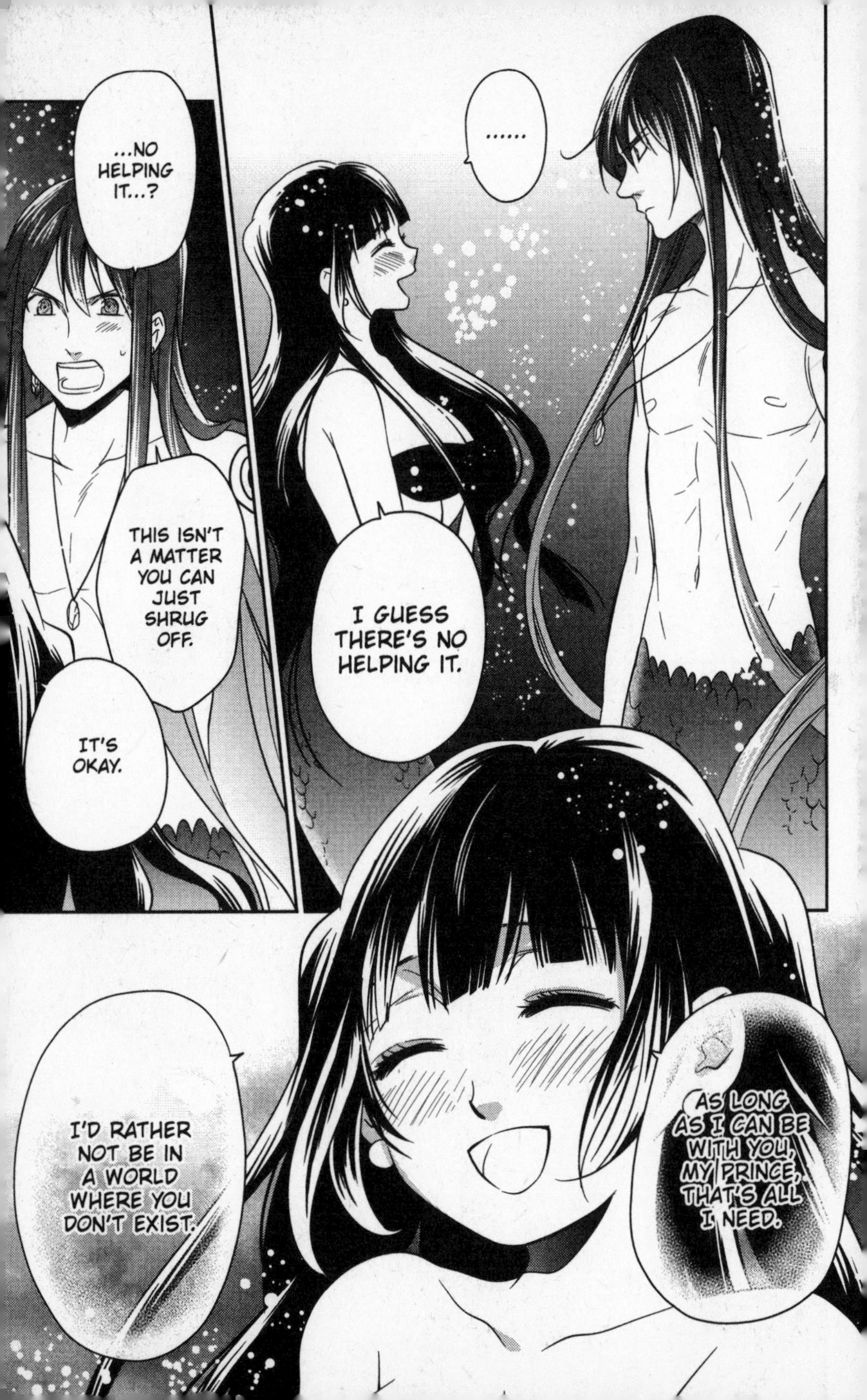
......
I GUESS THERE'S NO HELPING IT.
...NO HELPING IT...?
THIS ISN'T A MATTER YOU CAN JUST SHRUG OFF.
IT'S OKAY.
AS LONG AS I CAN BE WITH YOU, MY PRINCE, THAT'S ALL I NEED.
I'D RATHER NOT BE IN A WORLD WHERE YOU DON'T EXIST.

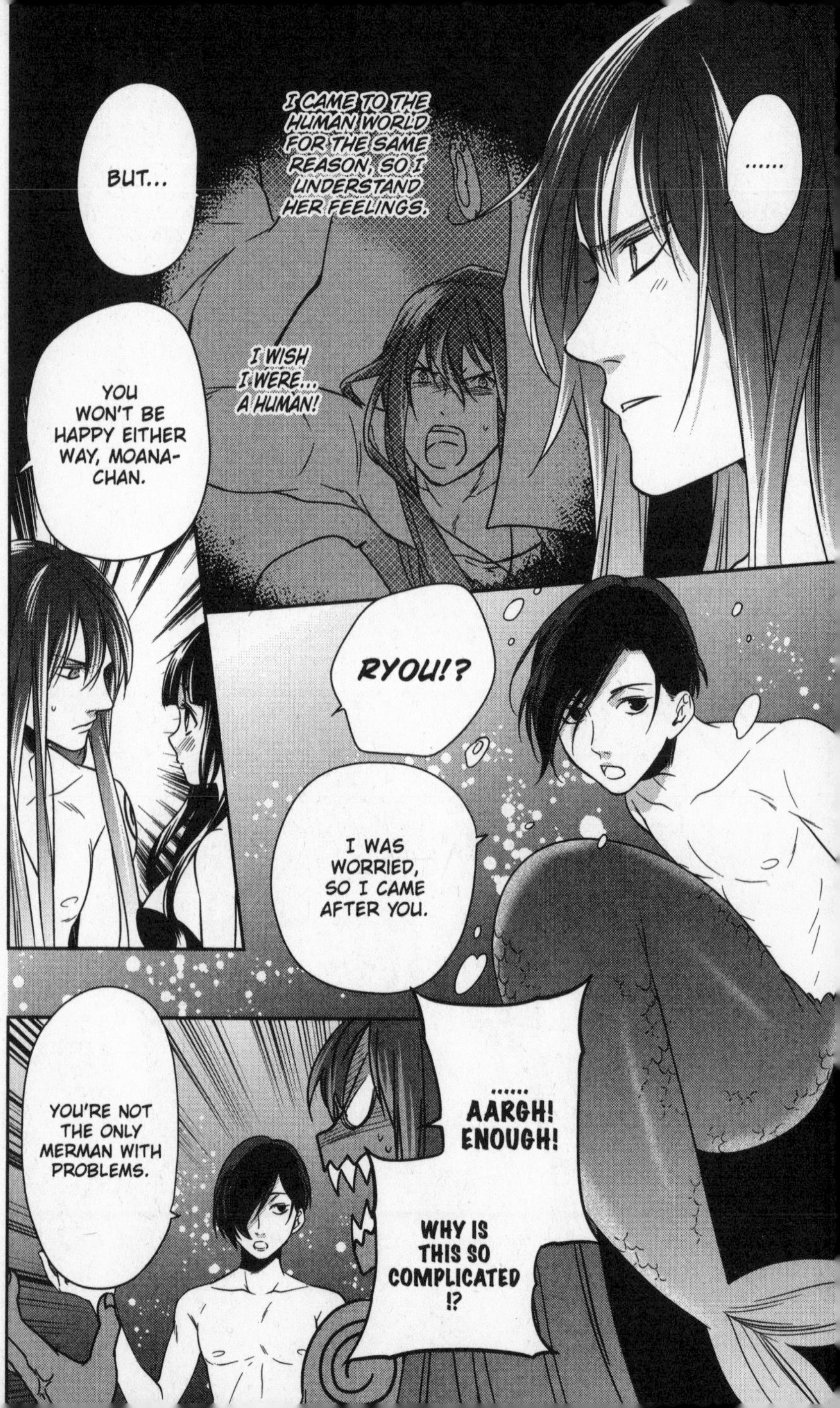
......
I CAME TO THE HUMAN WORLD FOR THE SAME REASON, SO I UNDERSTAND HER FEELINGS.
BUT...
I WISH I WERE... A HUMAN!
YOU WON'T BE HAPPY EITHER WAY, MOANA-CHAN.
RYOU!?
I WAS WORRIED, SO I CAME AFTER YOU.
......
AARGH! ENOUGH!
WHY IS THIS SO COMPLICATED !?
YOU'RE NOT THE ONLY MERMAN WITH PROBLEMS.

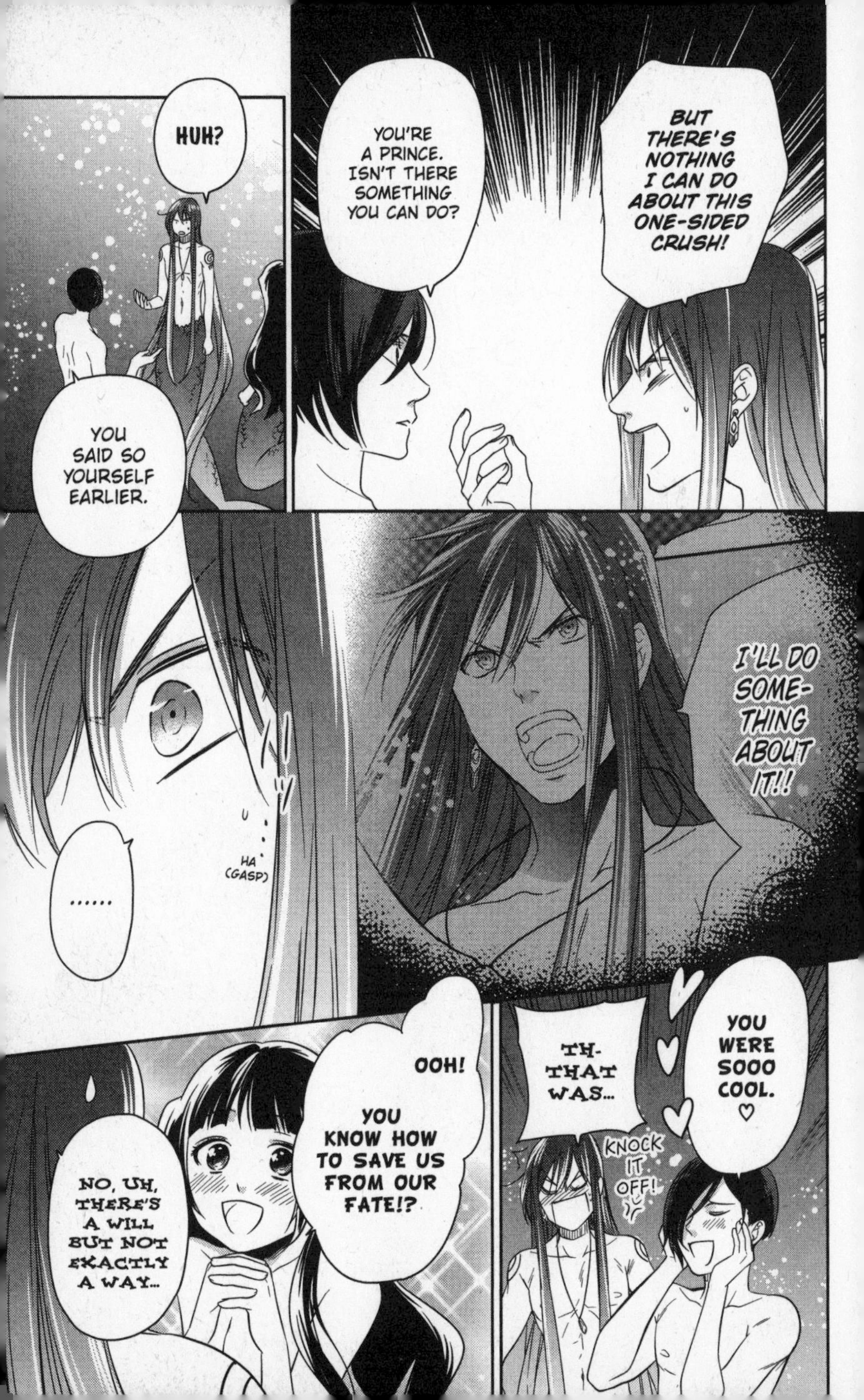
BUT THERE'S NOTHING I CAN DO ABOUT THIS ONE-SIDED CRUSH!
YOU'RE A PRINCE. ISN'T THERE SOMETHING YOU CAN DO?
HUH?
YOU SAID SO YOURSELF EARLIER.
I'LL DO SOMETHING ABOUT IT!!
U
HA (GASP)
......
YOU WERE SOOO COOL. ♡
TH-THAT WAS...
KNOCK IT OFF!
OOH!
YOU KNOW HOW TO SAVE US FROM OUR FATE!?
NO, UH, THERE'S A WILL BUT NOT EXACTLY A WAY...

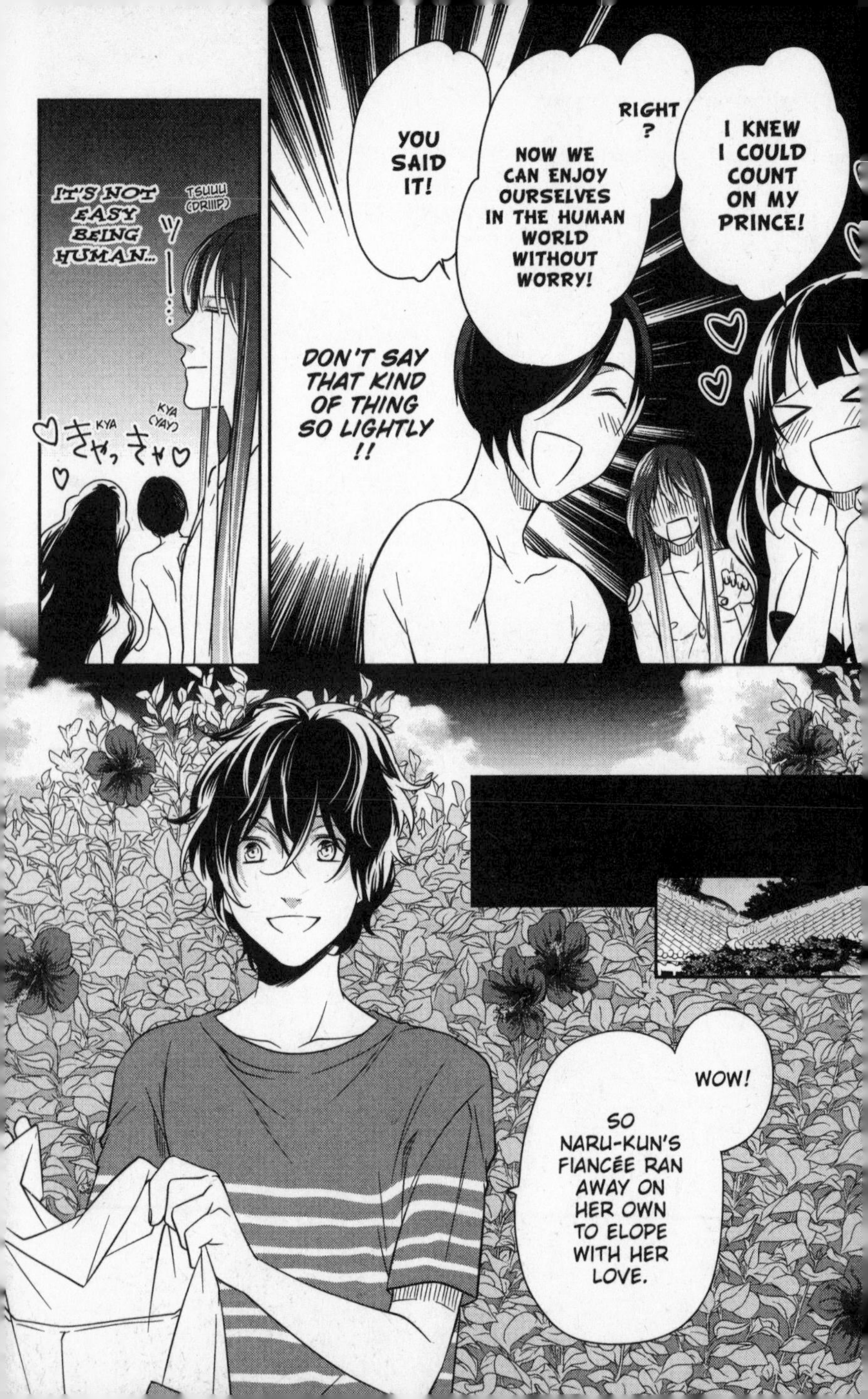
I KNEW I COULD COUNT ON MY PRINCE!
RIGHT?
NOW WE CAN ENJOY OURSELVES IN THE HUMAN WORLD WITHOUT WORRY!
YOU SAID IT!
DON'T SAY THAT KIND OF THING SO LIGHTLY!!
IT'S NOT EASY BEING HUMAN...
ツー…
TSUUU (DRIIIP)
♡きゃっきゃ♡
KYA KYA (YAY)
[redacted]
WOW!
SO NARU-KUN'S FIANCÉE RAN AWAY ON HER OWN TO ELOPE WITH HER LOVE.

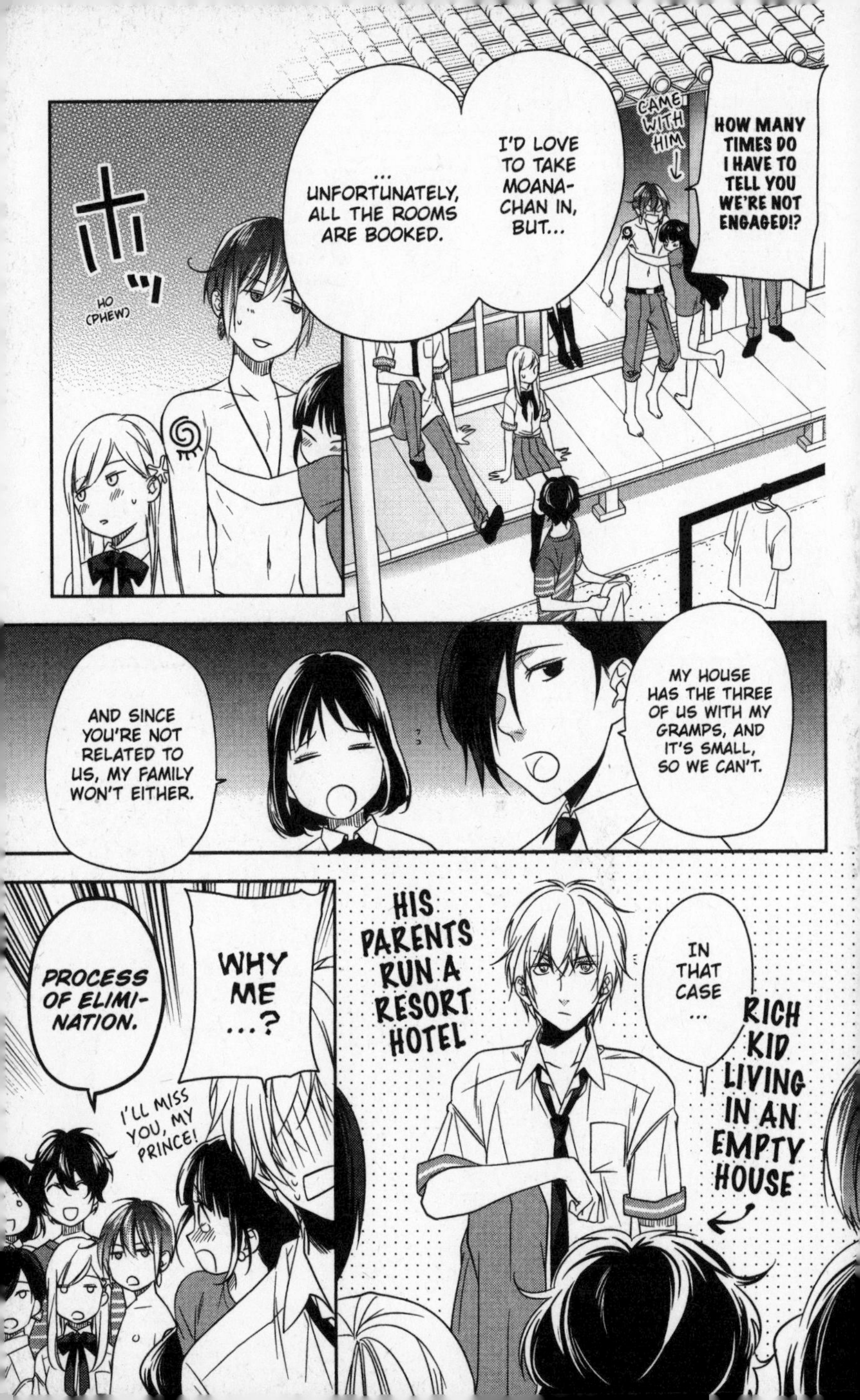
HOW MANY TIMES DO I HAVE TO TELL YOU WE'RE NOT ENGAGED!?
CAME WITH HIM
I'D LOVE TO TAKE MOANA-CHAN IN, BUT...
...UNFORTUNATELY, ALL THE ROOMS ARE BOOKED.
ホッ
HO (PHEW)
MY HOUSE HAS THE THREE OF US WITH MY GRAMPS, AND IT'S SMALL, SO WE CAN'T.
AND SINCE YOU'RE NOT RELATED TO US, MY FAMILY WON'T EITHER.
IN THAT CASE...
RICH KID LIVING IN AN EMPTY HOUSE
HIS PARENTS RUN A RESORT HOTEL
WHY ME...?
PROCESS OF ELIMINATION.
I'LL MISS YOU, MY PRINCE!

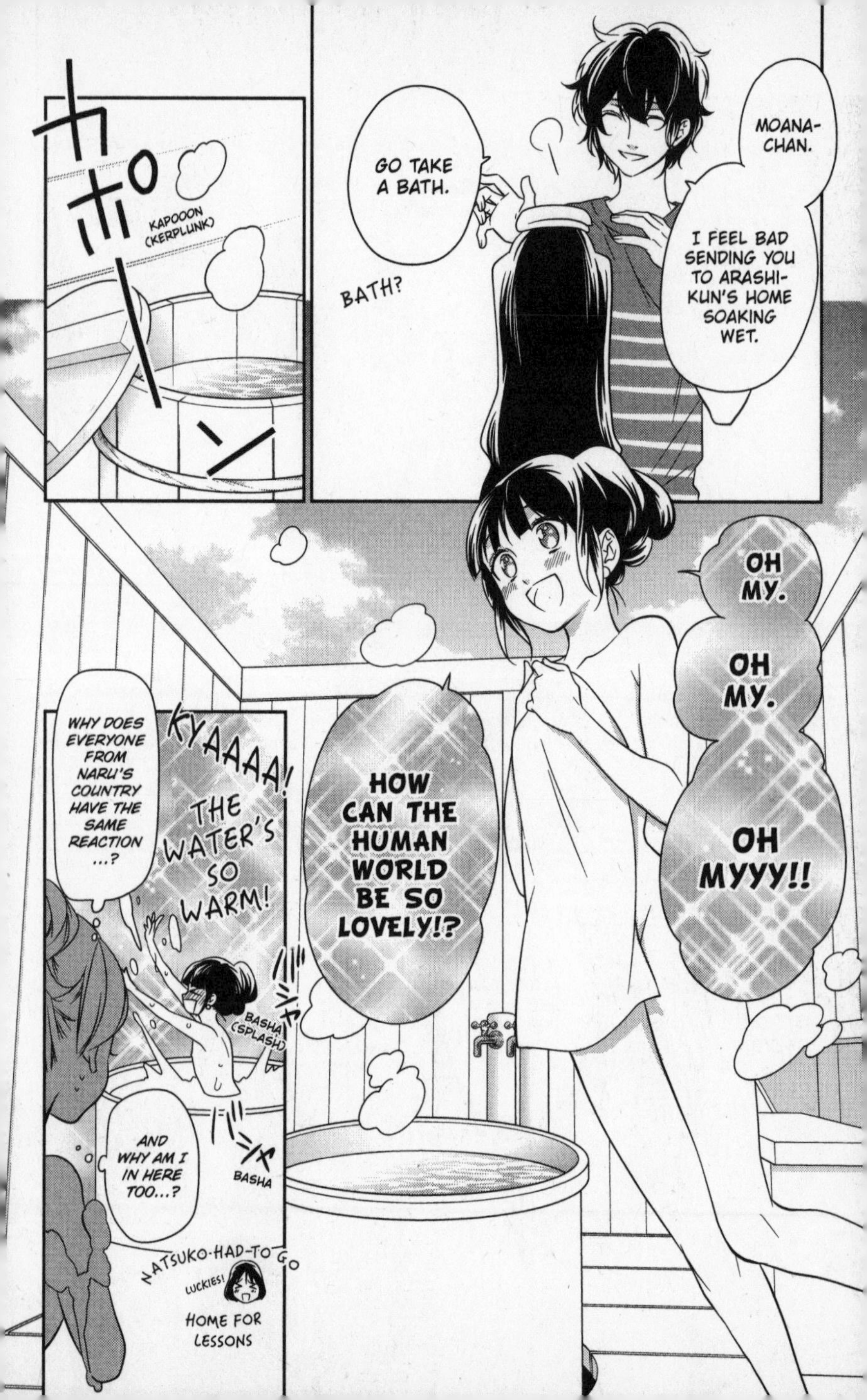
MOANA-CHAN.
I FEEL BAD SENDING YOU TO ARASHI-KUN'S HOME SOAKING WET.
GO TAKE A BATH.
BATH?
KAPOOON (KERPLUNK)
OH MY.
OH MY.
OH MYYY!!
HOW CAN THE HUMAN WORLD BE SO LOVELY!?
KYAAAAA! THE WATER'S SO WARM!
WHY DOES EVERYONE FROM NARU'S COUNTRY HAVE THE SAME REACTION ...?
BASHA (SPLASH)
AND WHY AM I IN HERE TOO...?
BASHA
NATSUKO-HAD-TO-GO HOME FOR LESSONS
LUCKIES!

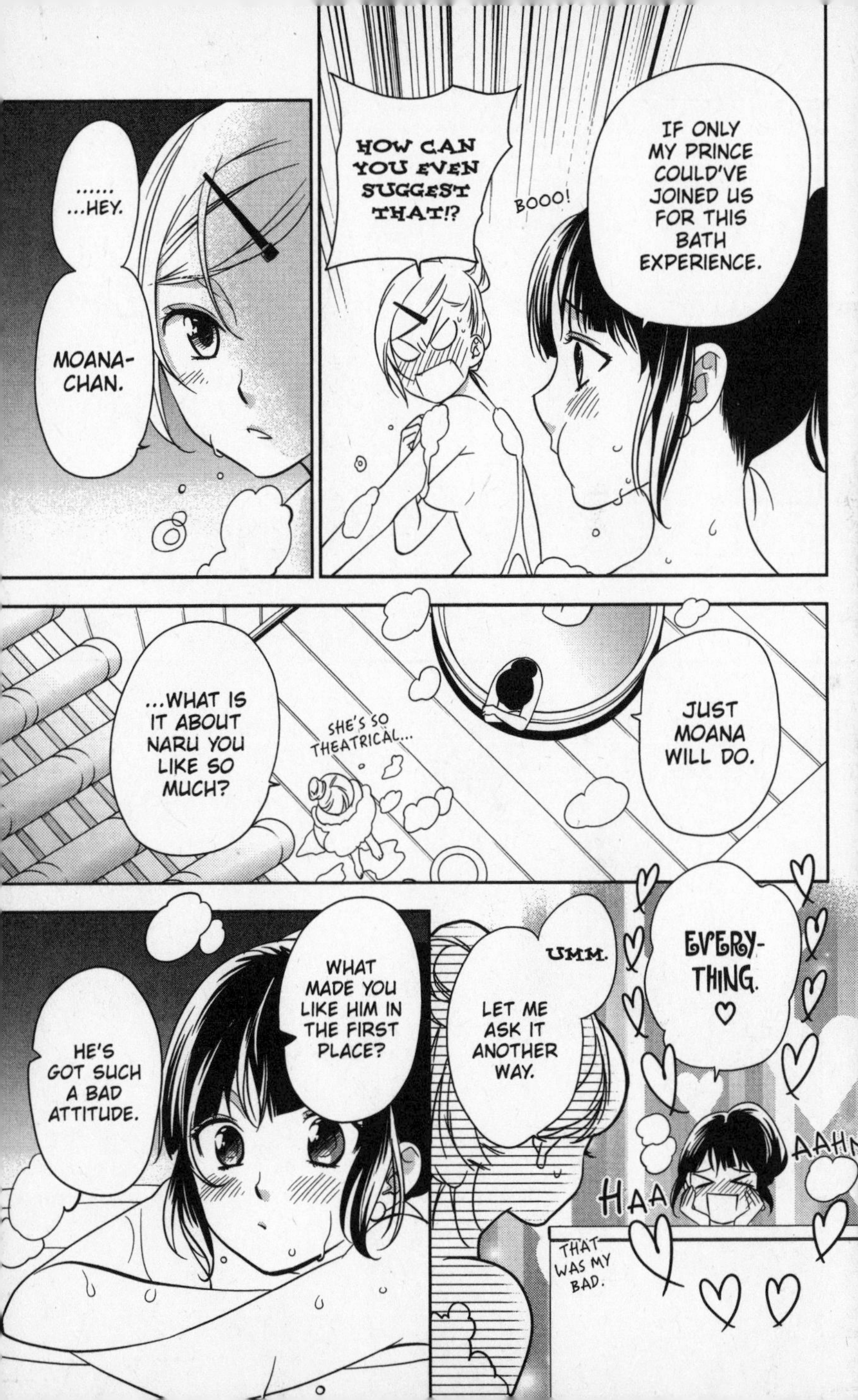
IF ONLY MY PRINCE COULD'VE JOINED US FOR THIS BATH EXPERIENCE.
BOOO!
HOW CAN YOU EVEN SUGGEST THAT!?
....HEY.
MOANA-CHAN.
JUST MOANA WILL DO.
SHE'S SO THEATRICAL...
...WHAT IS IT ABOUT NARU YOU LIKE SO MUCH?
EVERY-THING. ♡
AAHN
HAA
THAT WAS MY BAD.
UMM.
LET ME ASK IT ANOTHER WAY.
WHAT MADE YOU LIKE HIM IN THE FIRST PLACE?
HE'S GOT SUCH A BAD ATTITUDE.

...IT'S QUITE SIMPLE.
AT FIRST, I DIDN'T WANT TO MARRY THE PRINCE.
"THAT GIRL— SHE'S ALWAYS BEEN PART OF THE LINEUP OF ELIGIBLE FIANCÉES FOR THE PRINCE, RIGHT?"
"WHAT'S WITH HER CHEST?"
"LOOK AT HER, PARADING THOSE AROUND. IT'S LIKE SHE'S TRYING TO SEDUCE THE PRINCE WITH THEM."
"THEY FAVOR HER BECAUSE HER FAMILY HAS CONNECTIONS TO THE ROYAL FAMILY."
"SHE DOESN'T KNOW HOW HARD THE REST OF US GIRLS HAVE TO TRY."

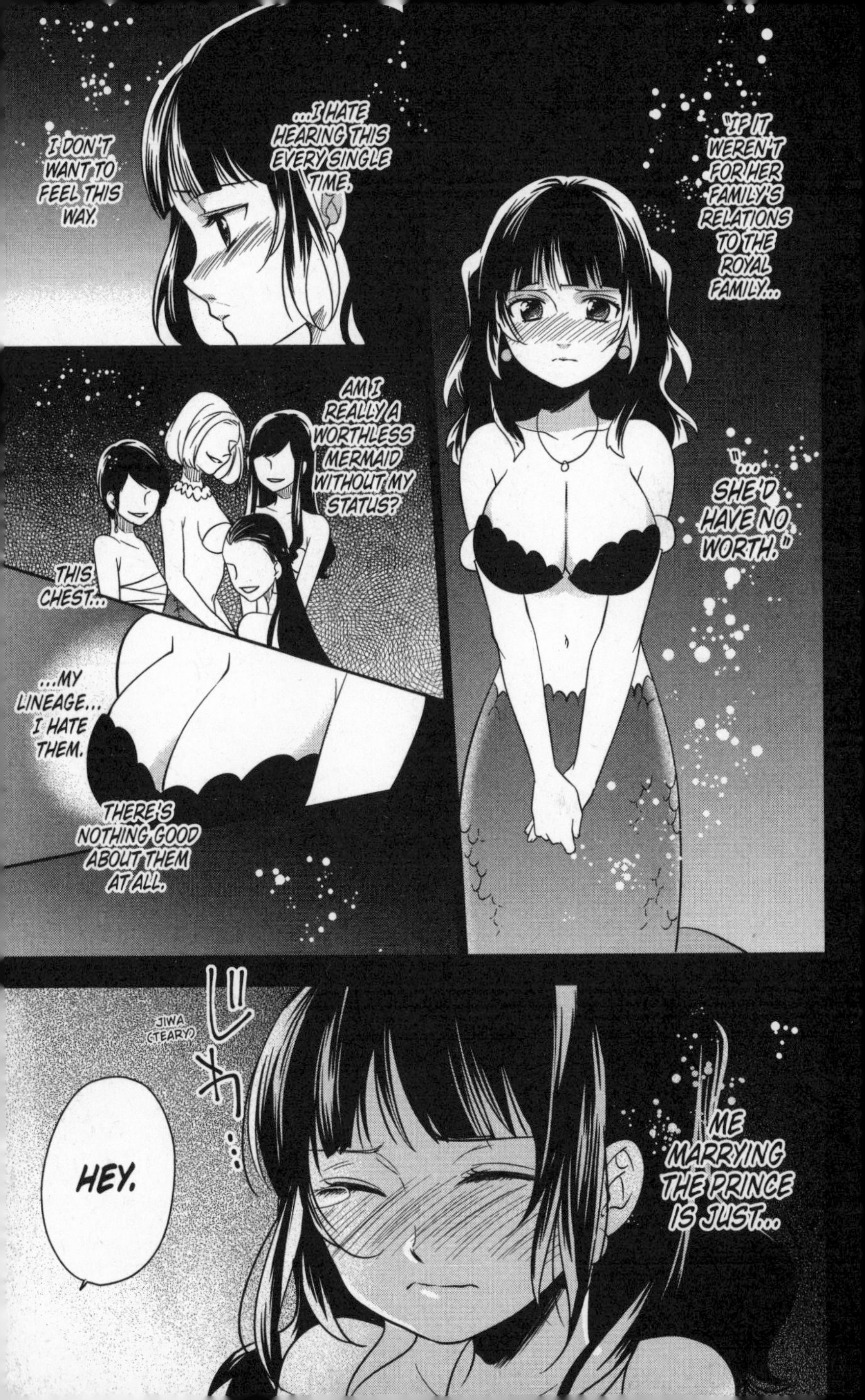
"IF IT WEREN'T FOR HER FAMILY'S RELATIONS TO THE ROYAL FAMILY...
"...SHE'D HAVE NO WORTH."
...I HATE HEARING THIS EVERY SINGLE TIME.
I DON'T WANT TO FEEL THIS WAY.
AM I REALLY A WORTHLESS MERMAID WITHOUT MY STATUS?
THIS CHEST...
...MY LINEAGE... I HATE THEM.
THERE'S NOTHING GOOD ABOUT THEM AT ALL.
ME MARRYING THE PRINCE IS JUST...
じわ…
JIWA (TEARY)
HEY.

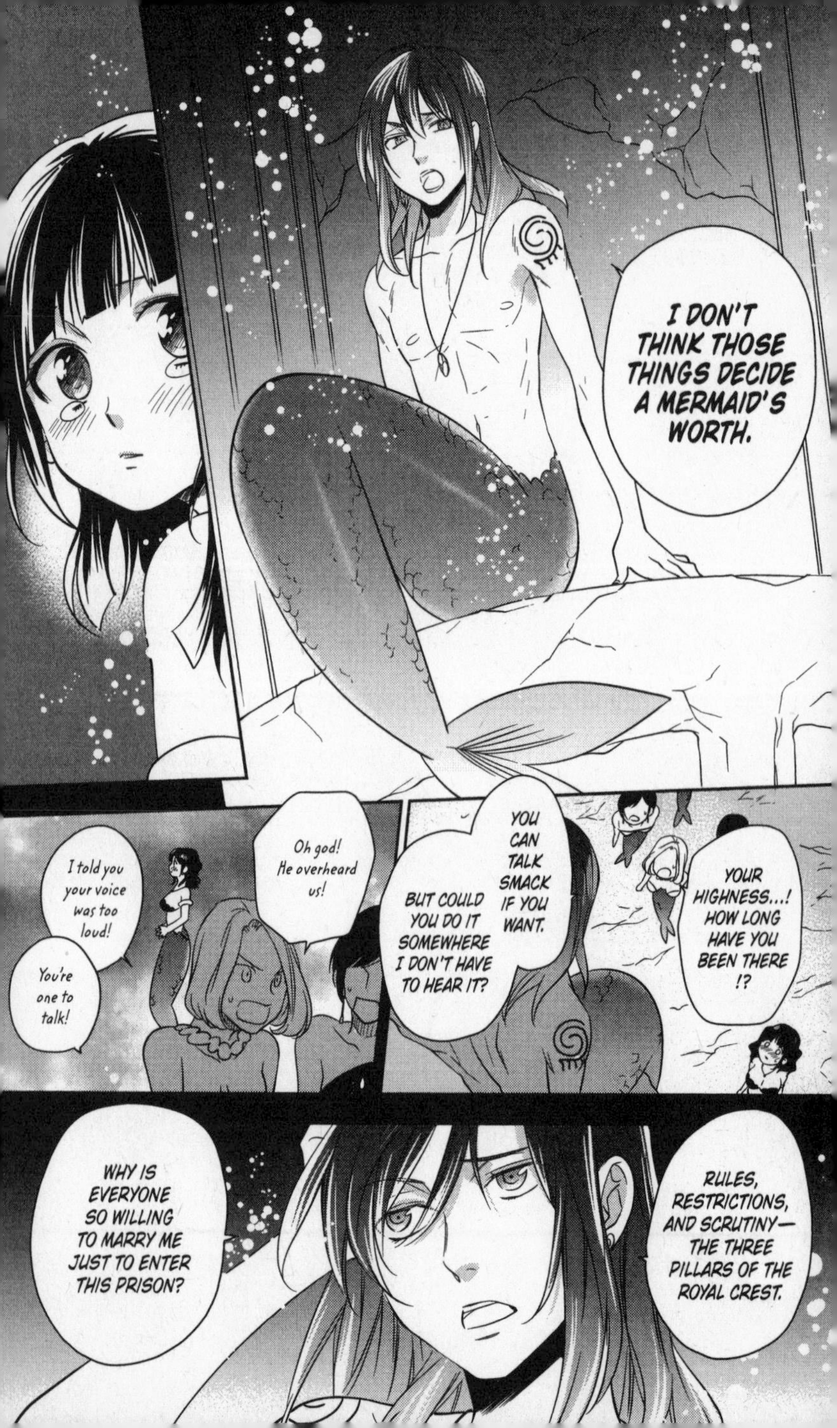
I DON'T THINK THOSE THINGS DECIDE A MERMAID'S WORTH.
YOUR HIGHNESS...! HOW LONG HAVE YOU BEEN THERE !?
YOU CAN TALK SMACK IF YOU WANT.
BUT COULD YOU DO IT SOMEWHERE I DON'T HAVE TO HEAR IT?
Oh god! He overheard us!
I told you your voice was too loud!
You're one to talk!
RULES, RESTRICTIONS, AND SCRUTINY—THE THREE PILLARS OF THE ROYAL CREST.
WHY IS EVERYONE SO WILLING TO MARRY ME JUST TO ENTER THIS PRISON?

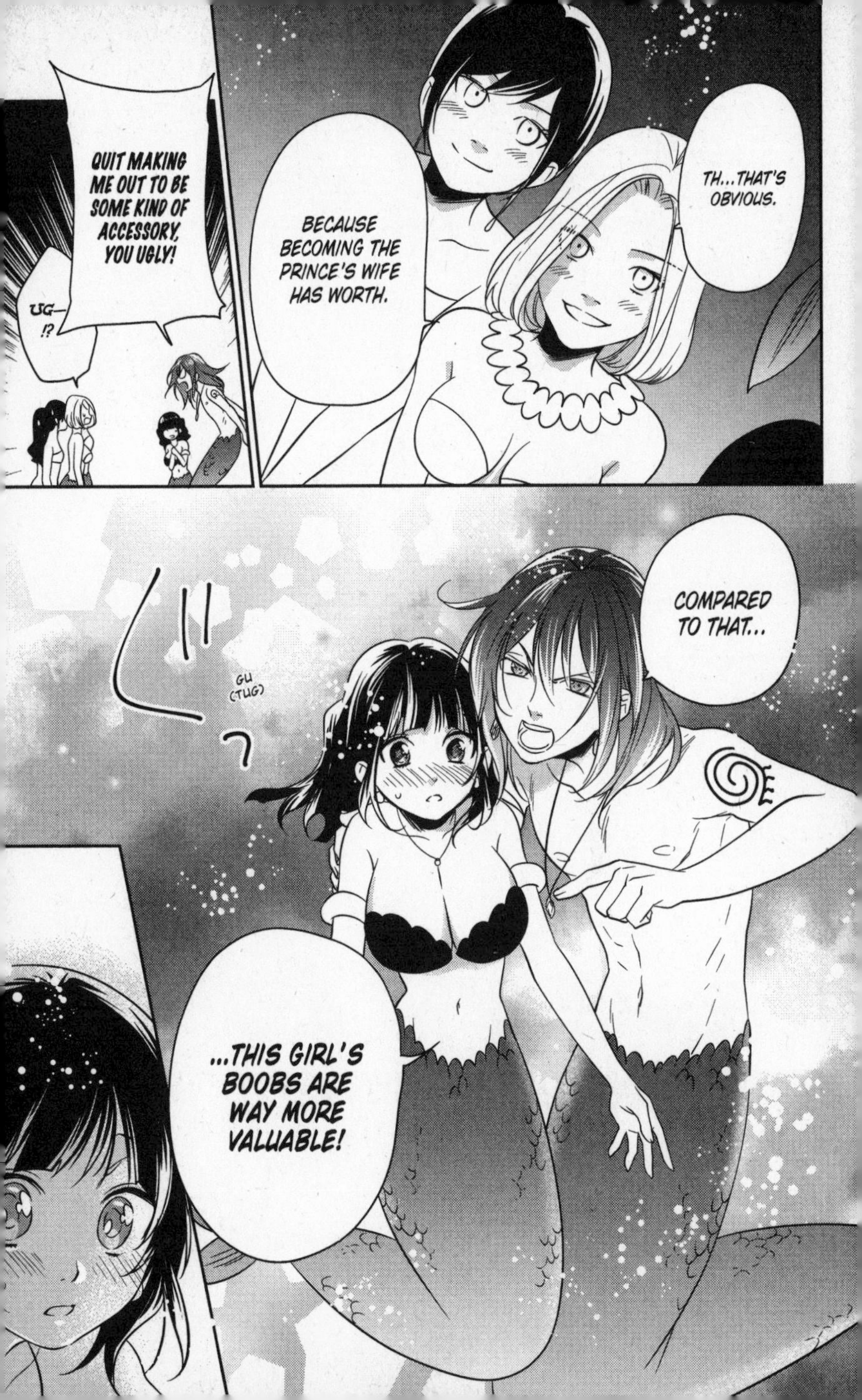
TH...THAT'S OBVIOUS.
BECAUSE BECOMING THE PRINCE'S WIFE HAS WORTH.
QUIT MAKING ME OUT TO BE SOME KIND OF ACCESSORY, YOU UGLY!
UG—!?
COMPARED TO THAT...
GU (TUG)
...THIS GIRL'S BOOBS ARE WAY MORE VALUABLE!

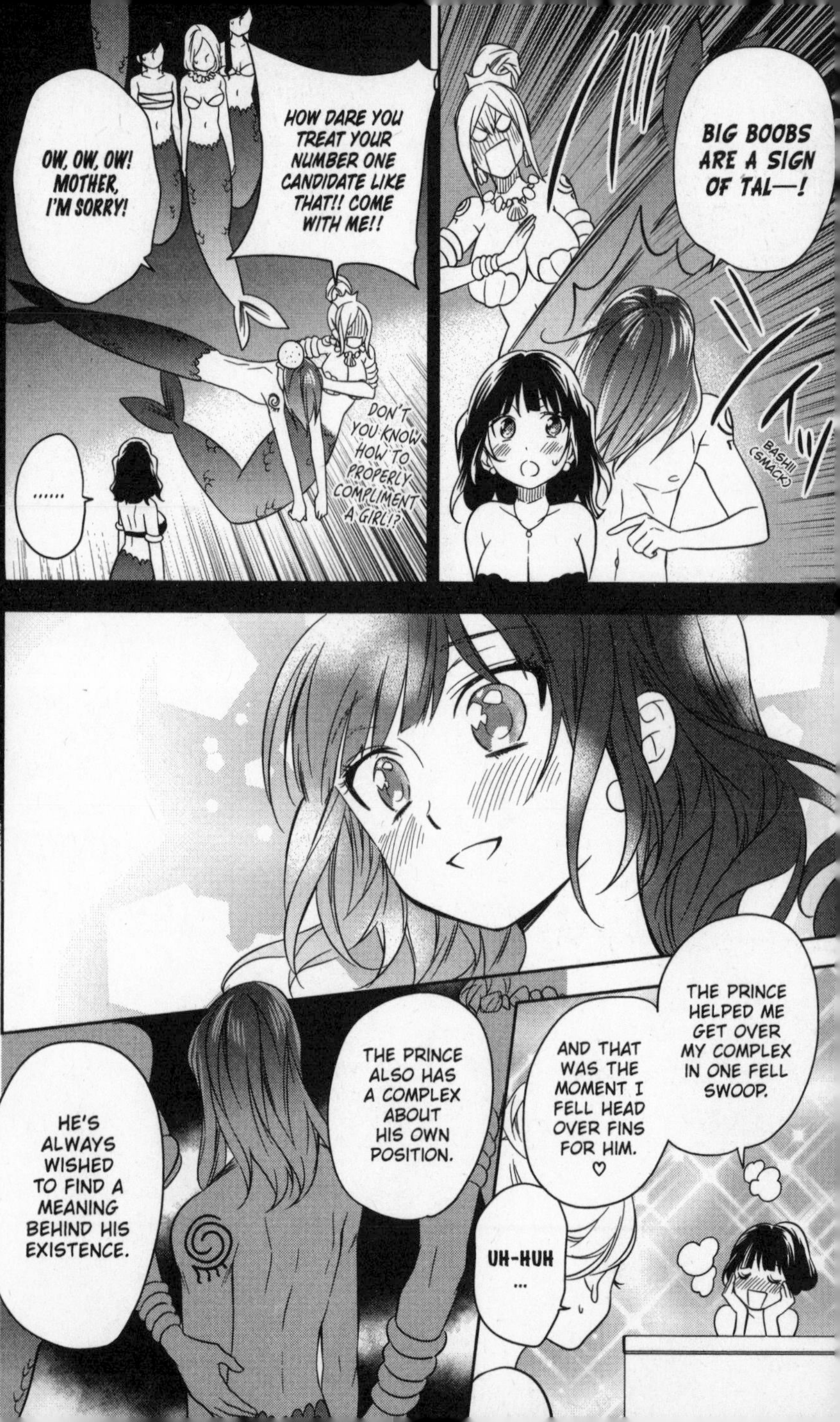
BIG BOOBS ARE A SIGN OF TAL—!
BASH!! (SMACK)
HOW DARE YOU TREAT YOUR NUMBER ONE CANDIDATE LIKE THAT!! COME WITH ME!!
OW, OW, OW! MOTHER, I'M SORRY!
DON'T YOU KNOW HOW TO PROPERLY COMPLIMENT A GIRL!?
......
THE PRINCE HELPED ME GET OVER MY COMPLEX IN ONE FELL SWOOP.
AND THAT WAS THE MOMENT I FELL HEAD OVER FINS FOR HIM. ♡
UH-HUH ...
THE PRINCE ALSO HAS A COMPLEX ABOUT HIS OWN POSITION.
HE'S ALWAYS WISHED TO FIND A MEANING BEHIND HIS EXISTENCE.

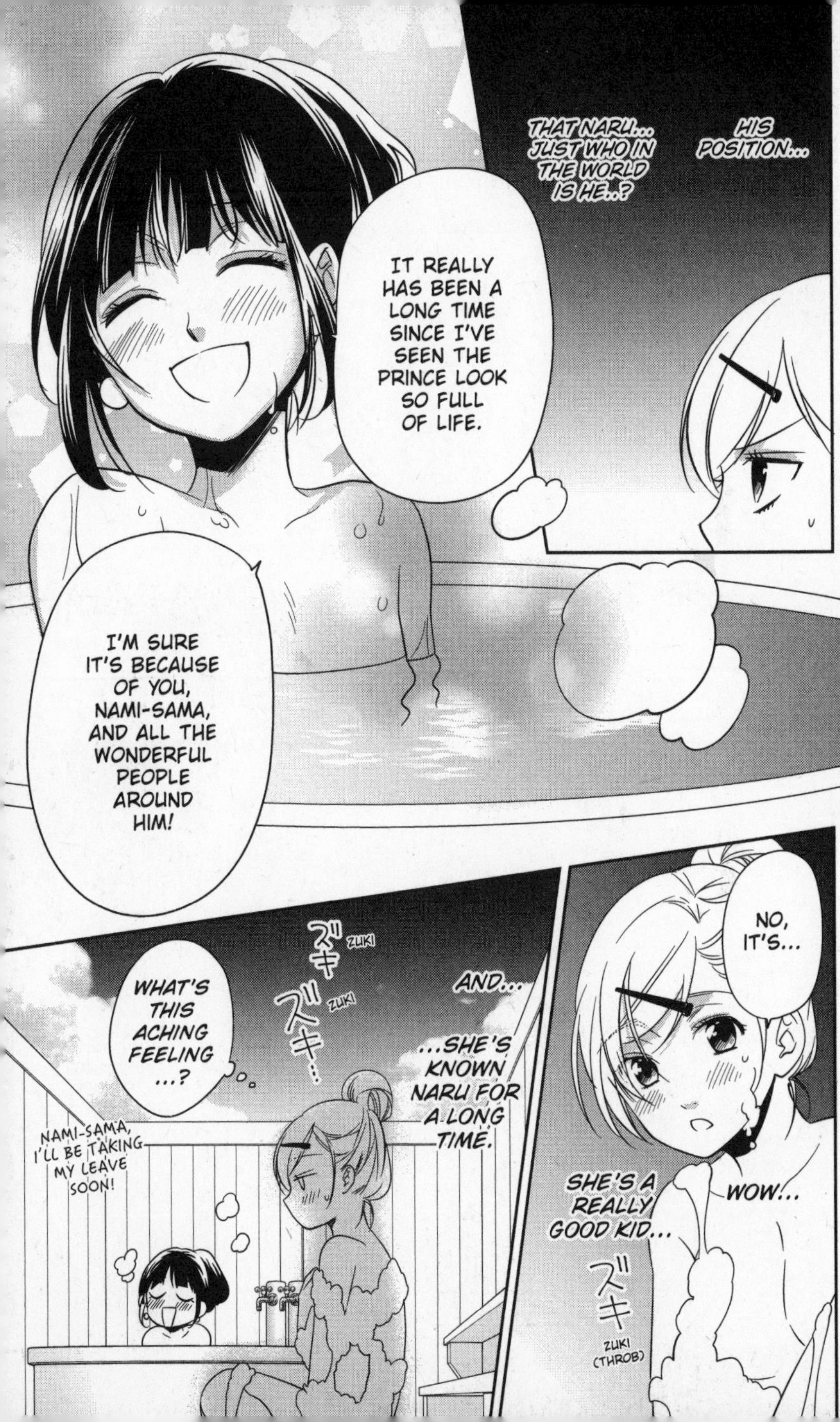
HIS POSITION...
THAT NARU... JUST WHO IN THE WORLD IS HE..?
IT REALLY HAS BEEN A LONG TIME SINCE I'VE SEEN THE PRINCE LOOK SO FULL OF LIFE.
I'M SURE IT'S BECAUSE OF YOU, NAMI-SAMA, AND ALL THE WONDERFUL PEOPLE AROUND HIM!
NO, IT'S...
WOW...
SHE'S A REALLY GOOD KID...
ズキ
ZUKI (THROB)
AND...
...SHE'S KNOWN NARU FOR A LONG TIME.
ズキ ZUKI
ズキ ZUKI
WHAT'S THIS ACHING FEELING ...?
NAMI-SAMA, I'LL BE TAKING MY LEAVE SOON!

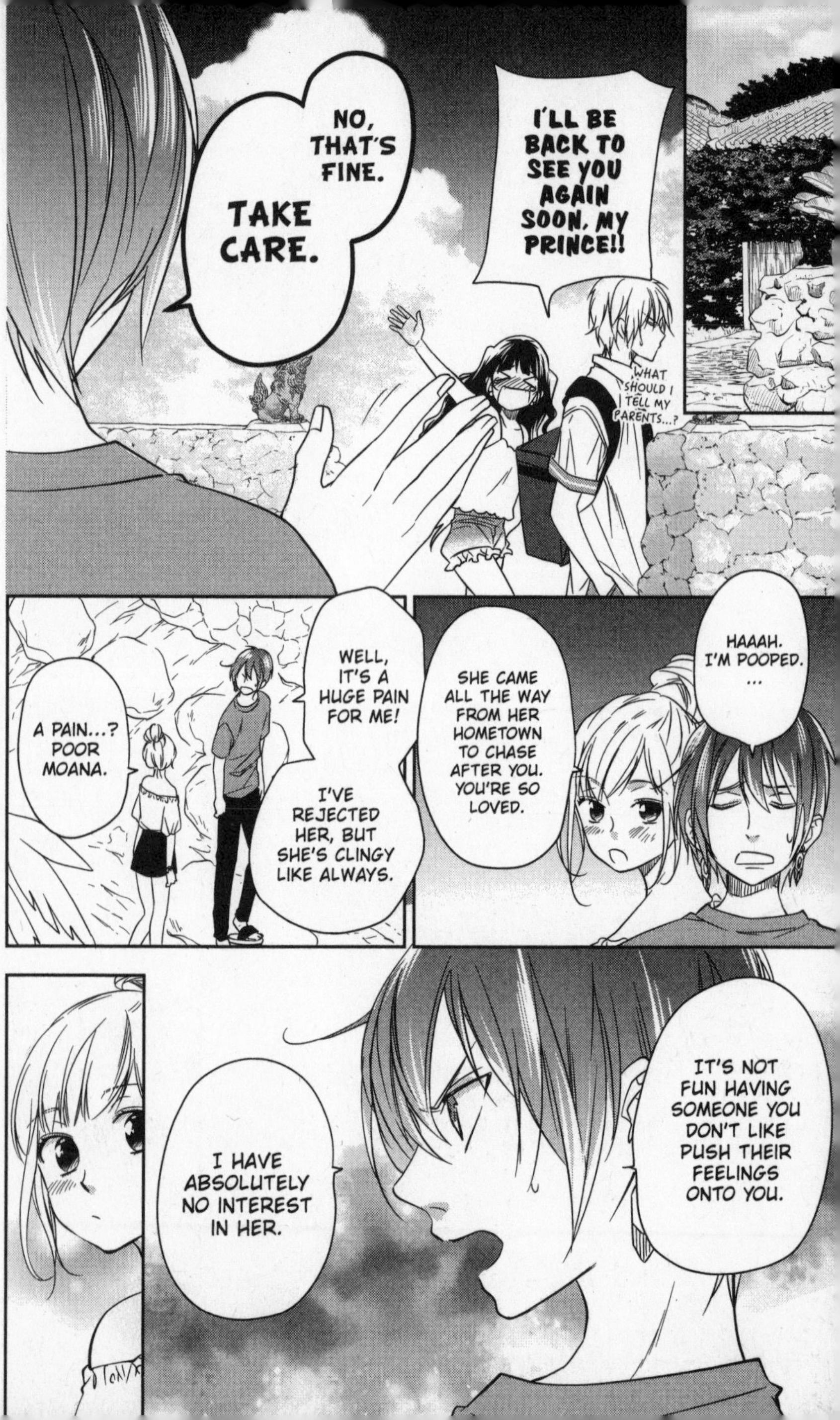
I'LL BE BACK TO SEE YOU AGAIN SOON, MY PRINCE!!
NO, THAT'S FINE.
TAKE CARE.
WHAT SHOULD I TELL MY PARENTS...?
HAAAH. I'M POOPED. ...
SHE CAME ALL THE WAY FROM HER HOMETOWN TO CHASE AFTER YOU. YOU'RE SO LOVED.
WELL, IT'S A HUGE PAIN FOR ME!
I'VE REJECTED HER, BUT SHE'S CLINGY LIKE ALWAYS.
A PAIN...? POOR MOANA.
IT'S NOT FUN HAVING SOMEONE YOU DON'T LIKE PUSH THEIR FEELINGS ONTO YOU.
I HAVE ABSOLUTELY NO INTEREST IN HER.

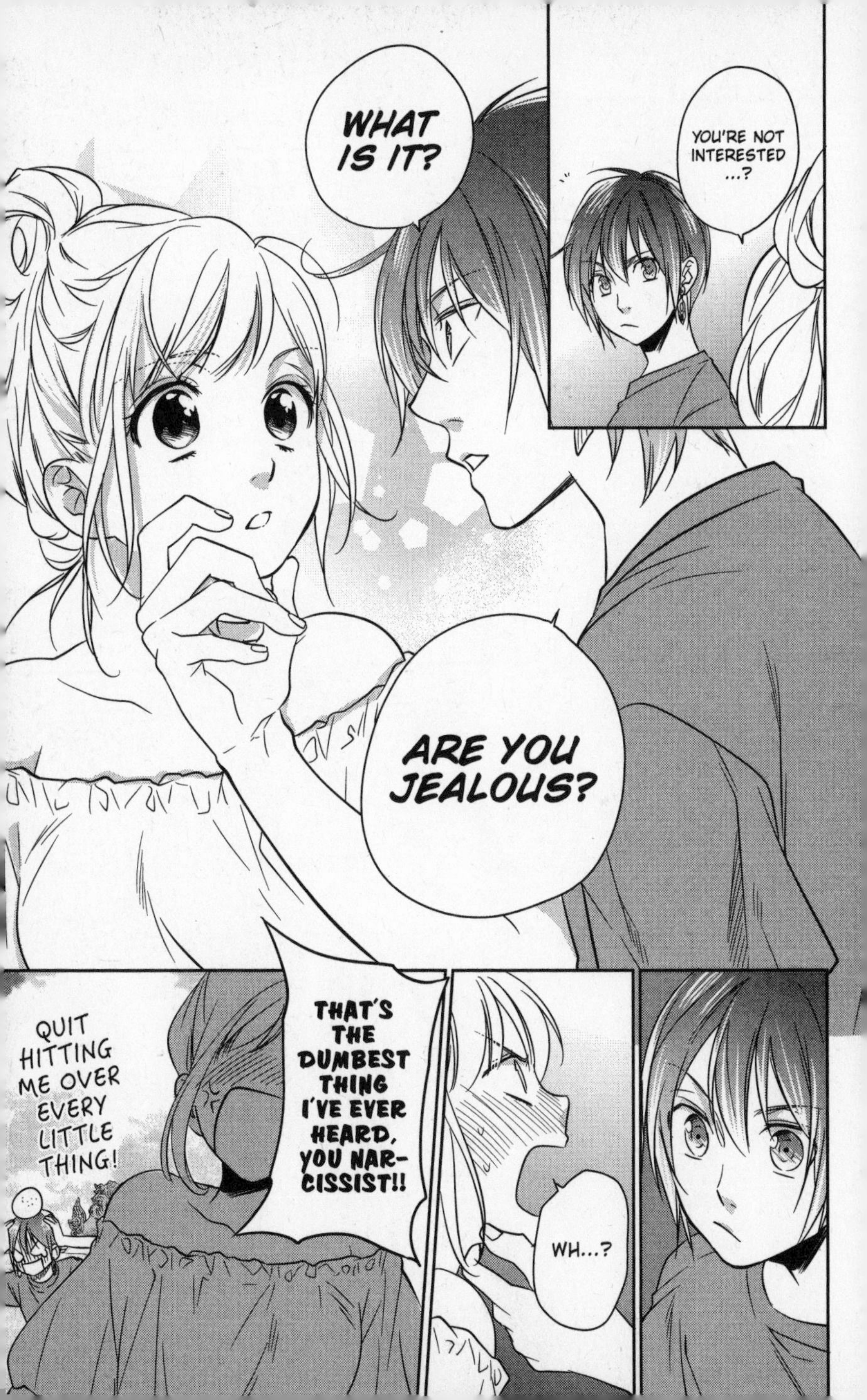
YOU'RE NOT INTERESTED ...?
WHAT IS IT?
ARE YOU JEALOUS?
WH...?
THAT'S THE DUMBEST THING I'VE EVER HEARD, YOU NAR-CISSIST!!
QUIT HITTING ME OVER EVERY LITTLE THING!

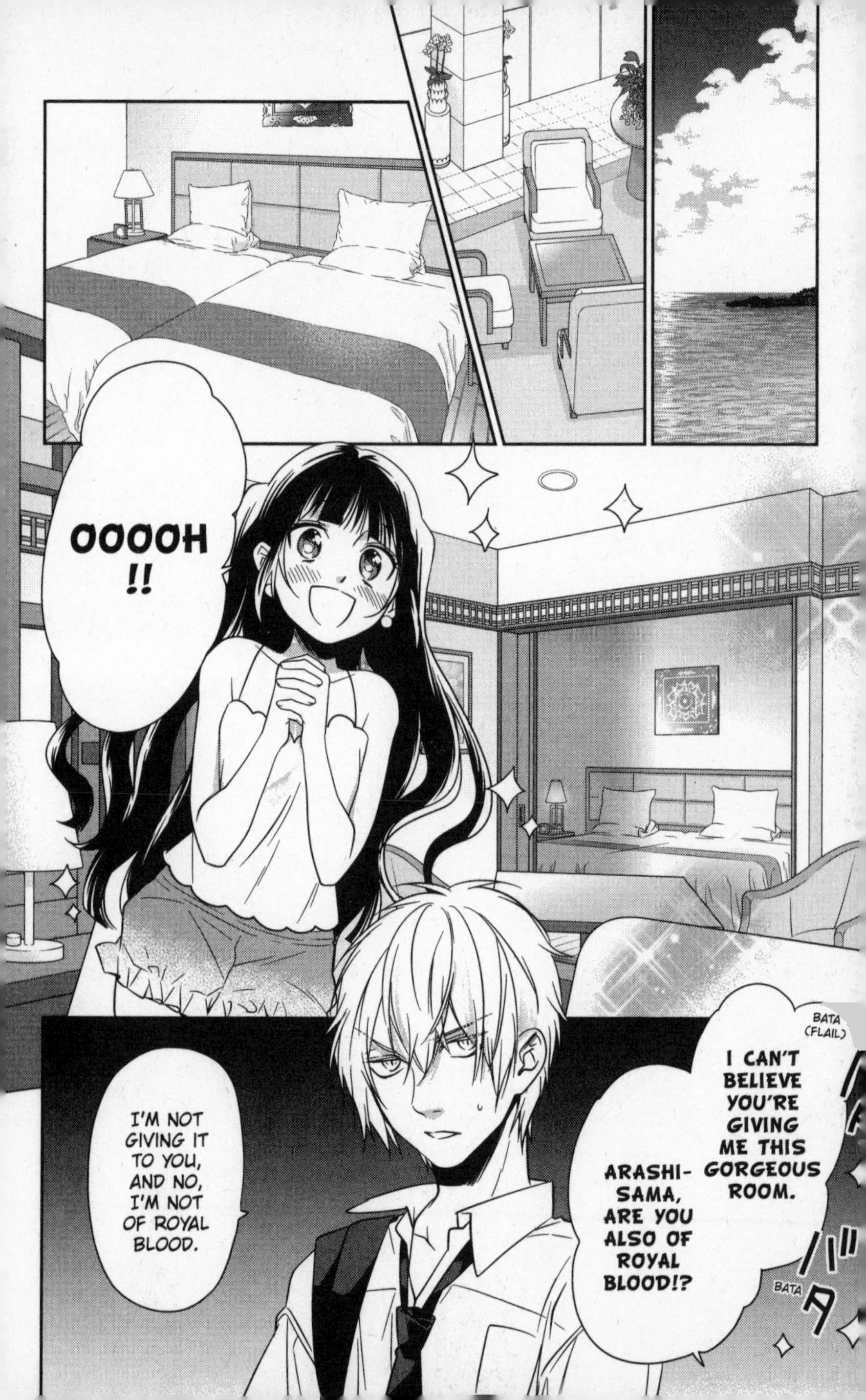
OOOOH !!
BATA (FLAIL)
I CAN'T BELIEVE YOU'RE GIVING ME THIS GORGEOUS ROOM.
ARASHI-SAMA, ARE YOU ALSO OF ROYAL BLOOD!?
BATA
I'M NOT GIVING IT TO YOU, AND NO, I'M NOT OF ROYAL BLOOD.

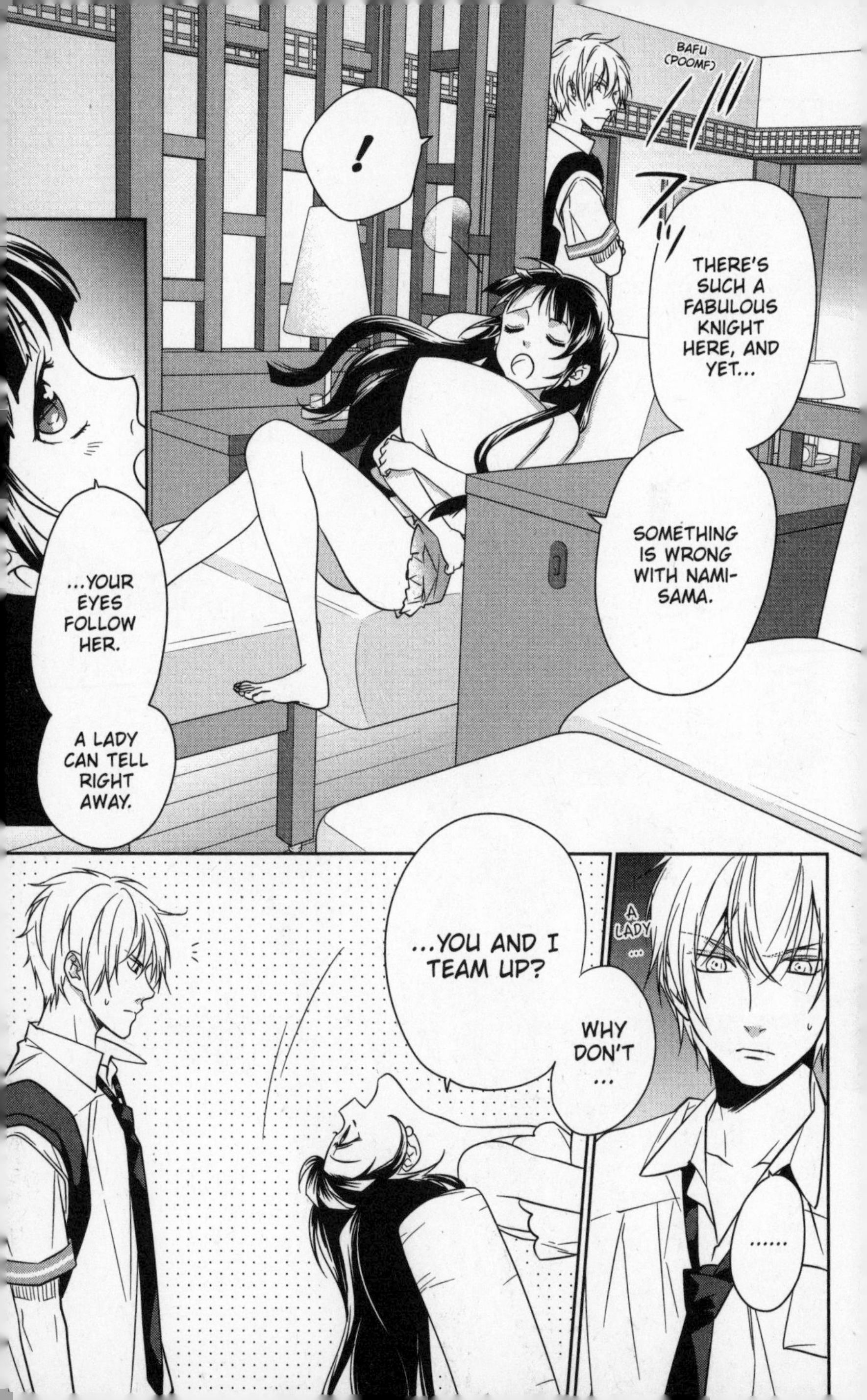
BAFU (POOMF)
!
THERE'S SUCH A FABULOUS KNIGHT HERE, AND YET...
SOMETHING IS WRONG WITH NAMI-SAMA.
...YOUR EYES FOLLOW HER.
A LADY CAN TELL RIGHT AWAY.
A LADY...
......
WHY DON'T...
...YOU AND I TEAM UP?

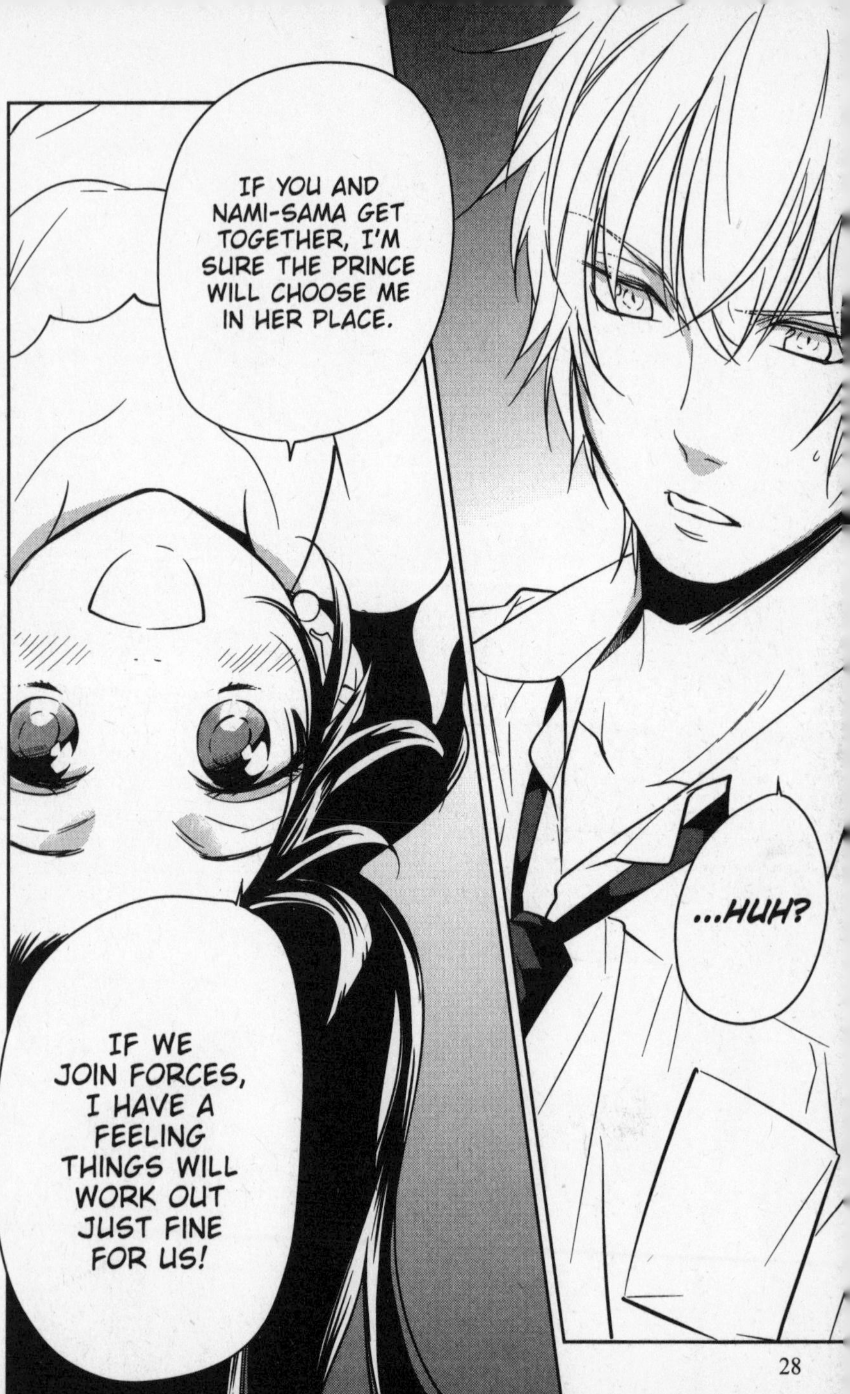
...HUH?
IF YOU AND NAMI-SAMA GET TOGETHER, I'M SURE THE PRINCE WILL CHOOSE ME IN HER PLACE.
IF WE JOIN FORCES, I HAVE A FEELING THINGS WILL WORK OUT JUST FINE FOR US!

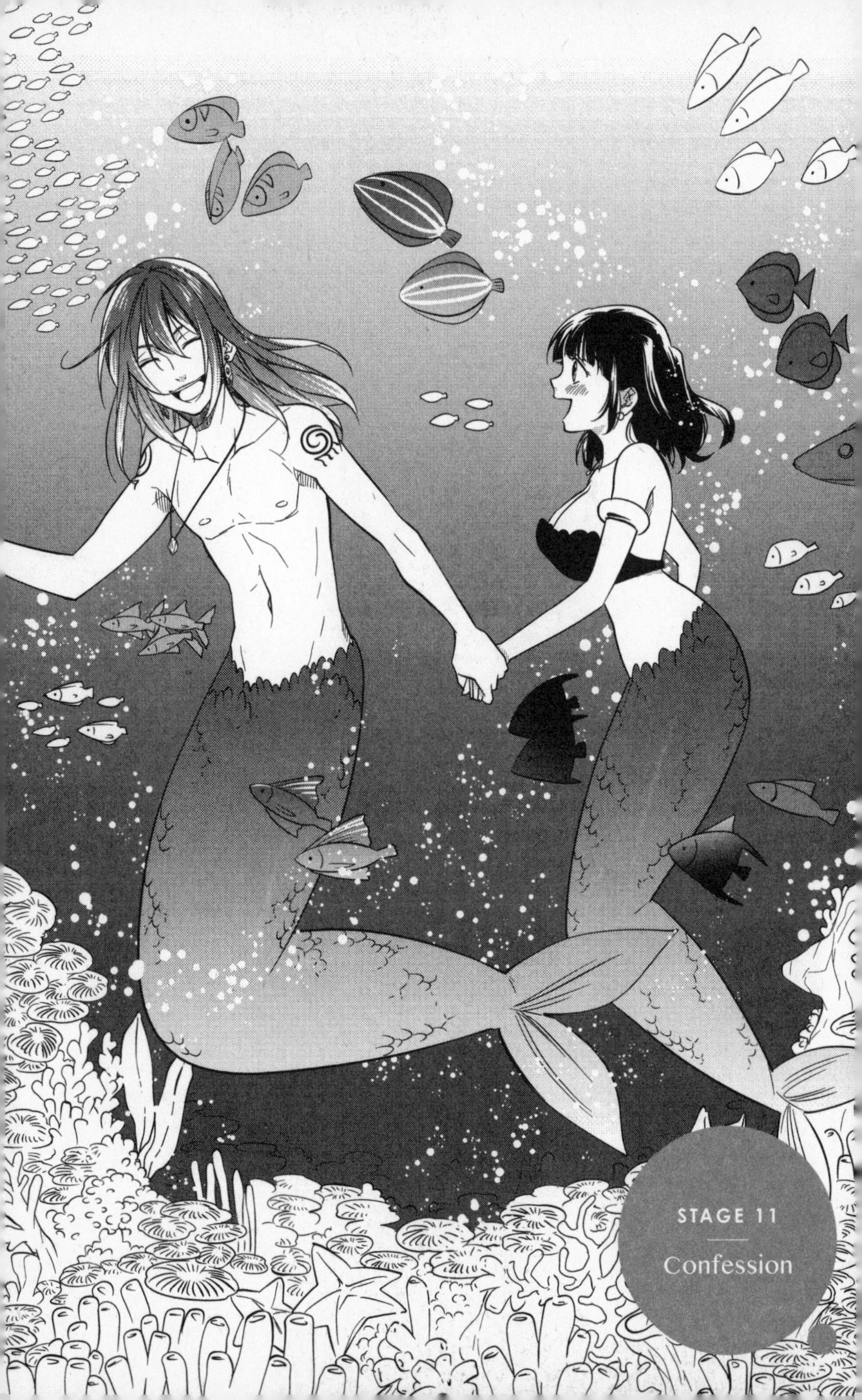
STAGE 11
Confession

MERMAID BOYS

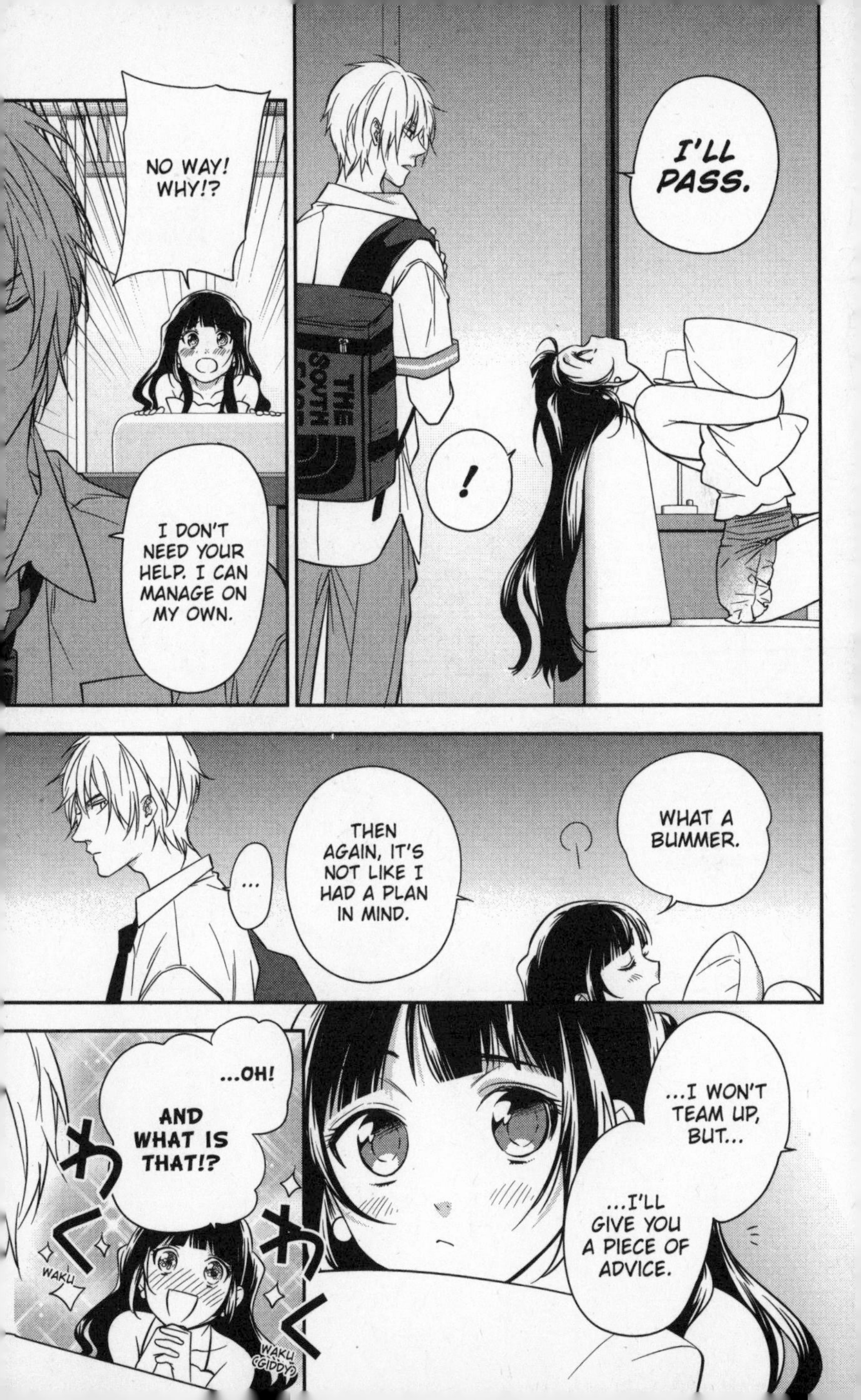
I'LL PASS.
!
NO WAY! WHY!?
I DON'T NEED YOUR HELP. I CAN MANAGE ON MY OWN.
WHAT A BUMMER.
THEN AGAIN, IT'S NOT LIKE I HAD A PLAN IN MIND.
...
...I WON'T TEAM UP, BUT...
...I'LL GIVE YOU A PIECE OF ADVICE.
...OH!
AND WHAT IS THAT!?
WAKU
WAKU (GIDDY)

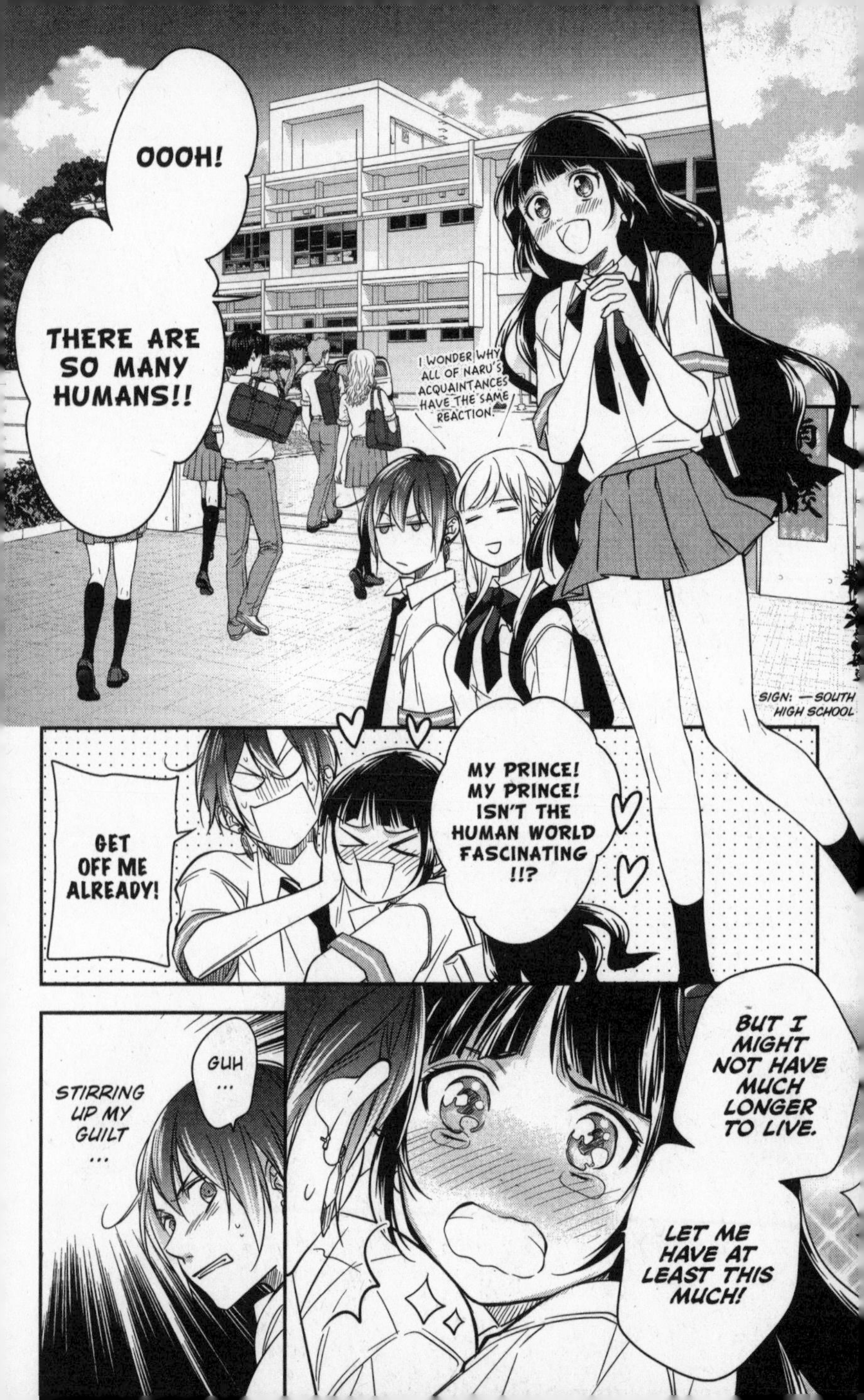
OOOH!
THERE ARE SO MANY HUMANS!!
I WONDER WHY ALL OF NARU'S ACQUAINTANCES HAVE THE SAME REACTION.
SIGN: —SOUTH HIGH SCHOOL
MY PRINCE! MY PRINCE! ISN'T THE HUMAN WORLD FASCINATING !!?
GET OFF ME ALREADY!
BUT I MIGHT NOT HAVE MUCH LONGER TO LIVE.
LET ME HAVE AT LEAST THIS MUCH!
GUH ...
STIRRING UP MY GUILT ...

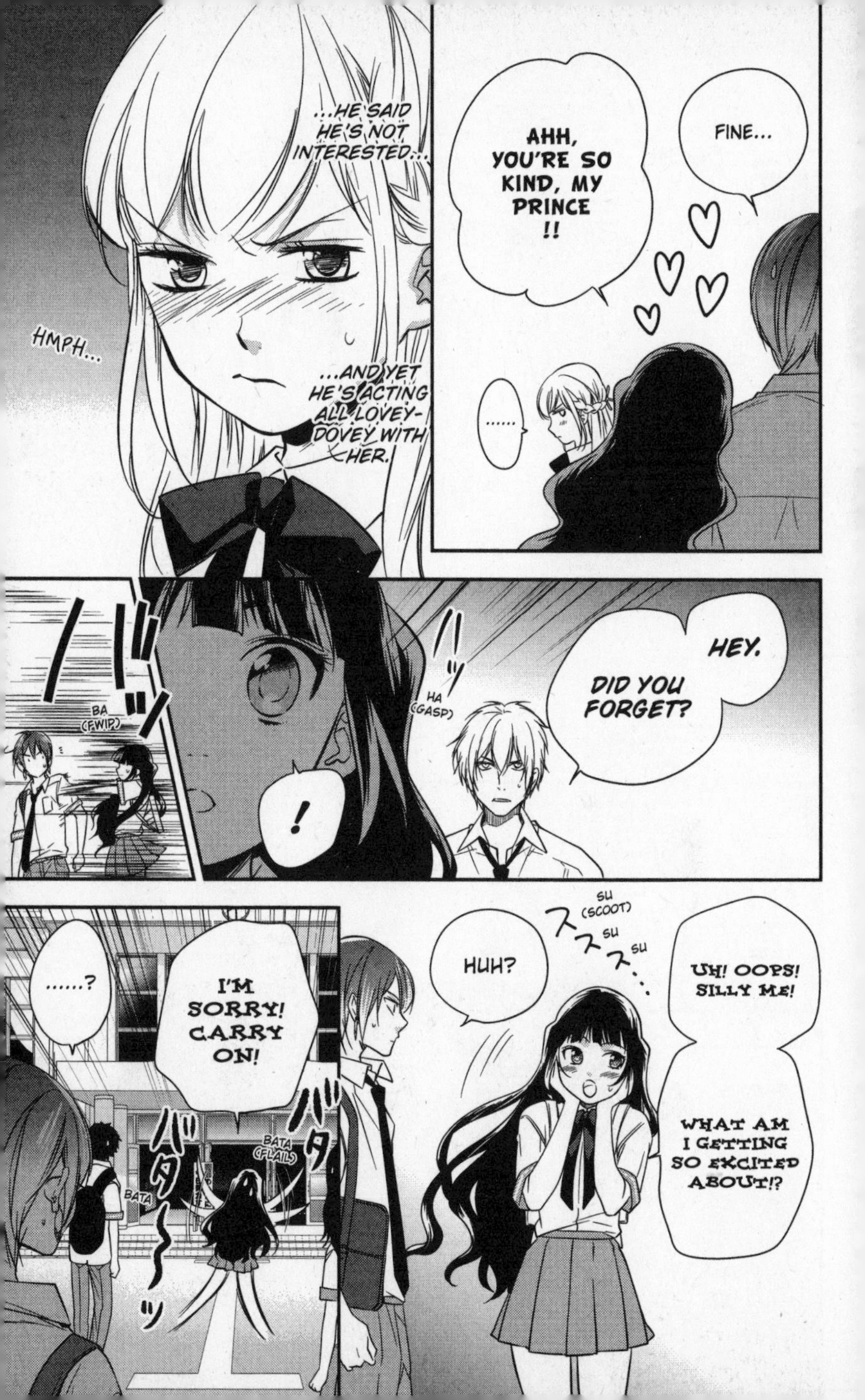
FINE...
AHH, YOU'RE SO KIND, MY PRINCE !!
......
...HE SAID HE'S NOT INTERESTED...
...AND YET HE'S ACTING ALL LOVEY-DOVEY WITH HER.
HMPH...
HEY.
DID YOU FORGET?
HA (GASP)
!
BA (FWIP)
UH! OOPS! SILLY ME!
SU (SCOOT) SU SU
HUH?
WHAT AM I GETTING SO EXCITED ABOUT!?
I'M SORRY! CARRY ON!
......?
BATA (FLAIL)
BATA

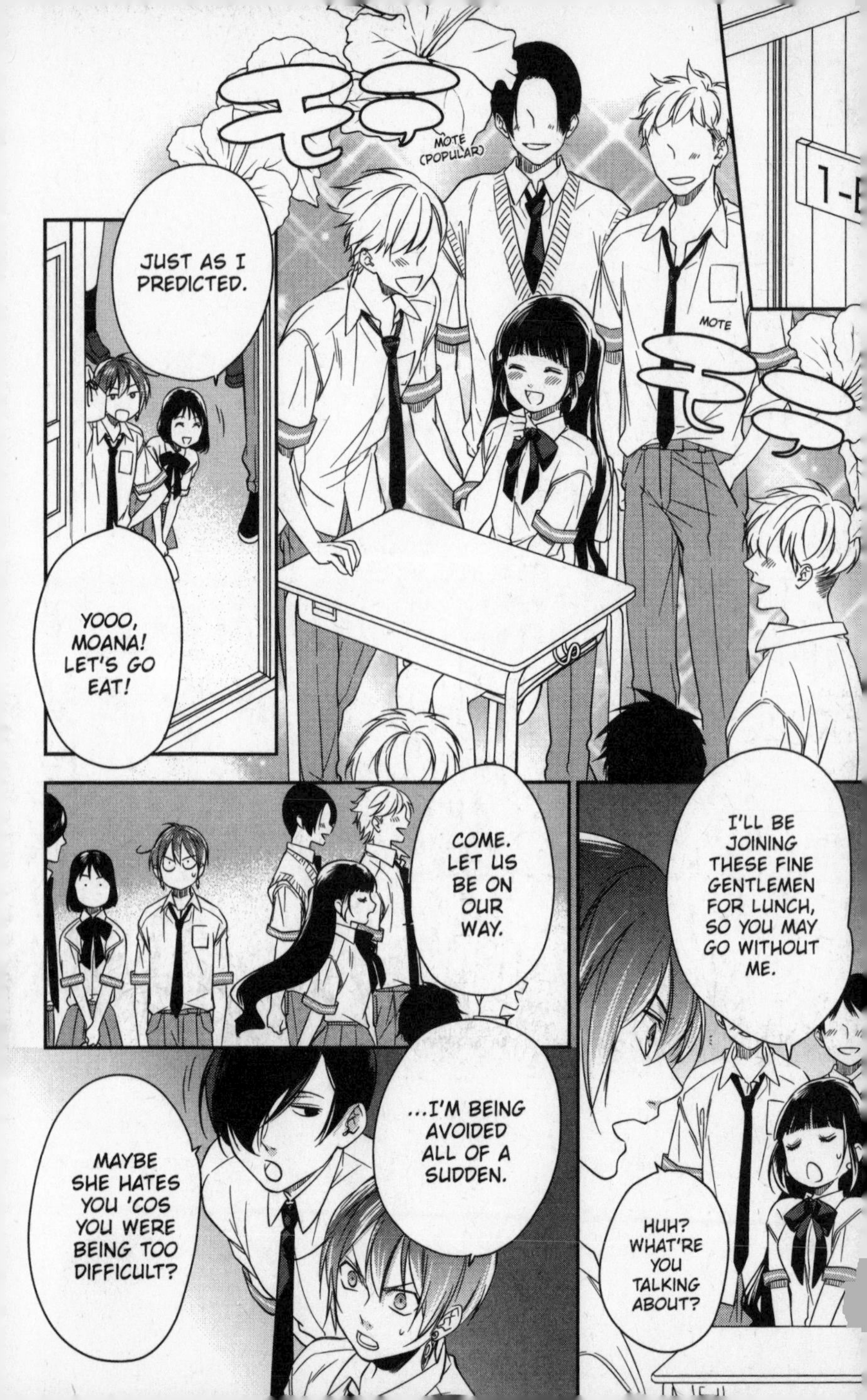
MOTE (POPULAR)
MOTE
JUST AS I PREDICTED.
YOOO, MOANA! LET'S GO EAT!
I'LL BE JOINING THESE FINE GENTLEMEN FOR LUNCH, SO YOU MAY GO WITHOUT ME.
HUH? WHAT'RE YOU TALKING ABOUT?
COME. LET US BE ON OUR WAY.
...I'M BEING AVOIDED ALL OF A SUDDEN.
MAYBE SHE HATES YOU 'COS YOU WERE BEING TOO DIFFICULT?

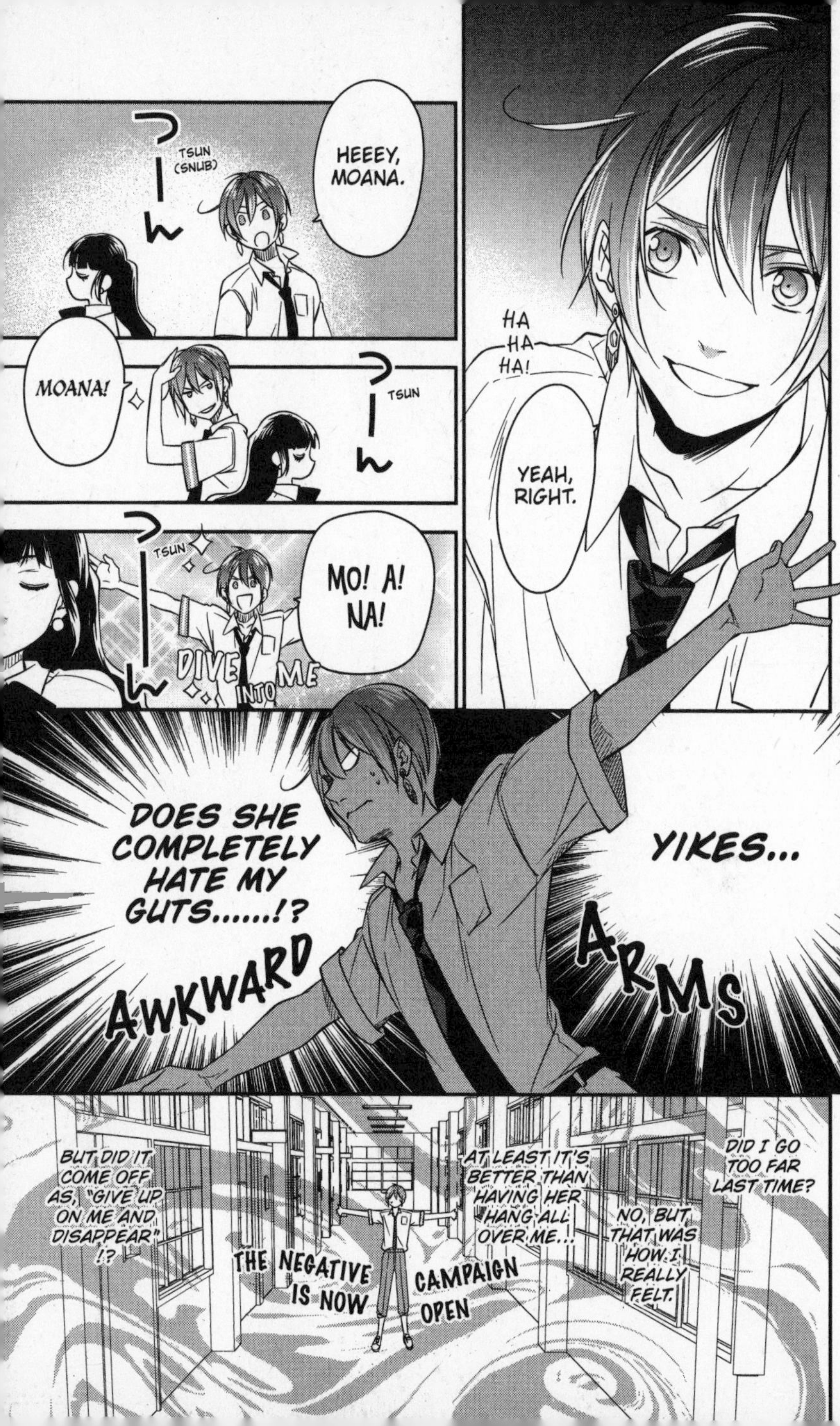
HA HA HA!
YEAH, RIGHT.
HEEEY, MOANA.
つーん
TSUN (SNUB)
つーん
TSUN
MOANA!
MO! A! NA!
つーん
TSUN
DIVE INTO ME
YIKES...
ARMS
DOES SHE COMPLETELY HATE MY GUTS......!?
AWKWARD
DID I GO TOO FAR LAST TIME?
NO, BUT THAT WAS HOW I REALLY FELT.
AT LEAST IT'S BETTER THAN HAVING HER HANG ALL OVER ME...
THE NEGATIVE CAMPAIGN IS NOW OPEN
BUT DID IT COME OFF AS, "GIVE UP ON ME AND DISAPPEAR"!?

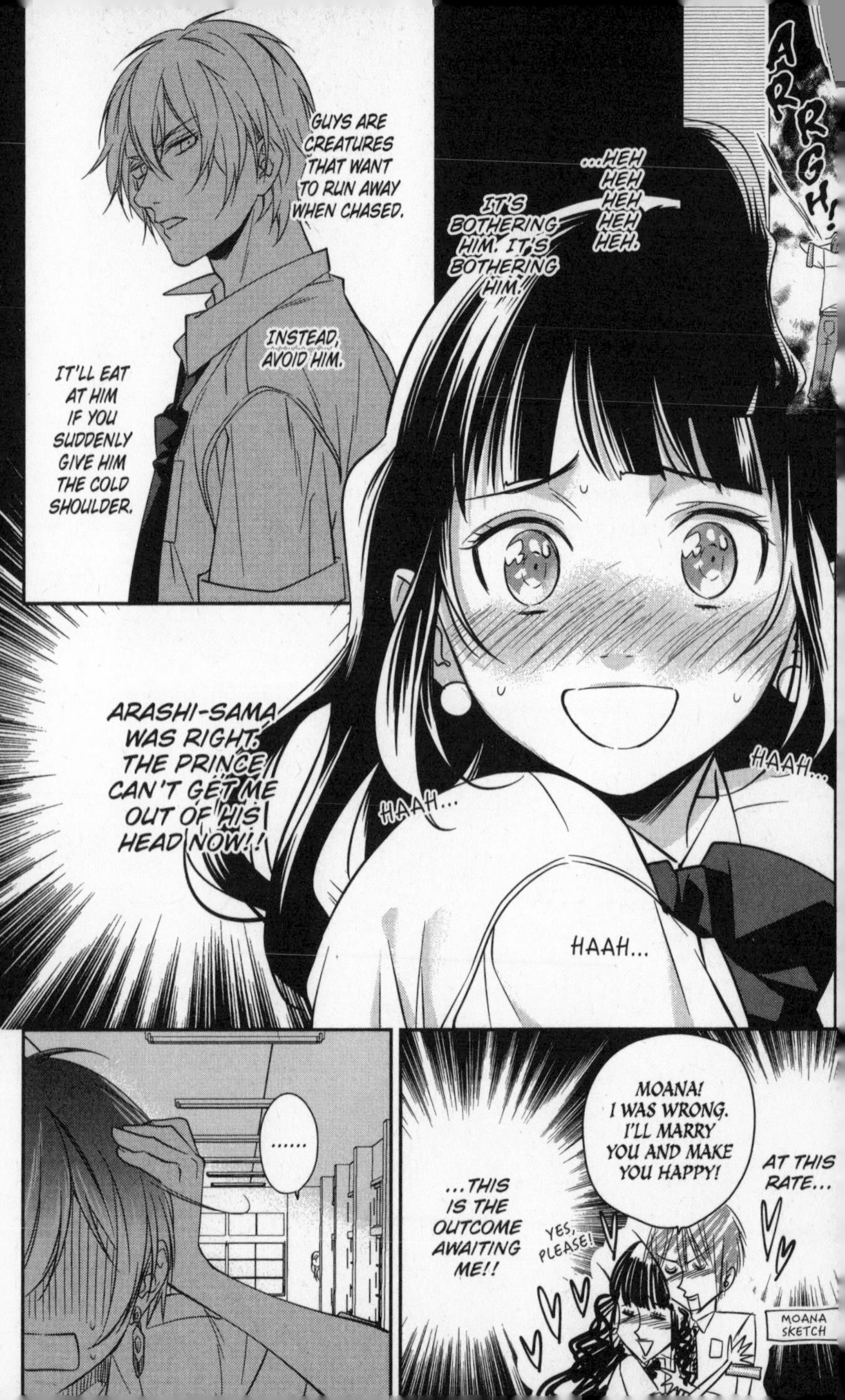
ARRGH!
...HEH HEH HEH HEH HEH.
IT'S BOTHERING HIM. IT'S BOTHERING HIM.
GUYS ARE CREATURES THAT WANT TO RUN AWAY WHEN CHASED.
INSTEAD, AVOID HIM.
IT'LL EAT AT HIM IF YOU SUDDENLY GIVE HIM THE COLD SHOULDER.
HAAH...
ARASHI-SAMA WAS RIGHT. THE PRINCE CAN'T GET ME OUT OF HIS HEAD NOW!!
HAAH...
HAAH...
AT THIS RATE...
MOANA! I WAS WRONG. I'LL MARRY YOU AND MAKE YOU HAPPY!
YES, PLEASE!
...THIS IS THE OUTCOME AWAITING ME!!
MOANA SKETCH
......

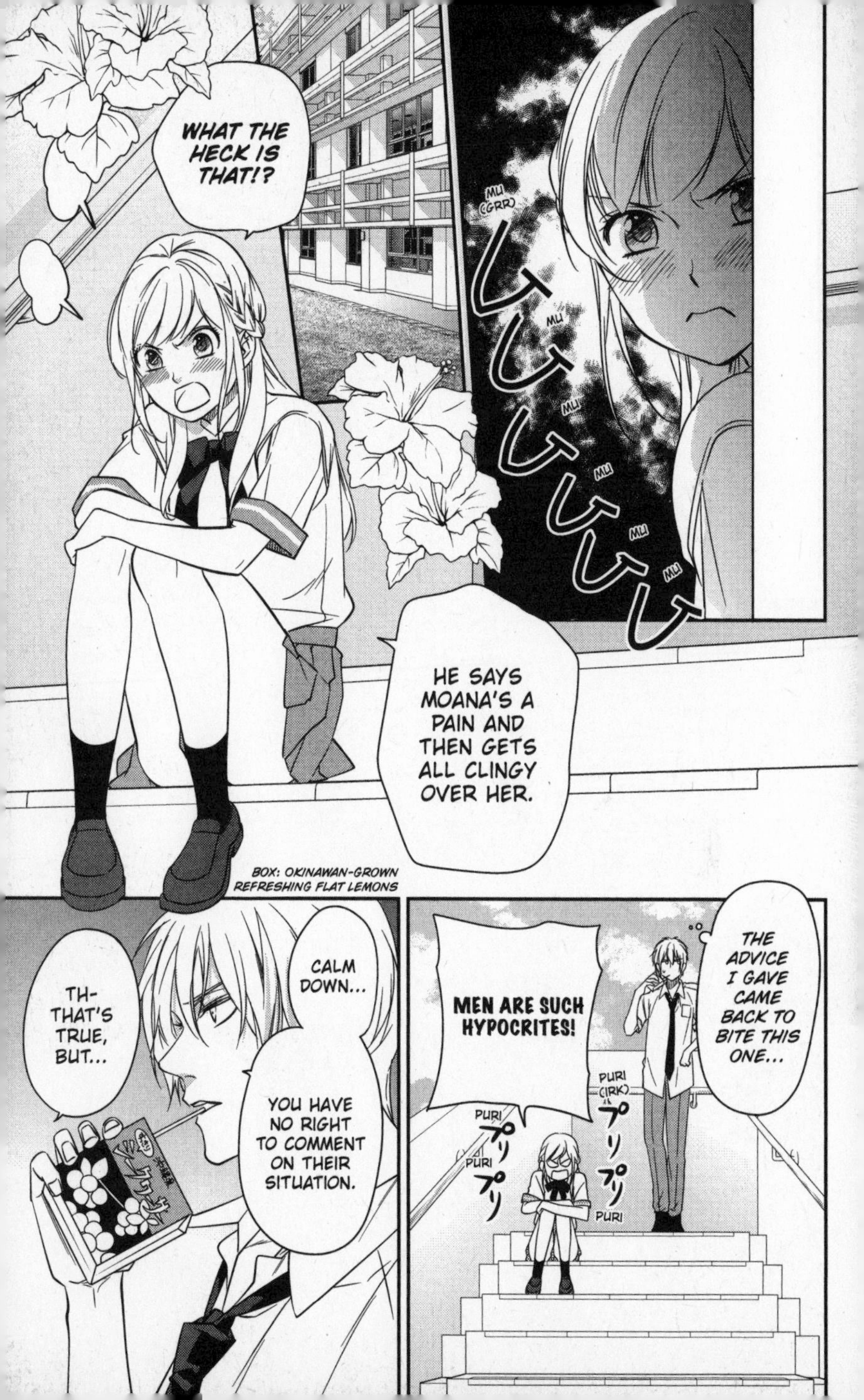
MU (GRR)
MU
MU
MU
MU
MU
WHAT THE HECK IS THAT!?
HE SAYS MOANA'S A PAIN AND THEN GETS ALL CLINGY OVER HER.
BOX: OKINAWAN-GROWN REFRESHING FLAT LEMONS
THE ADVICE I GAVE CAME BACK TO BITE THIS ONE...
MEN ARE SUCH HYPOCRITES!
PURI (IRK)
PURI
PURI
PURI
CALM DOWN...
YOU HAVE NO RIGHT TO COMMENT ON THEIR SITUATION.
TH-THAT'S TRUE, BUT...

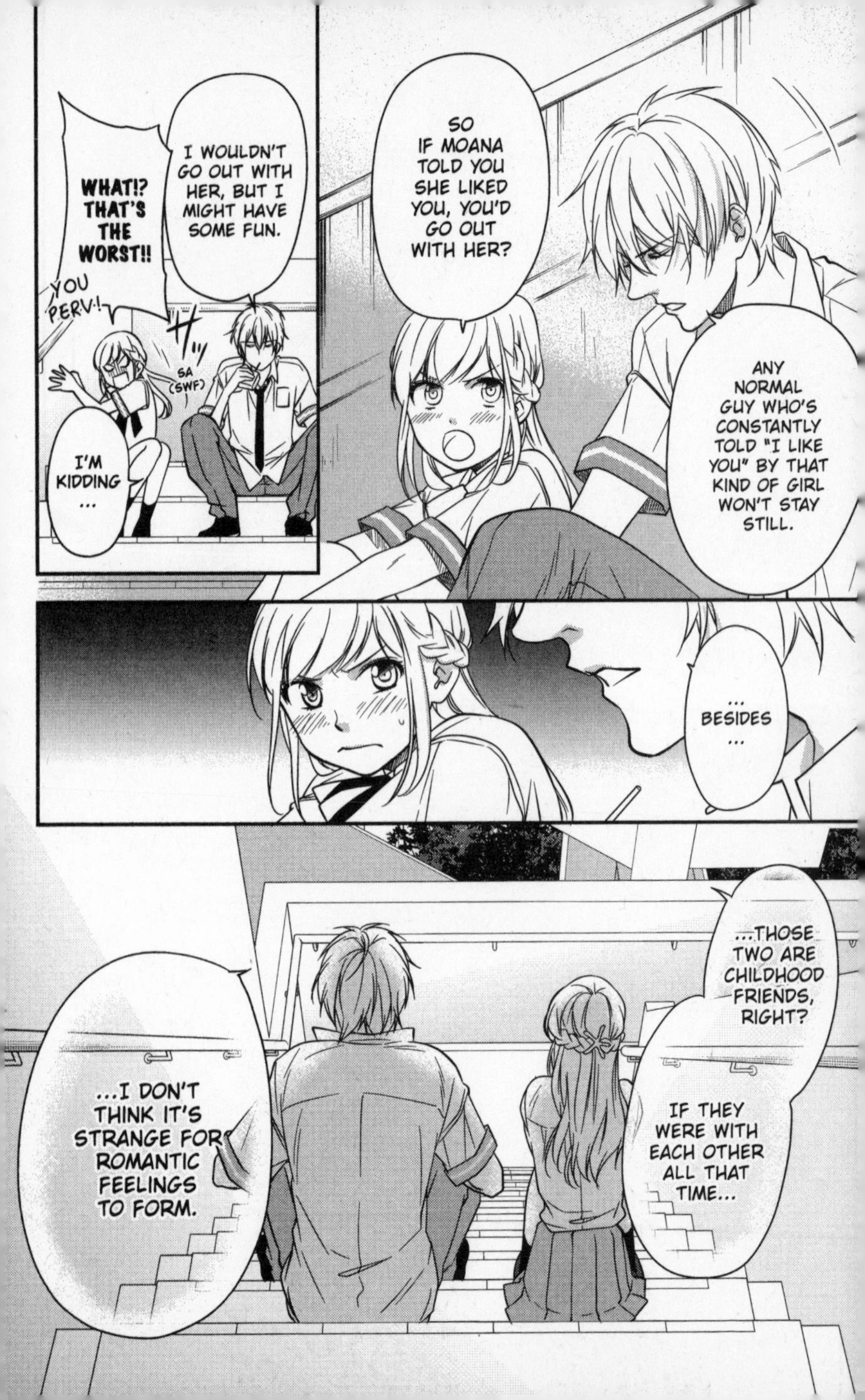
SO IF MOANA TOLD YOU SHE LIKED YOU, YOU'D GO OUT WITH HER?
ANY NORMAL GUY WHO'S CONSTANTLY TOLD "I LIKE YOU" BY THAT KIND OF GIRL WON'T STAY STILL.
I WOULDN'T GO OUT WITH HER, BUT I MIGHT HAVE SOME FUN.
WHAT!? THAT'S THE WORST!!
YOU PERV!
SA (SWF)
I'M KIDDING...
...BESIDES...
...THOSE TWO ARE CHILDHOOD FRIENDS, RIGHT?
IF THEY WERE WITH EACH OTHER ALL THAT TIME...
...I DON'T THINK IT'S STRANGE FOR ROMANTIC FEELINGS TO FORM.

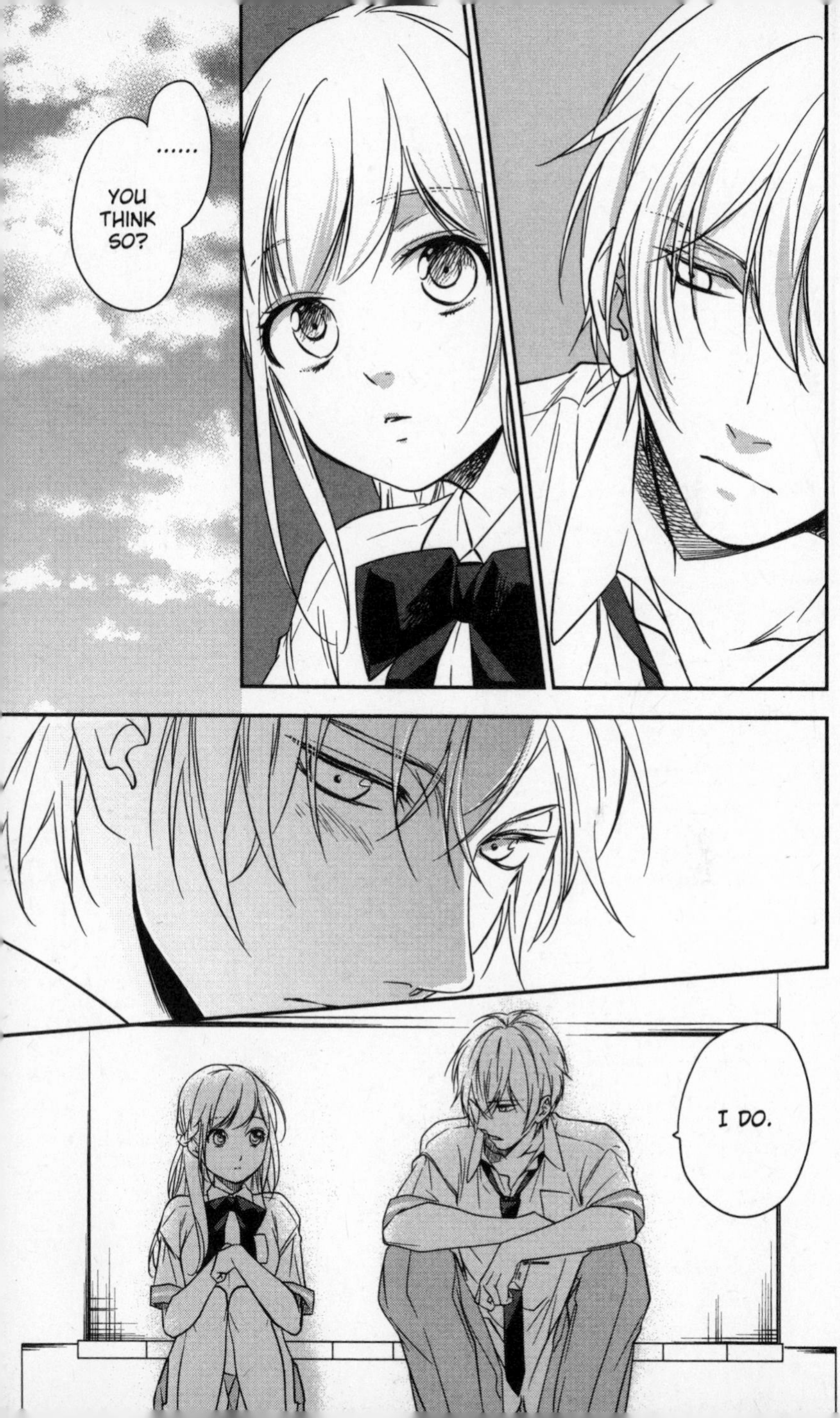
...... YOU THINK SO?
I DO.

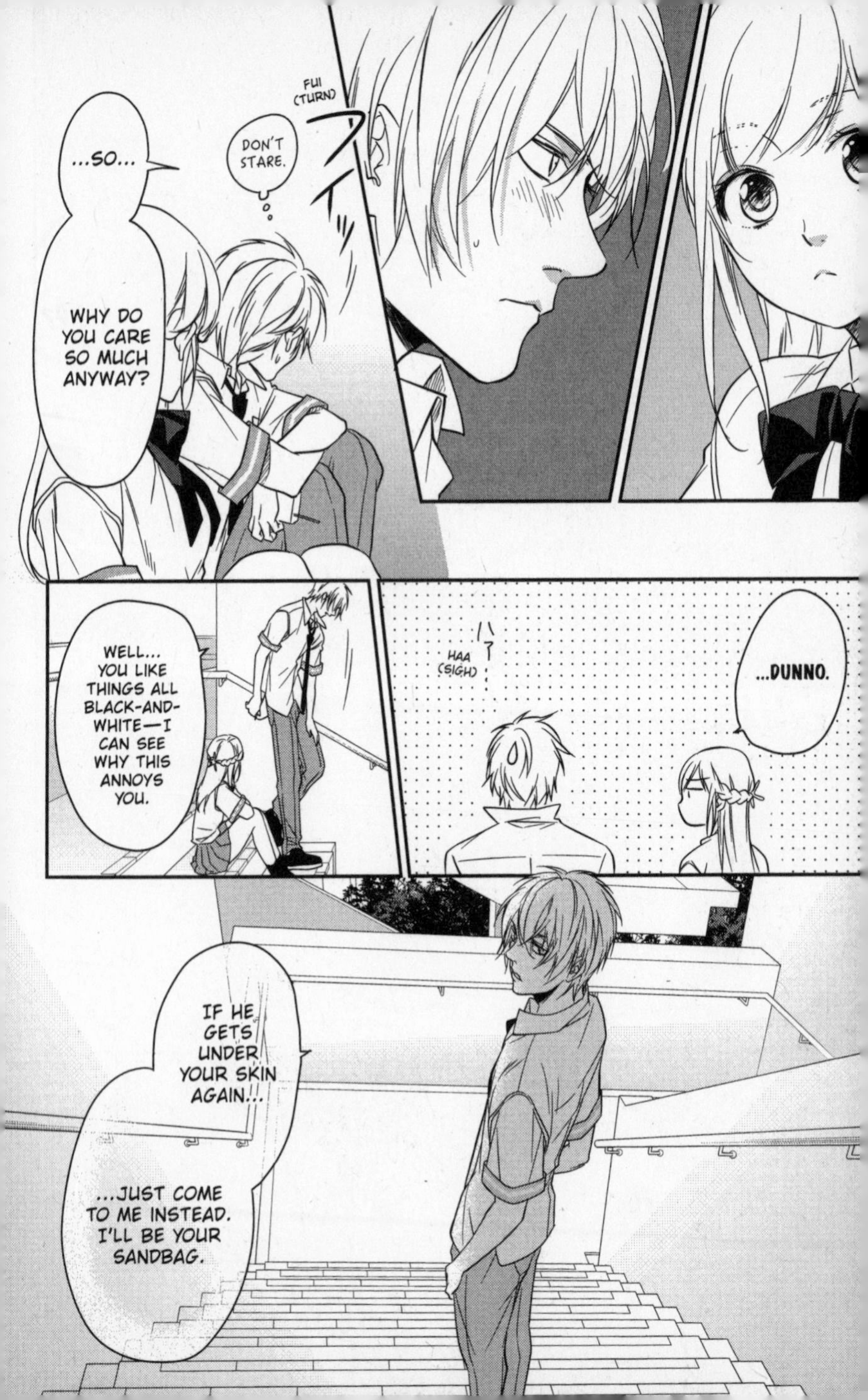
FUI (TURN)
DON'T STARE.
...SO...
WHY DO YOU CARE SO MUCH ANYWAY?
...DUNNO.
HAA (SIGH)
WELL... YOU LIKE THINGS ALL BLACK-AND-WHITE—I CAN SEE WHY THIS ANNOYS YOU.
IF HE GETS UNDER YOUR SKIN AGAIN...
...JUST COME TO ME INSTEAD. I'LL BE YOUR SANDBAG.

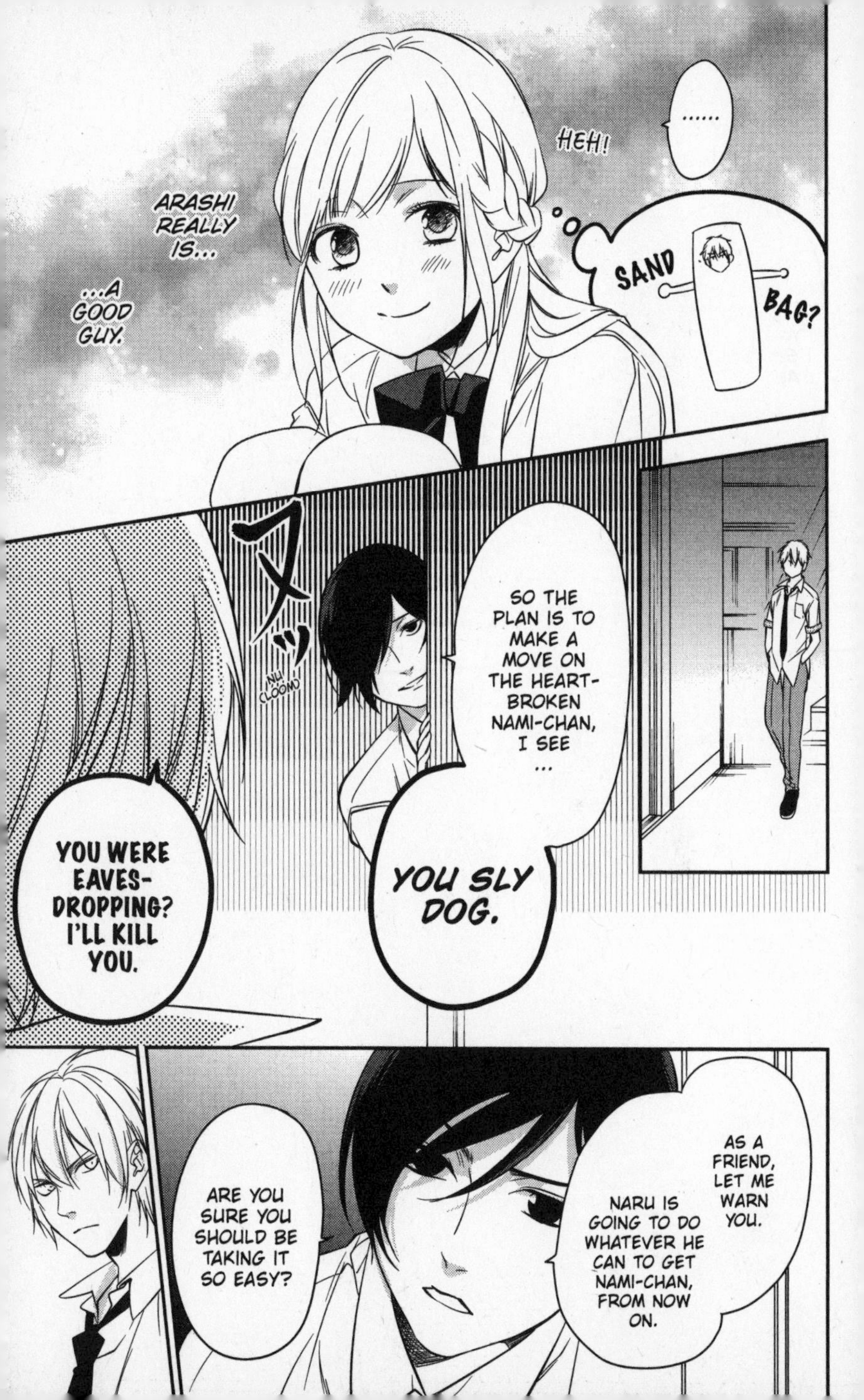
......
SAND BAG?
HEH!
ARASHI REALLY IS...
...A GOOD GUY.
SO THE PLAN IS TO MAKE A MOVE ON THE HEART-BROKEN NAMI-CHAN, I SEE ...
ヌッ
NU (LOOM)
YOU SLY DOG.
YOU WERE EAVES-DROPPING? I'LL KILL YOU.
AS A FRIEND, LET ME WARN YOU.
NARU IS GOING TO DO WHATEVER HE CAN TO GET NAMI-CHAN, FROM NOW ON.
ARE YOU SURE YOU SHOULD BE TAKING IT SO EASY?

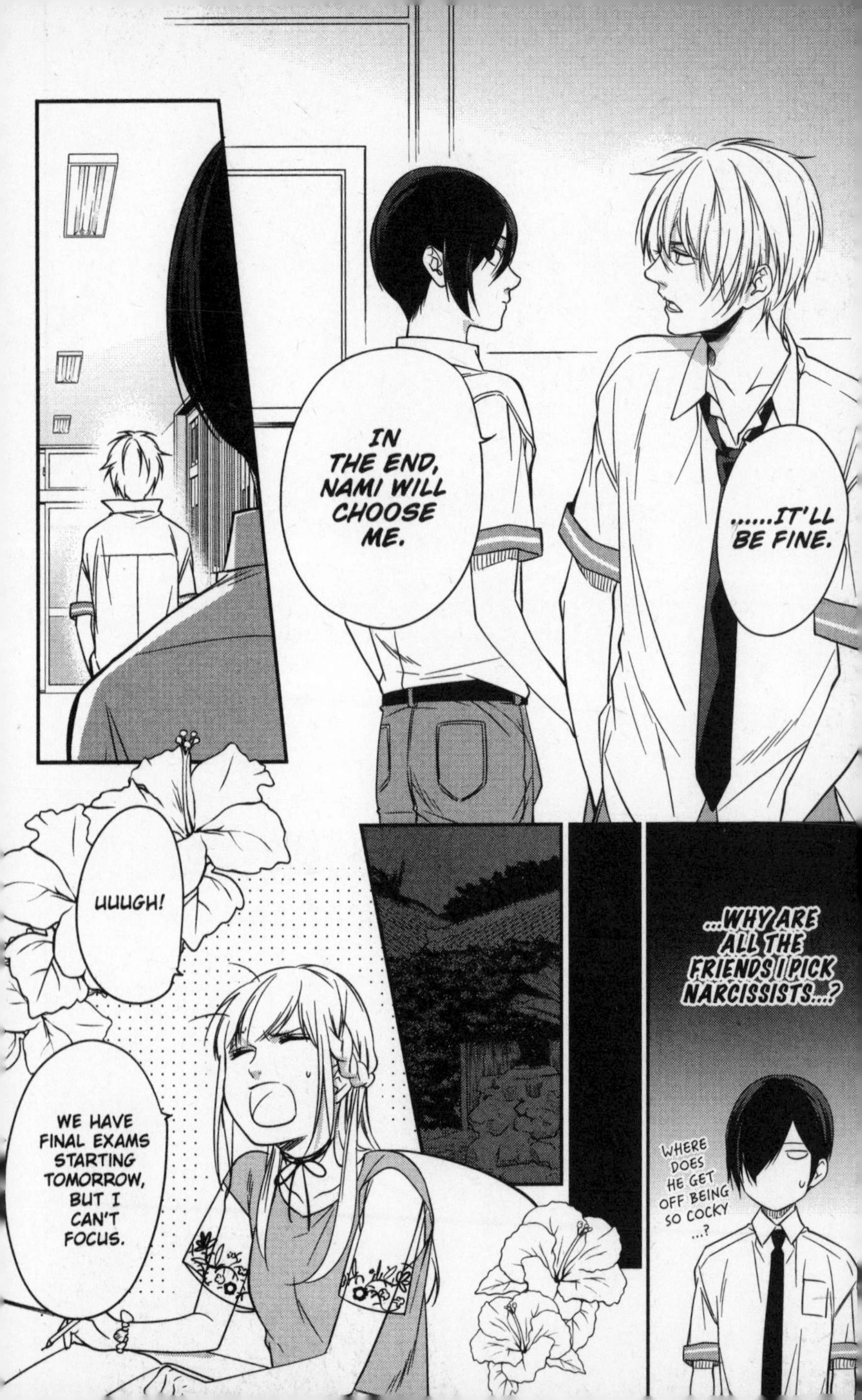
......IT'LL BE FINE.
IN THE END, NAMI WILL CHOOSE ME.
...WHY ARE ALL THE FRIENDS I PICK NARCISSISTS...?
WHERE DOES HE GET OFF BEING SO COCKY ...?
UUUGH!
WE HAVE FINAL EXAMS STARTING TOMORROW, BUT I CAN'T FOCUS.

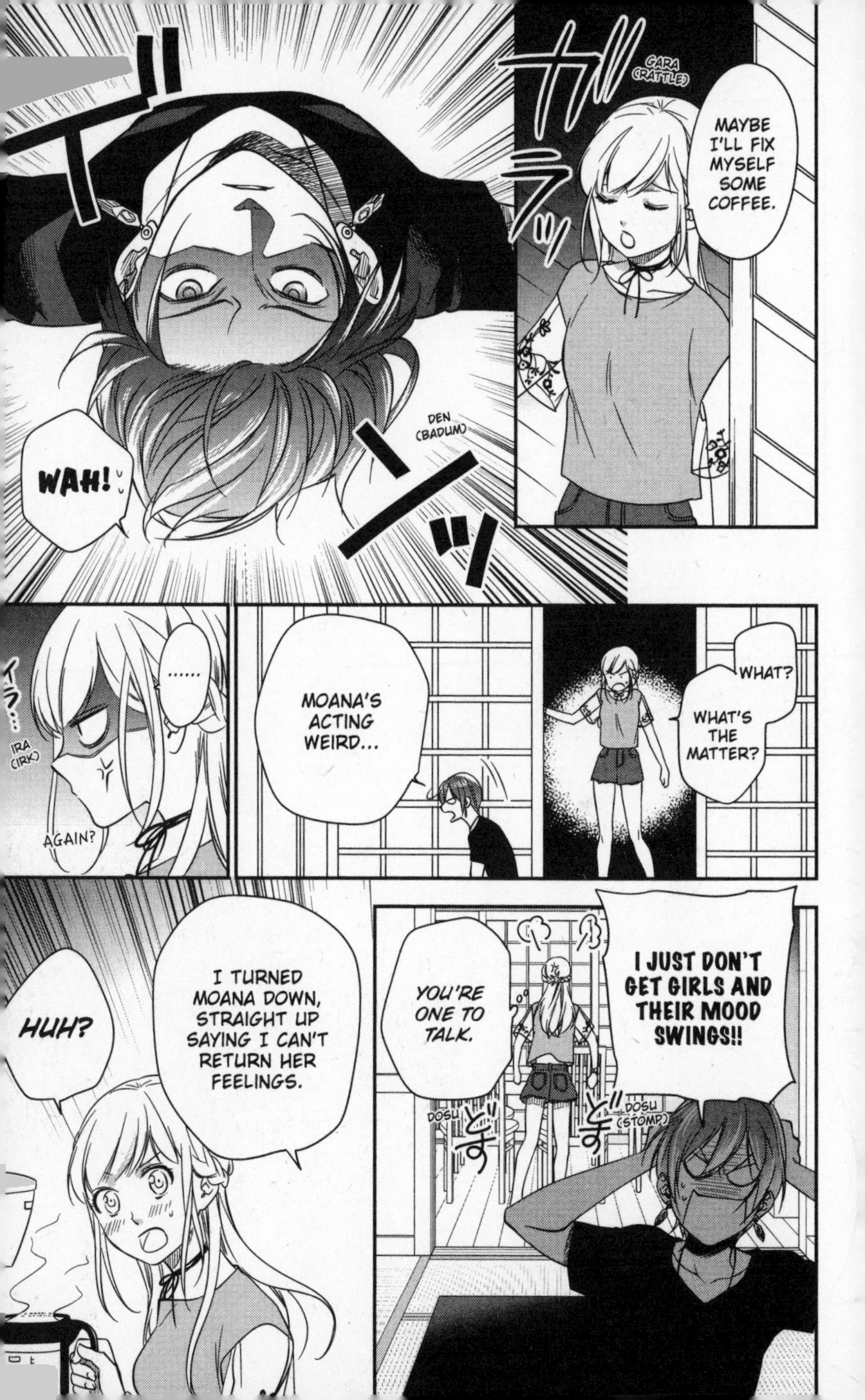
GARA (RATTLE)
MAYBE I'LL FIX MYSELF SOME COFFEE.
DEN (BADUM)
WAH!
WHAT?
WHAT'S THE MATTER?
MOANA'S ACTING WEIRD...
......
IRA (IRK)
AGAIN?
I JUST DON'T GET GIRLS AND THEIR MOOD SWINGS!!
DOSU (STOMP)
DOSU
YOU'RE ONE TO TALK.
I TURNED MOANA DOWN, STRAIGHT UP SAYING I CAN'T RETURN HER FEELINGS.
HUH?

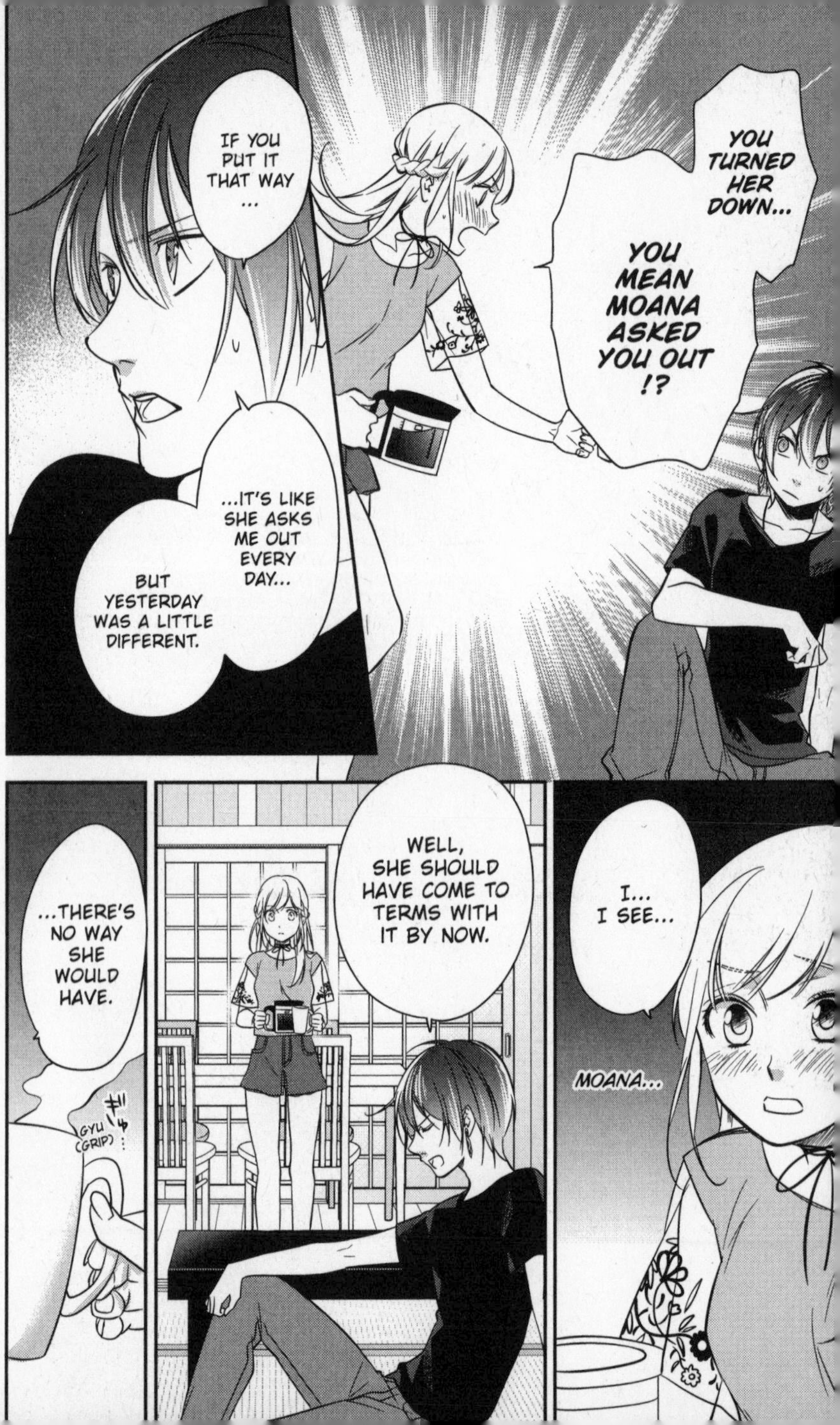
YOU TURNED HER DOWN...
YOU MEAN MOANA ASKED YOU OUT!?
IF YOU PUT IT THAT WAY ...
...IT'S LIKE SHE ASKS ME OUT EVERY DAY...
BUT YESTERDAY WAS A LITTLE DIFFERENT.
I... I SEE...
MOANA...
WELL, SHE SHOULD HAVE COME TO TERMS WITH IT BY NOW.
...THERE'S NO WAY SHE WOULD HAVE.
GYU (GRIP)

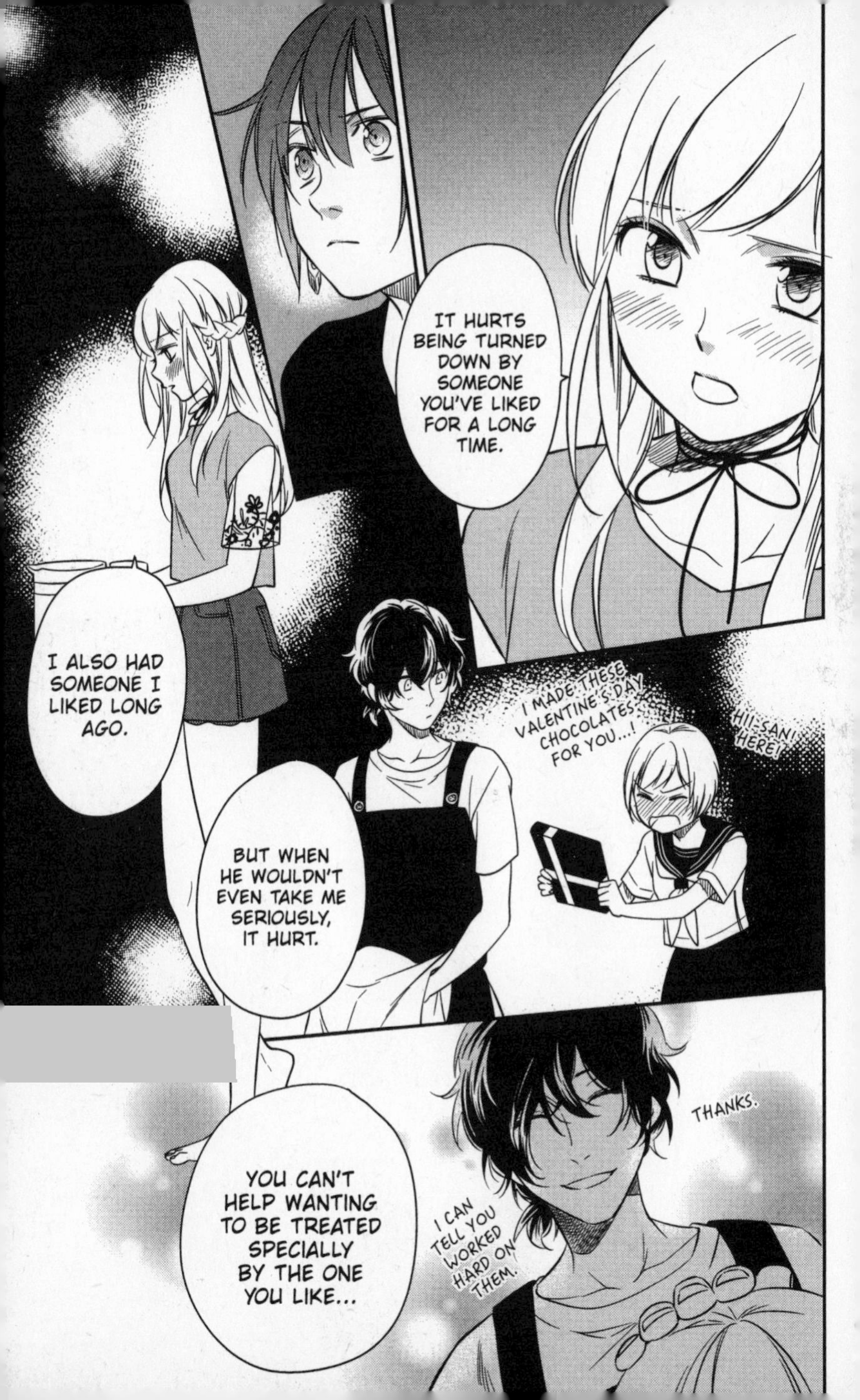
IT HURTS BEING TURNED DOWN BY SOMEONE YOU'VE LIKED FOR A LONG TIME.
I ALSO HAD SOMEONE I LIKED LONG AGO.
HII-SAN! HERE!
I MADE THESE VALENTINE'S DAY CHOCOLATES FOR YOU...!
BUT WHEN HE WOULDN'T EVEN TAKE ME SERIOUSLY, IT HURT.
THANKS.
I CAN TELL YOU WORKED HARD ON THEM.
YOU CAN'T HELP WANTING TO BE TREATED SPECIALLY BY THE ONE YOU LIKE...

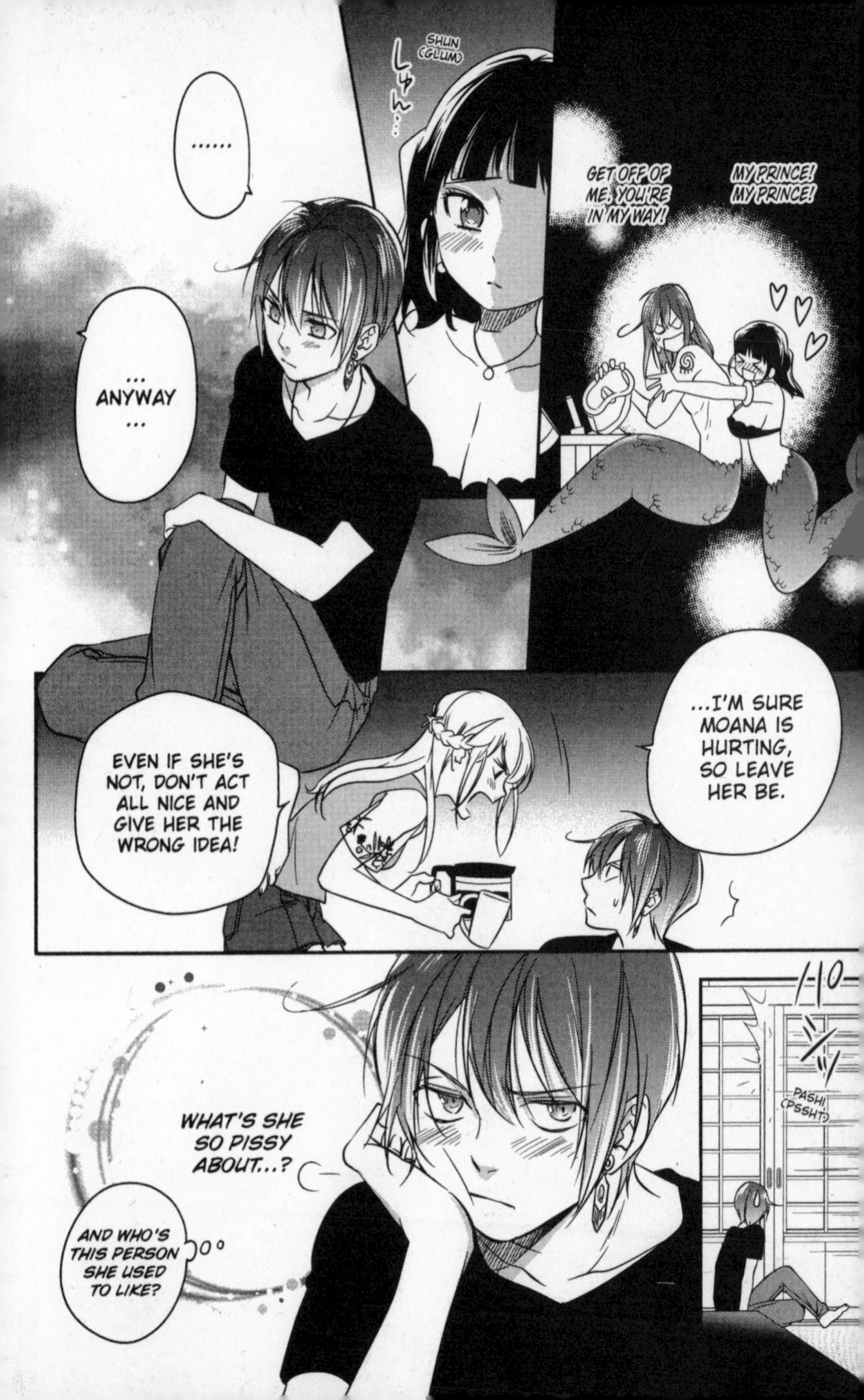
MY PRINCE! MY PRINCE!
GET OFF OF ME, YOU'RE IN MY WAY!
しゅん…
SHUN (GLUM)
......
... ANYWAY ...
...I'M SURE MOANA IS HURTING, SO LEAVE HER BE.
EVEN IF SHE'S NOT, DON'T ACT ALL NICE AND GIVE HER THE WRONG IDEA!
PASHI (PSSHT)
WHAT'S SHE SO PISSY ABOUT...?
AND WHO'S THIS PERSON SHE USED TO LIKE?

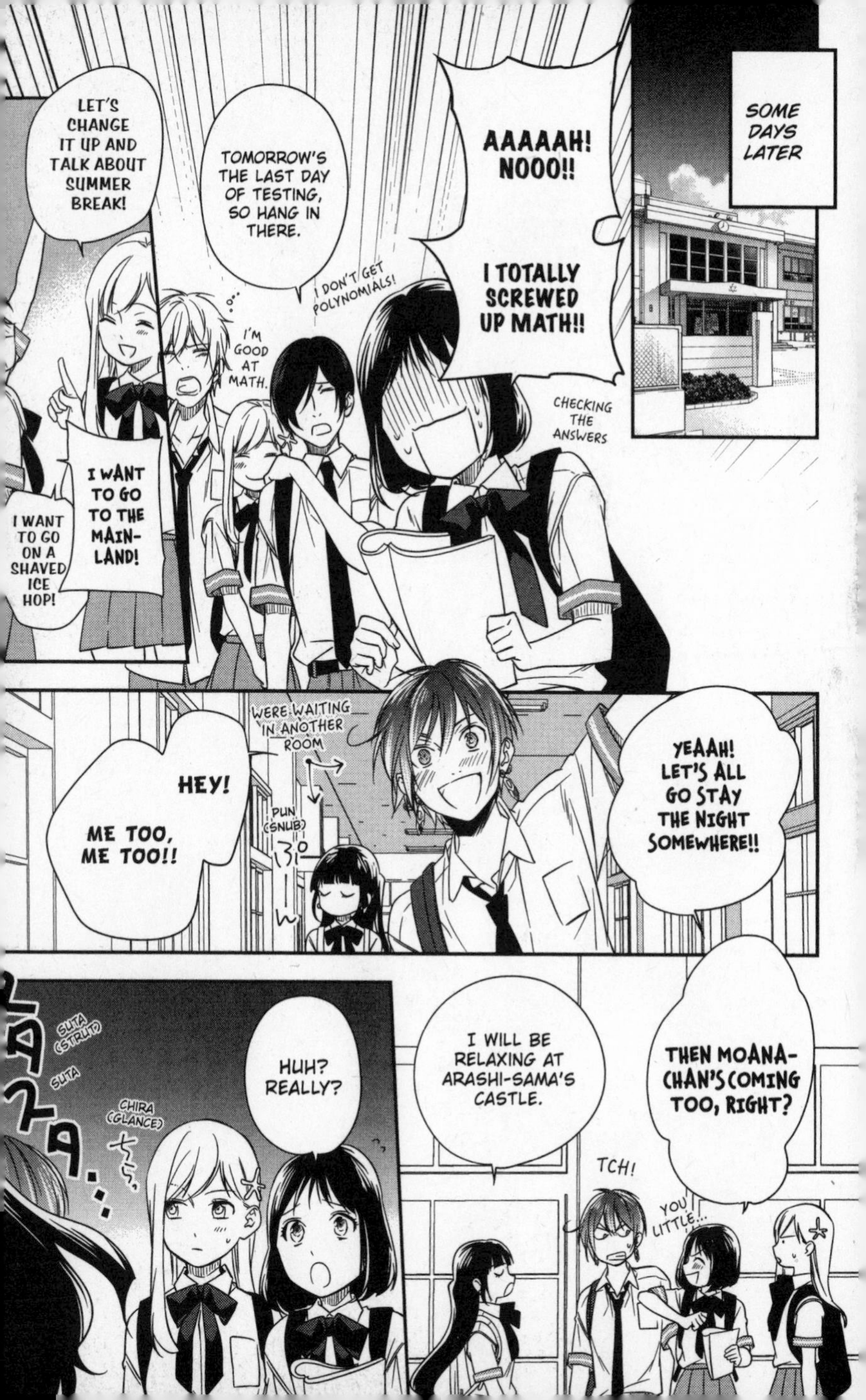

SOME DAYS LATER
AAAAAH! NOOO!!
I TOTALLY SCREWED UP MATH!!
CHECKING THE ANSWERS
I DON'T GET POLYNOMIALS!
TOMORROW'S THE LAST DAY OF TESTING, SO HANG IN THERE.
I'M GOOD AT MATH.
LET'S CHANGE IT UP AND TALK ABOUT SUMMER BREAK!
I WANT TO GO TO THE MAIN-LAND!
I WANT TO GO ON A SHAVED ICE HOP!
YEAAH! LET'S ALL GO STAY THE NIGHT SOMEWHERE!!
WERE WAITING IN ANOTHER ROOM
PUN (SNUB)
HEY!
ME TOO, ME TOO!!
THEN MOANA-CHAN'S COMING TOO, RIGHT?
I WILL BE RELAXING AT ARASHI-SAMA'S CASTLE.
TCH!
YOU LITTLE...
HUH? REALLY?
CHIRA (GLANCE)
SUTA (STRUT)
SUTA

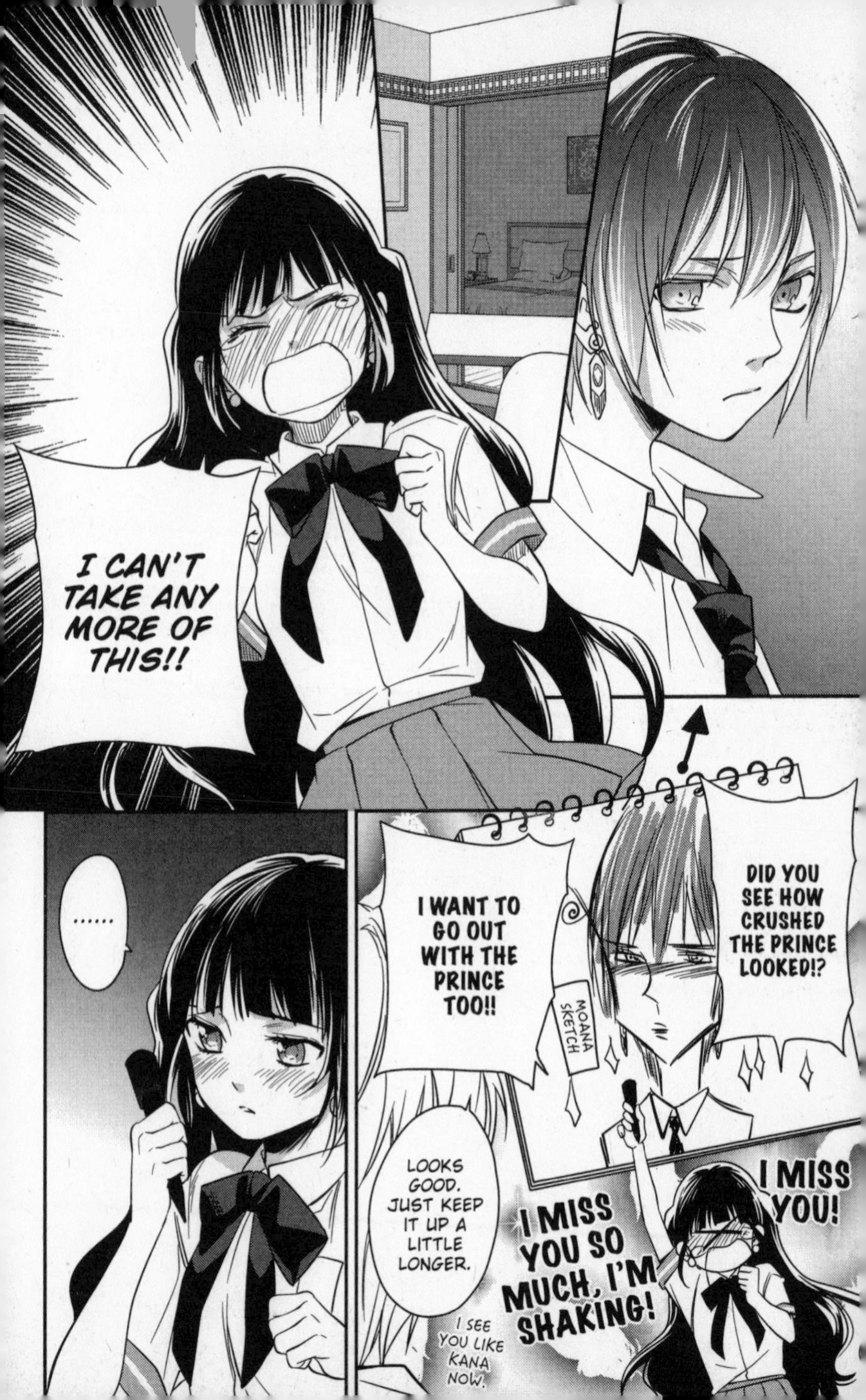
I CAN'T TAKE ANY MORE OF THIS!!
DID YOU SEE HOW CRUSHED THE PRINCE LOOKED!?
I WANT TO GO OUT WITH THE PRINCE TOO!!
MOANA SKETCH
I MISS YOU!
I MISS YOU SO MUCH, I'M SHAKING!
LOOKS GOOD. JUST KEEP IT UP A LITTLE LONGER.
I SEE YOU LIKE KANA NOW.
......

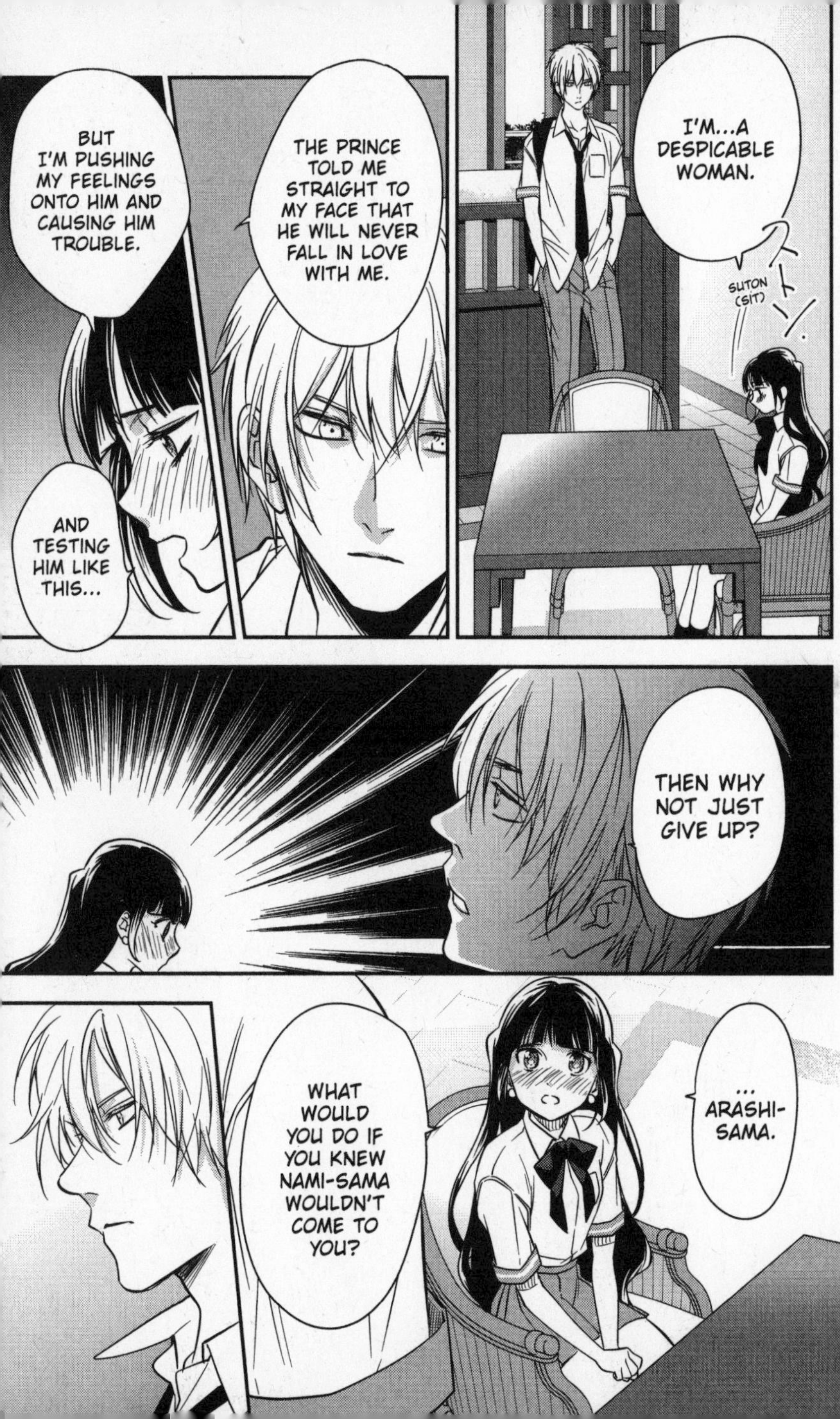
I'M...A DESPICABLE WOMAN.
SUTON (SIT)
THE PRINCE TOLD ME STRAIGHT TO MY FACE THAT HE WILL NEVER FALL IN LOVE WITH ME.
BUT I'M PUSHING MY FEELINGS ONTO HIM AND CAUSING HIM TROUBLE.
AND TESTING HIM LIKE THIS...
THEN WHY NOT JUST GIVE UP?
...ARASHI-SAMA.
WHAT WOULD YOU DO IF YOU KNEW NAMI-SAMA WOULDN'T COME TO YOU?

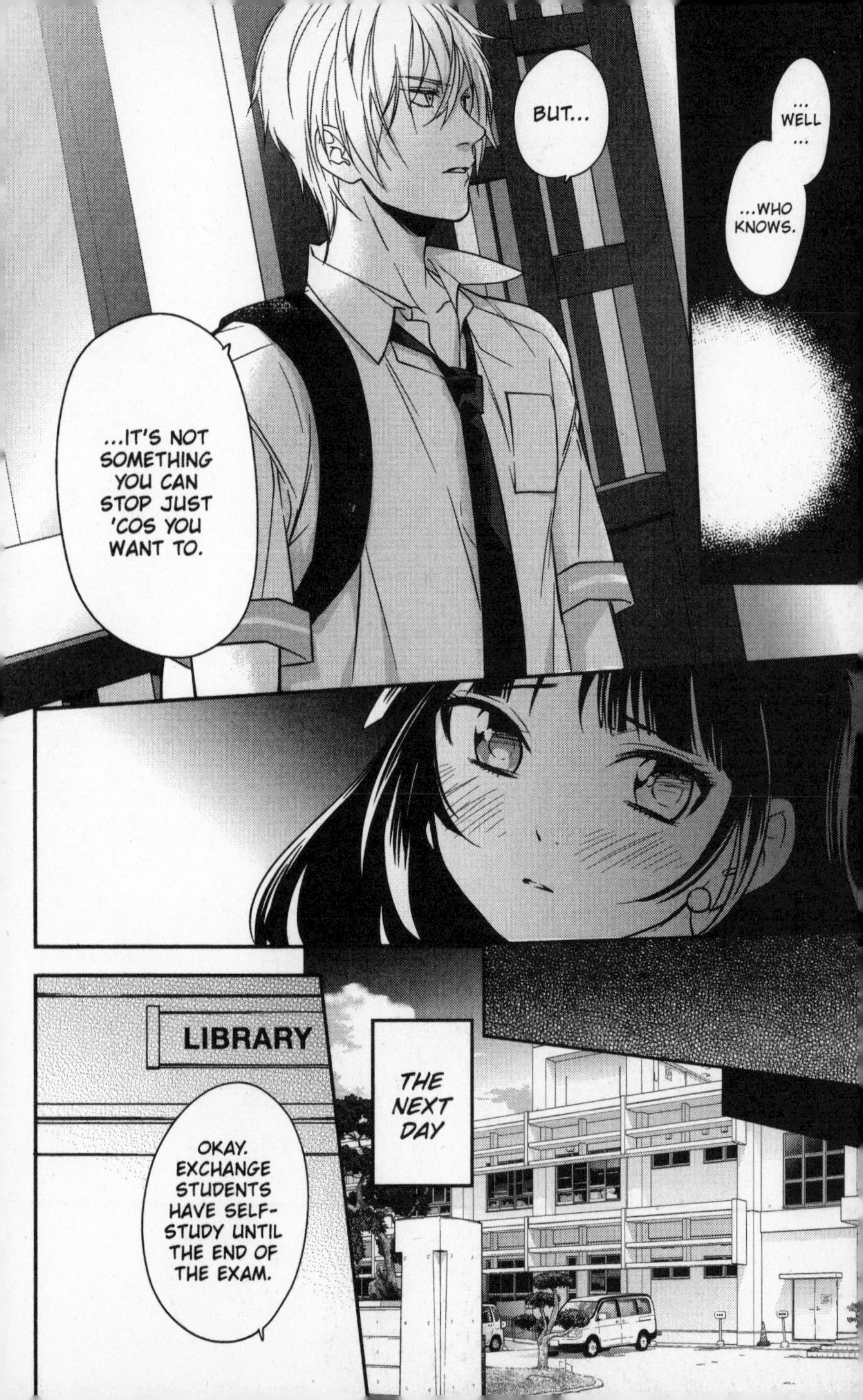
... WELL ... ...WHO KNOWS.
BUT...
...IT'S NOT SOMETHING YOU CAN STOP JUST 'COS YOU WANT TO.
THE NEXT DAY
LIBRARY
OKAY. EXCHANGE STUDENTS HAVE SELF-STUDY UNTIL THE END OF THE EXAM.

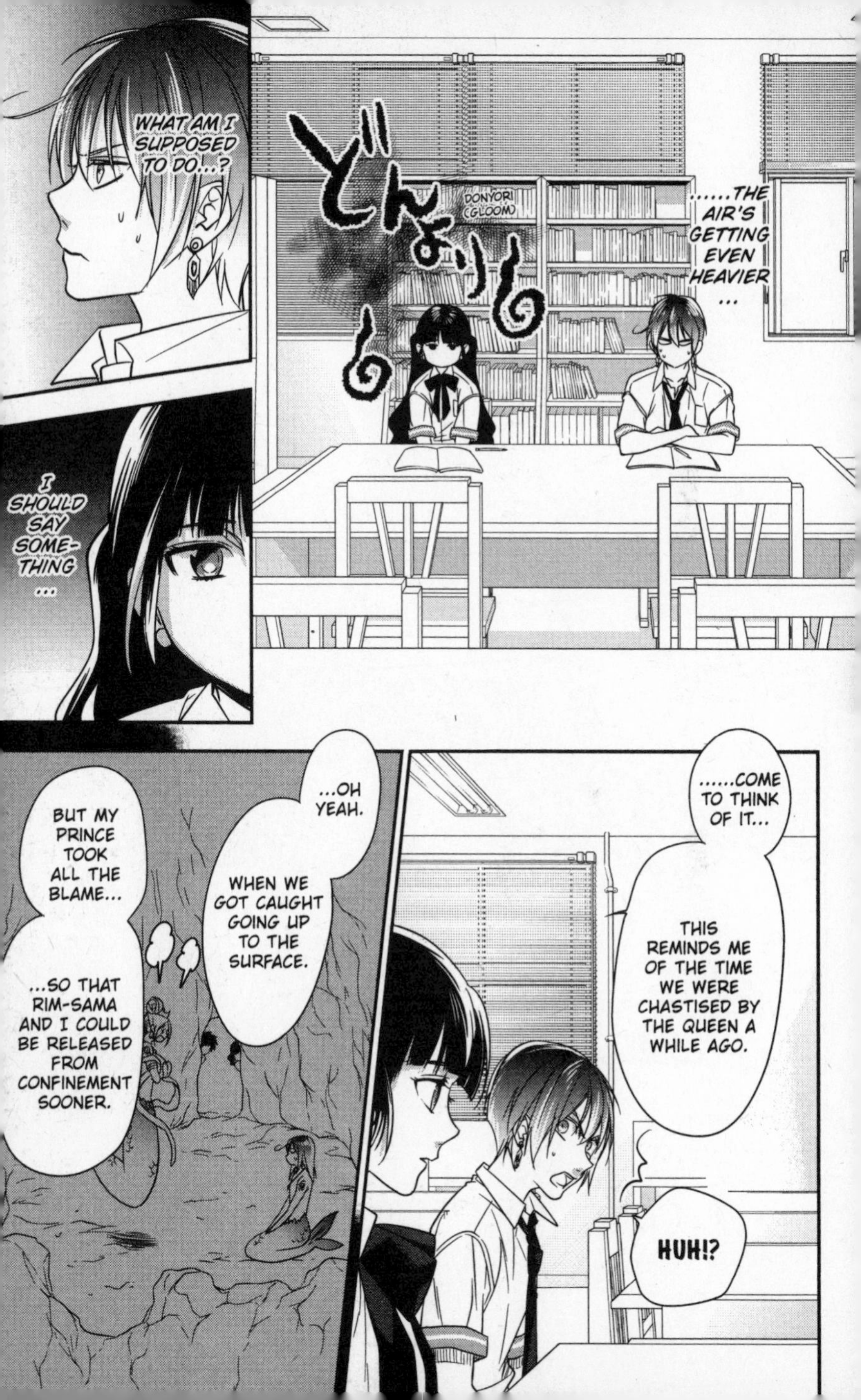
どんより
DONYORI (GLOOM)
......THE AIR'S GETTING EVEN HEAVIER...
WHAT AM I SUPPOSED TO DO...?
I SHOULD SAY SOMETHING...
......COME TO THINK OF IT...
THIS REMINDS ME OF THE TIME WE WERE CHASTISED BY THE QUEEN A WHILE AGO.
HUH!?
...OH YEAH.
WHEN WE GOT CAUGHT GOING UP TO THE SURFACE.
BUT MY PRINCE TOOK ALL THE BLAME...
...SO THAT RIM-SAMA AND I COULD BE RELEASED FROM CONFINEMENT SOONER.

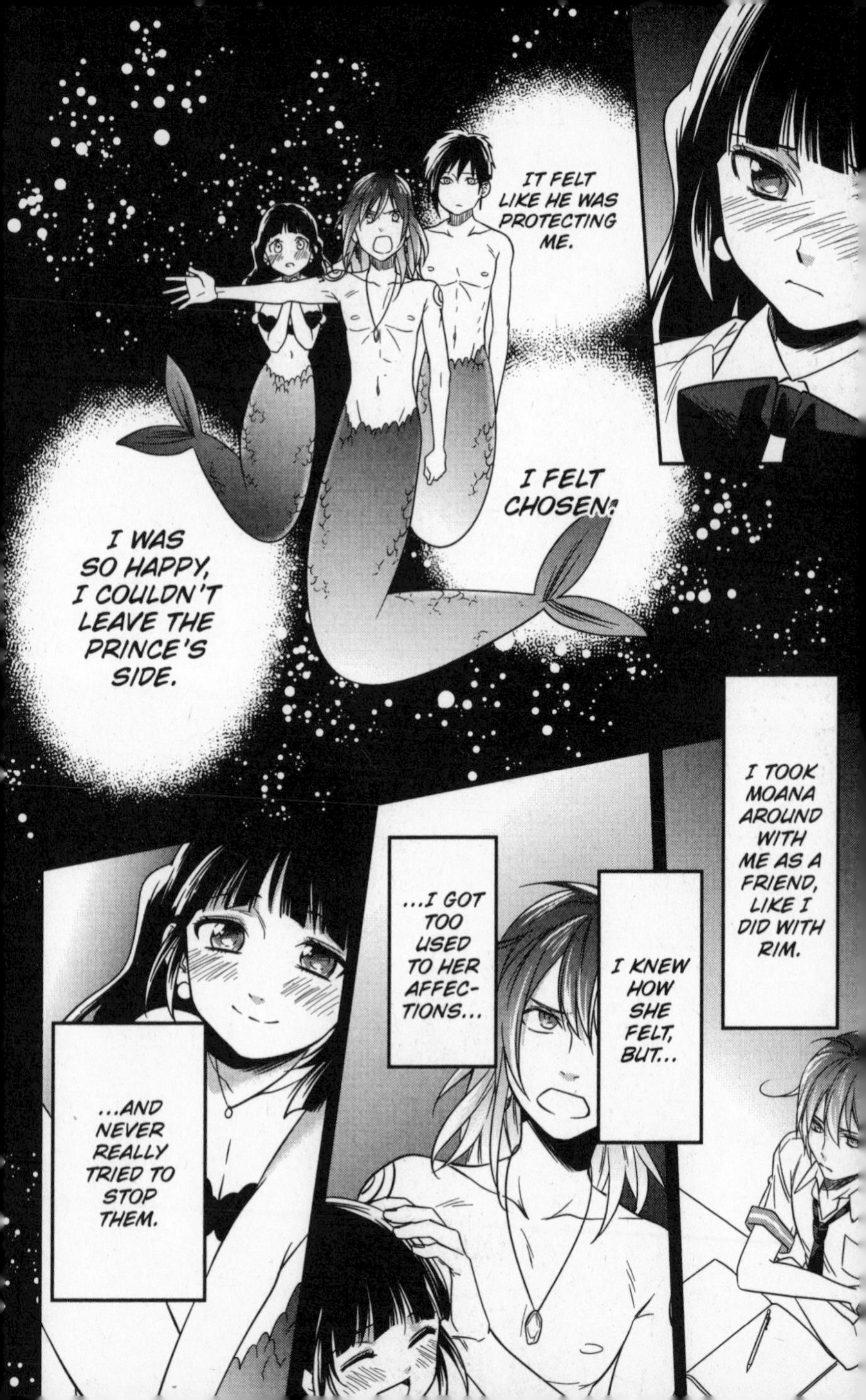
IT FELT LIKE HE WAS PROTECTING ME.
I FELT CHOSEN.
I WAS SO HAPPY, I COULDN'T LEAVE THE PRINCE'S SIDE.
I TOOK MOANA AROUND WITH ME AS A FRIEND, LIKE I DID WITH RIM.
I KNEW HOW SHE FELT, BUT...
...I GOT TOO USED TO HER AFFECTIONS...
...AND NEVER REALLY TRIED TO STOP THEM.

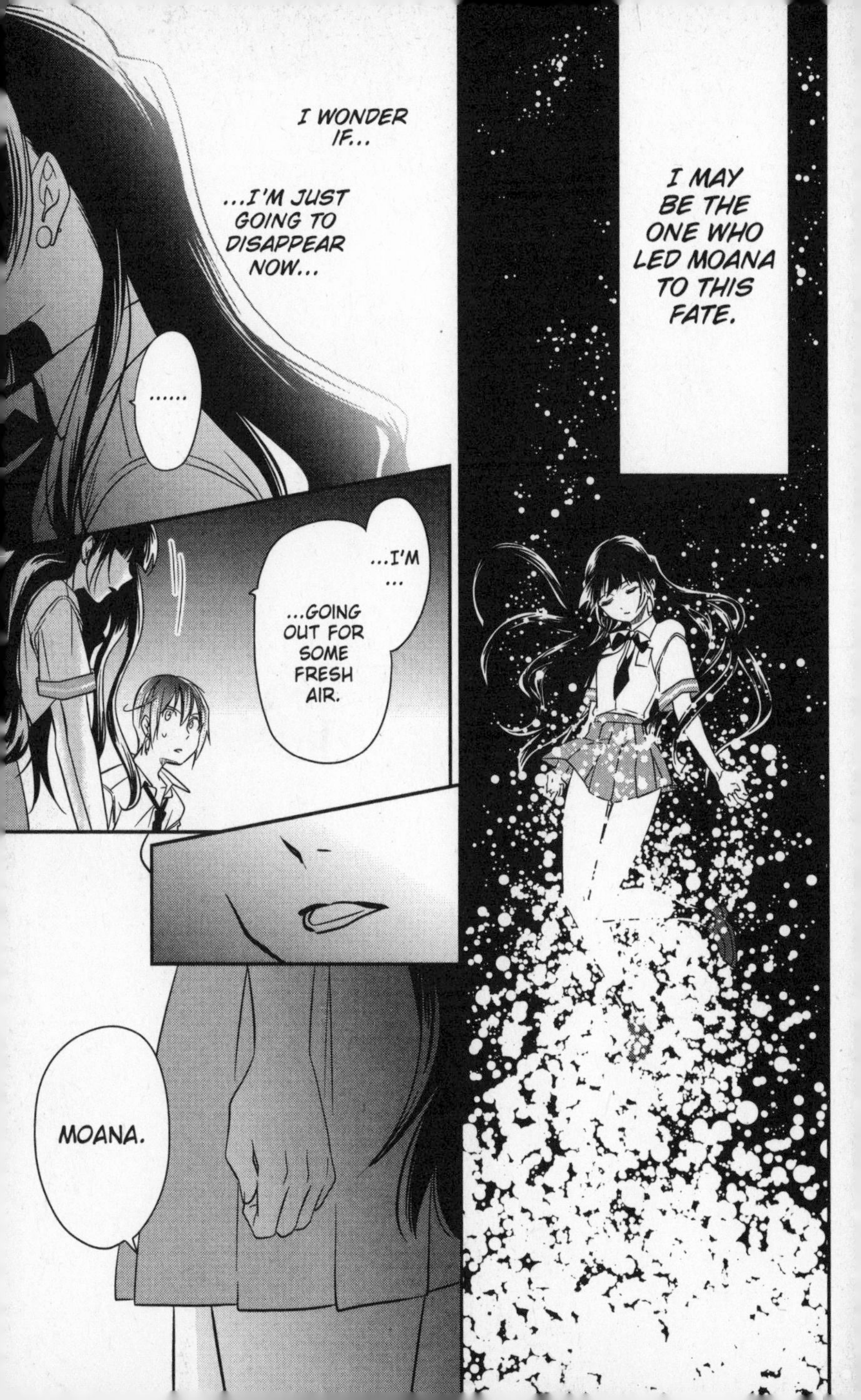
I MAY BE THE ONE WHO LED MOANA TO THIS FATE.
I WONDER IF...
...I'M JUST GOING TO DISAPPEAR NOW...
......
...I'M ...
...GOING OUT FOR SOME FRESH AIR.
MOANA.

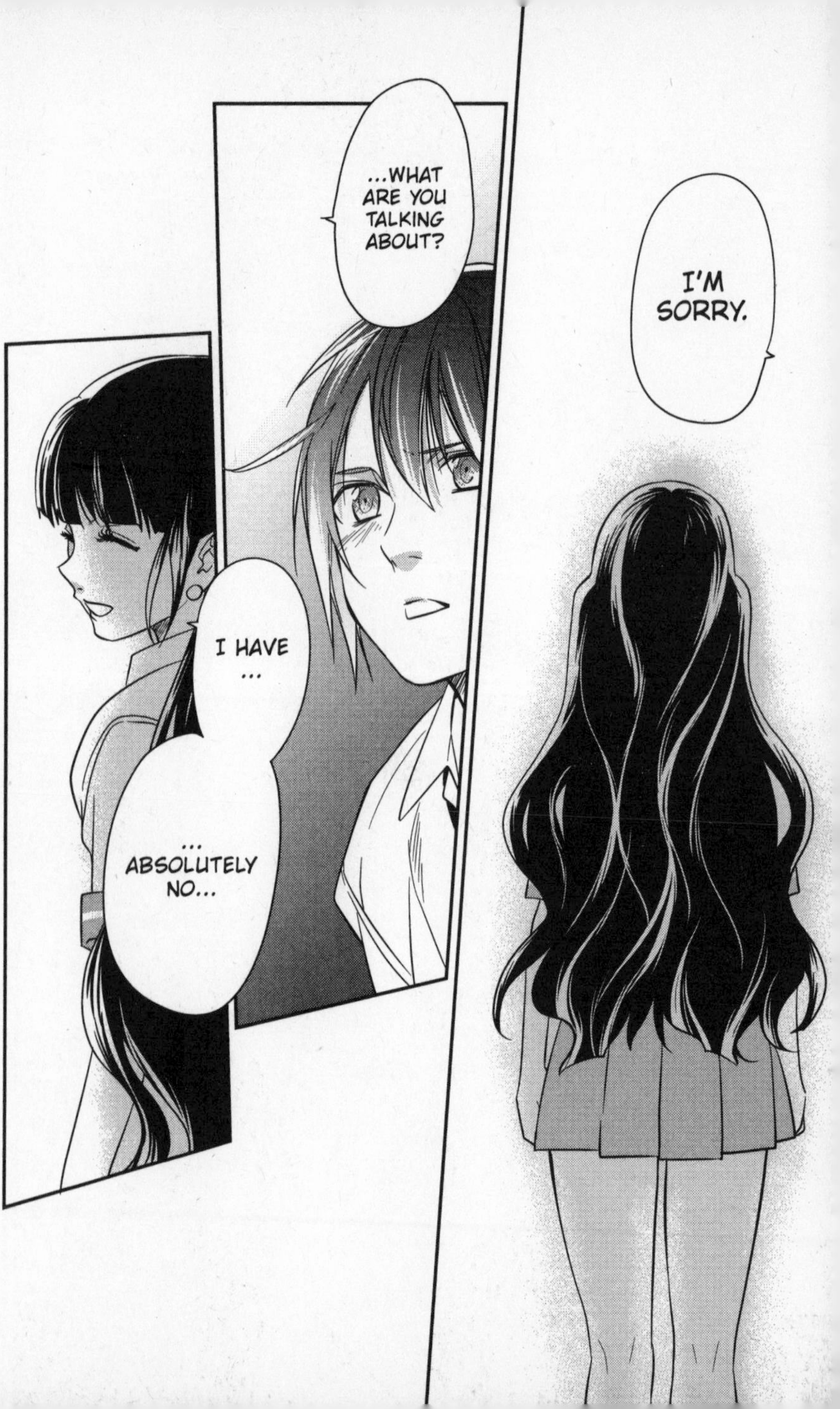
I'M SORRY.
...WHAT ARE YOU TALKING ABOUT?
I HAVE ...
... ABSOLUTELY NO...

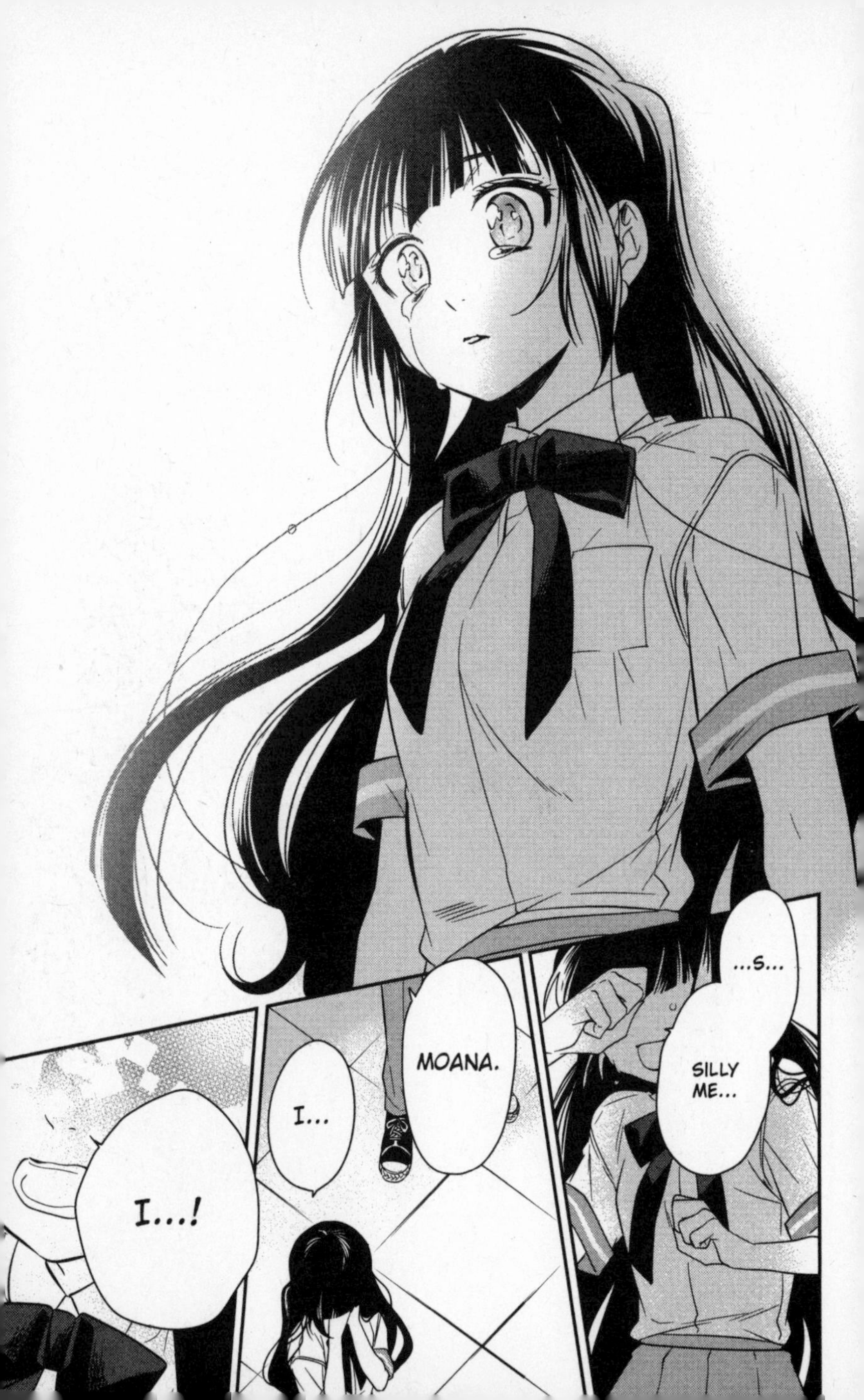
...S...
SILLY ME...
MOANA.
I...
I...!

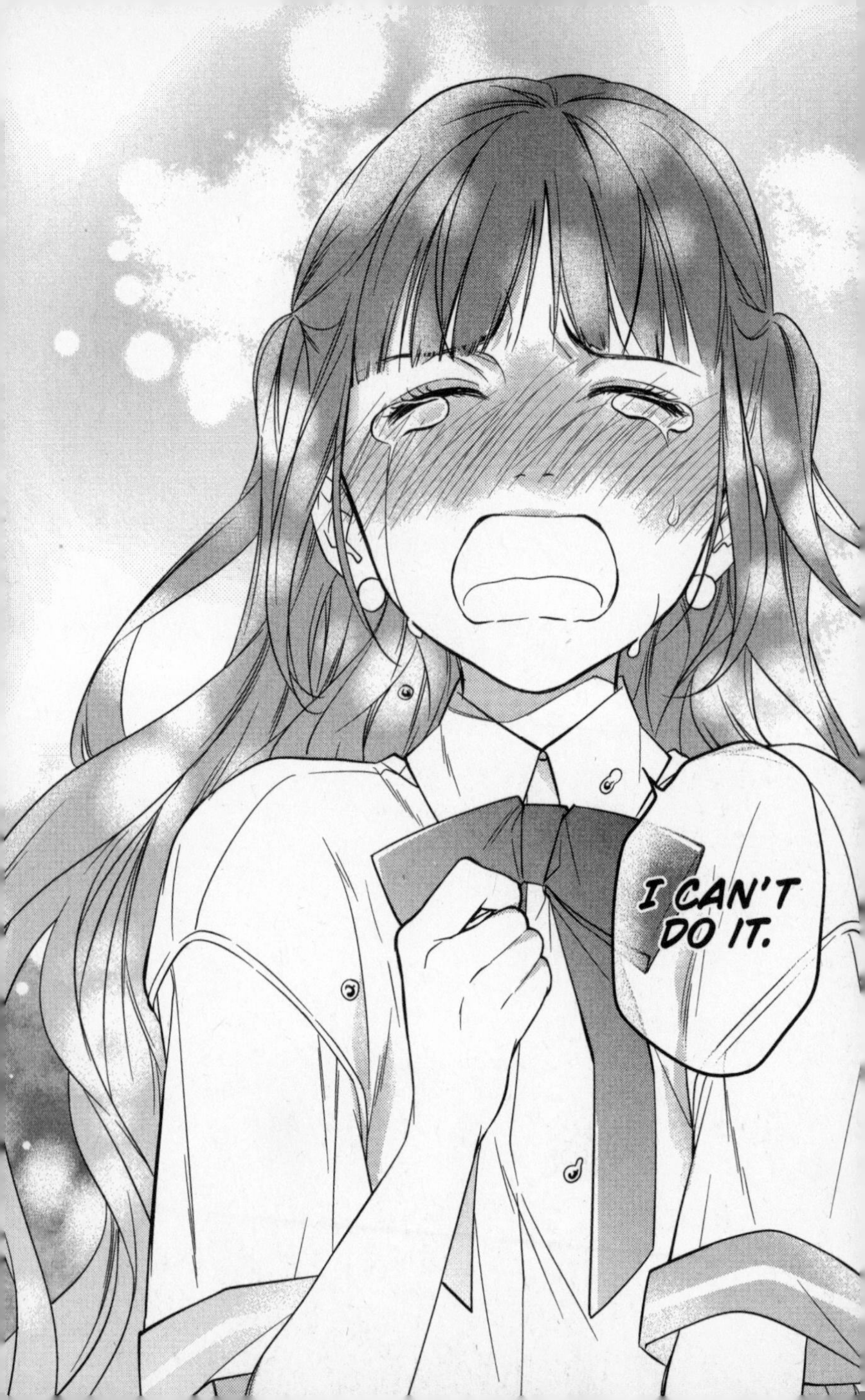
I CAN'T DO IT.

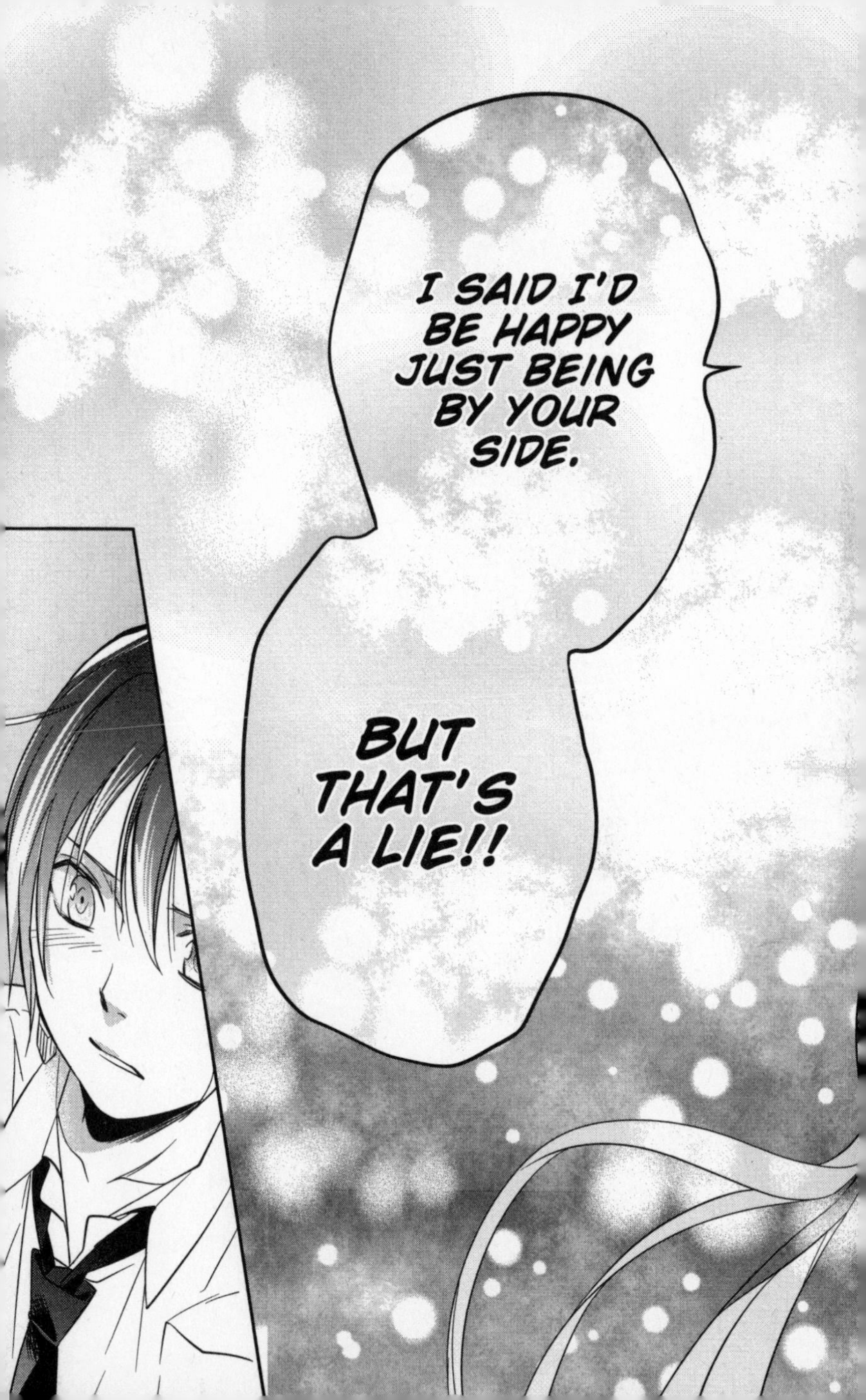
I SAID I'D BE HAPPY JUST BEING BY YOUR SIDE.
BUT THAT'S A LIE!!

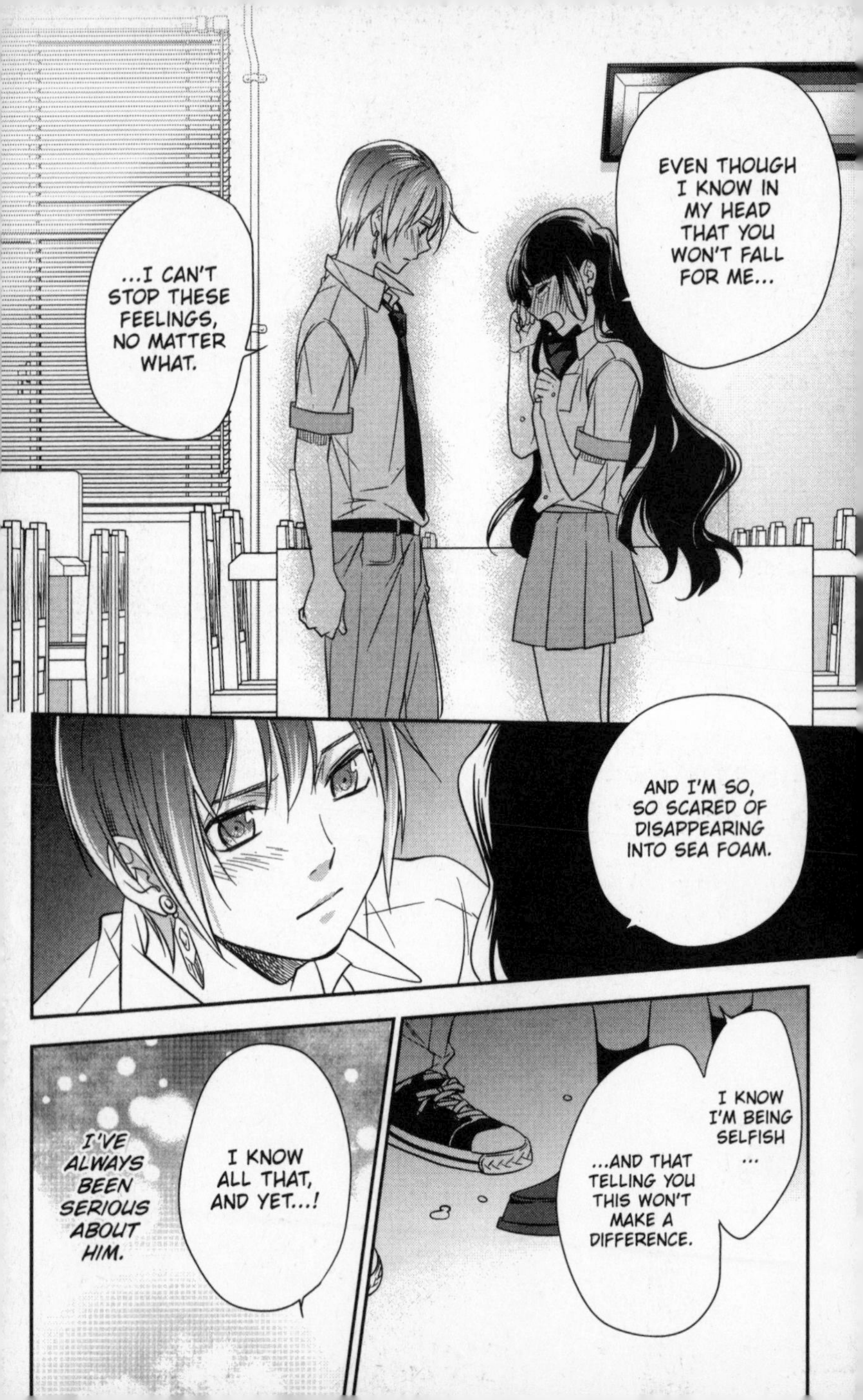
EVEN THOUGH I KNOW IN MY HEAD THAT YOU WON'T FALL FOR ME...
...I CAN'T STOP THESE FEELINGS, NO MATTER WHAT.
AND I'M SO, SO SCARED OF DISAPPEARING INTO SEA FOAM.
I KNOW I'M BEING SELFISH ...
...AND THAT TELLING YOU THIS WON'T MAKE A DIFFERENCE.
I KNOW ALL THAT, AND YET...!
I'VE ALWAYS BEEN SERIOUS ABOUT HIM.

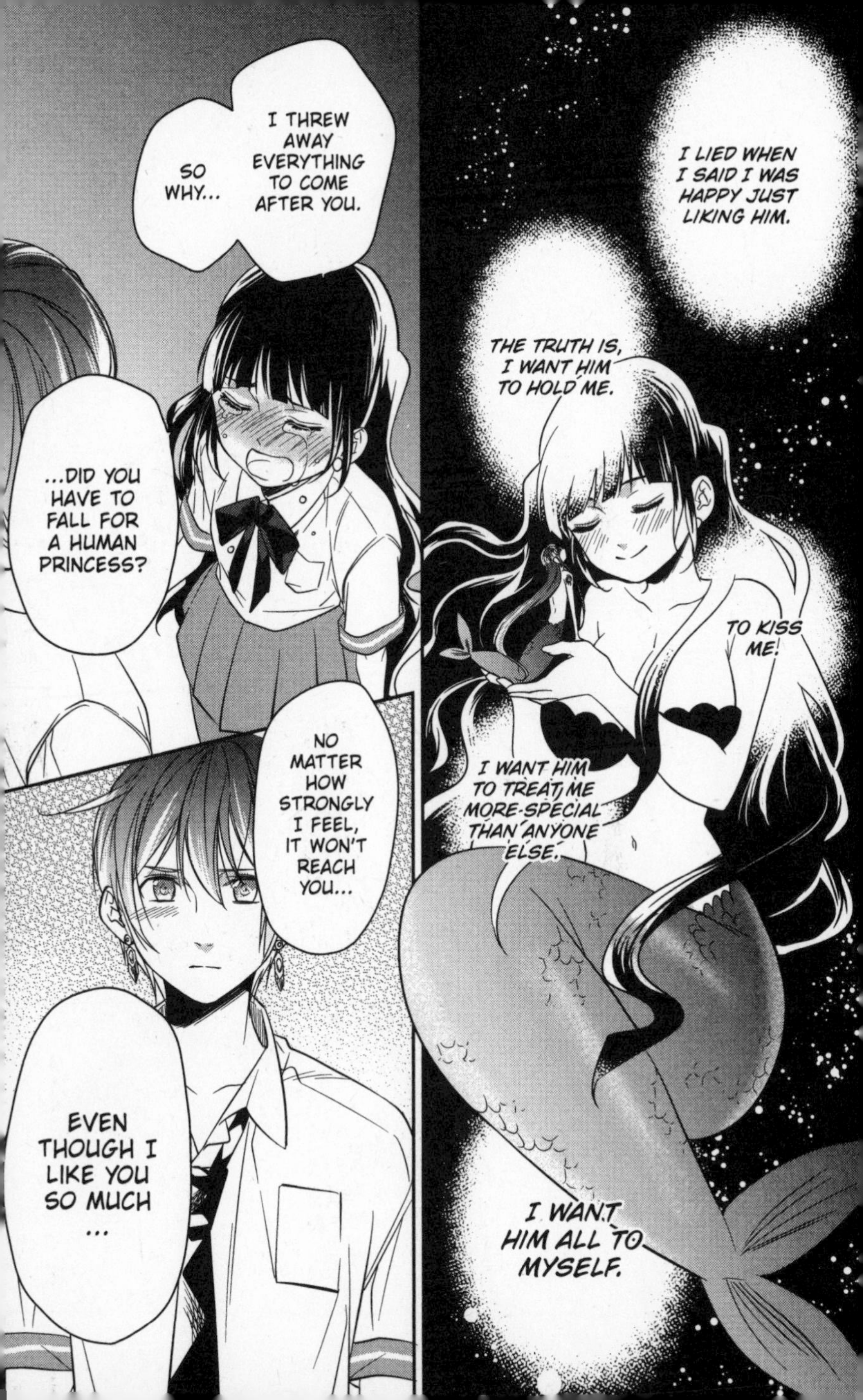
I LIED WHEN I SAID I WAS HAPPY JUST LIKING HIM.
THE TRUTH IS, I WANT HIM TO HOLD ME.
TO KISS ME.
I WANT HIM TO TREAT ME MORE SPECIAL THAN ANYONE ELSE.
I WANT HIM ALL TO MYSELF.
I THREW AWAY EVERYTHING TO COME AFTER YOU.
SO WHY...
...DID YOU HAVE TO FALL FOR A HUMAN PRINCESS?
NO MATTER HOW STRONGLY I FEEL, IT WON'T REACH YOU...
EVEN THOUGH I LIKE YOU SO MUCH ...

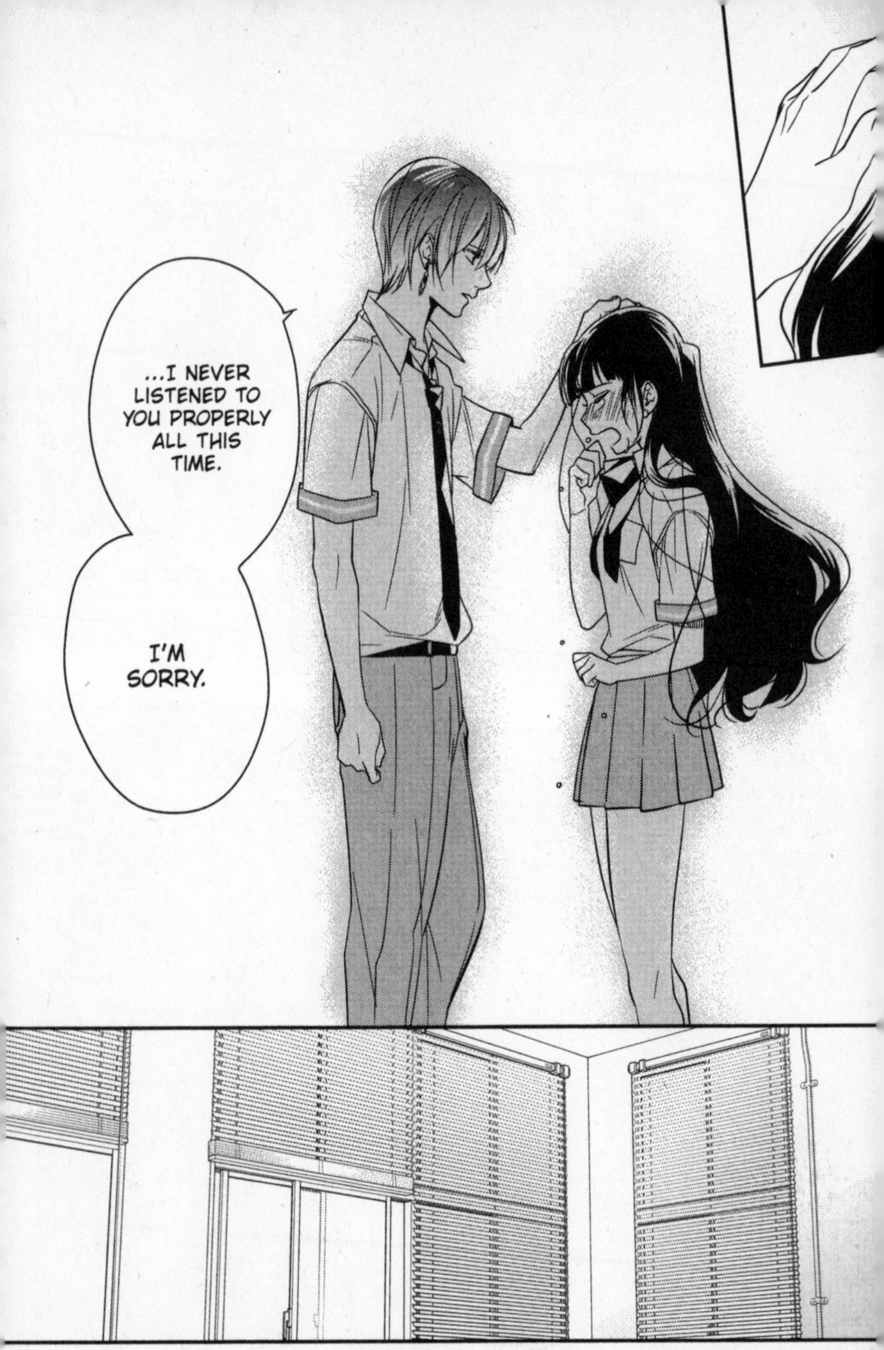
...I NEVER LISTENED TO YOU PROPERLY ALL THIS TIME.
I'M SORRY.

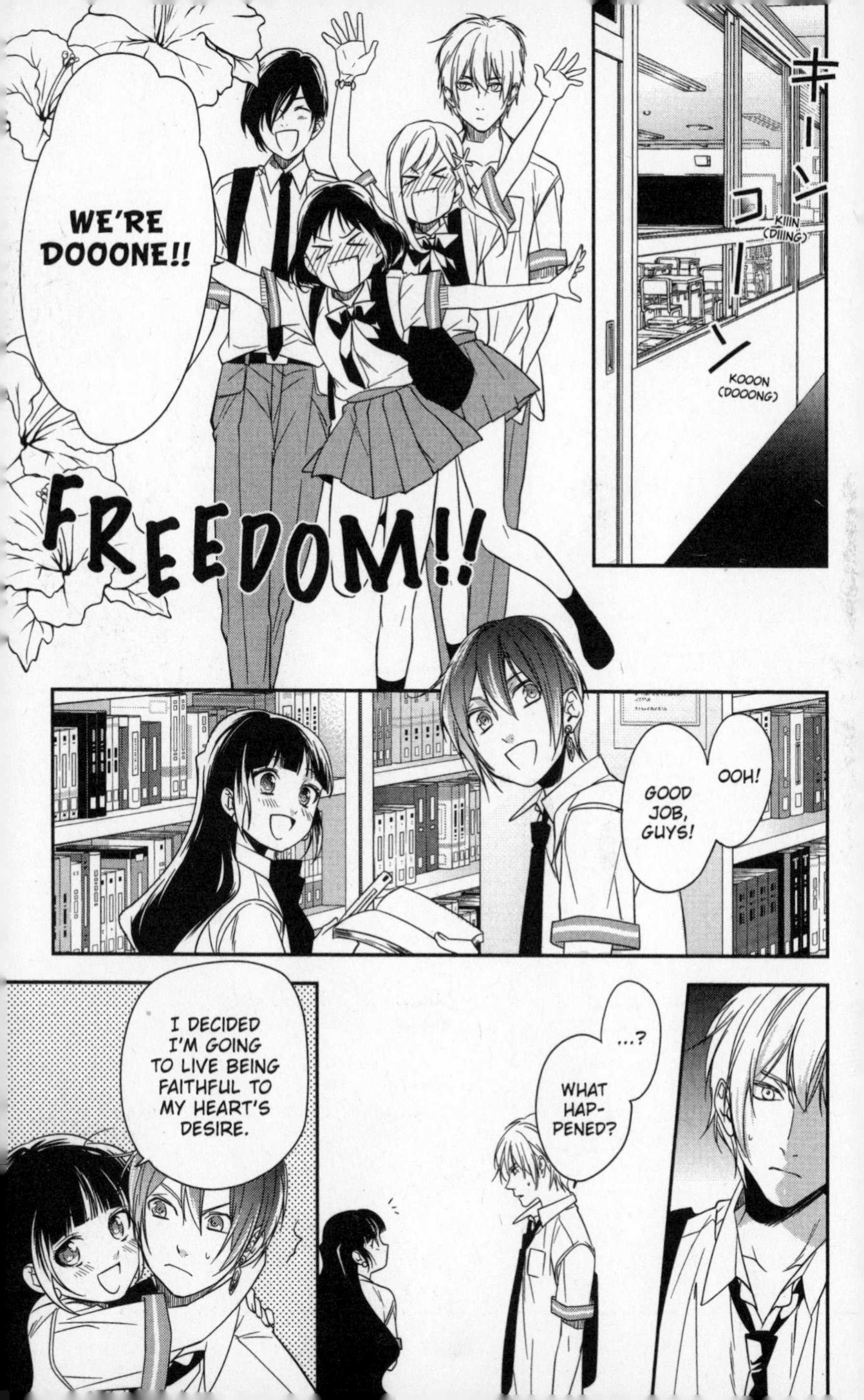
キーンコーン
KIIN (DIIING)
KOOON (DOOONG)
WE'RE DOOONE!!
FREEDOM!!
OOH! GOOD JOB, GUYS!
...?
WHAT HAP-PENED?
I DECIDED I'M GOING TO LIVE BEING FAITHFUL TO MY HEART'S DESIRE.

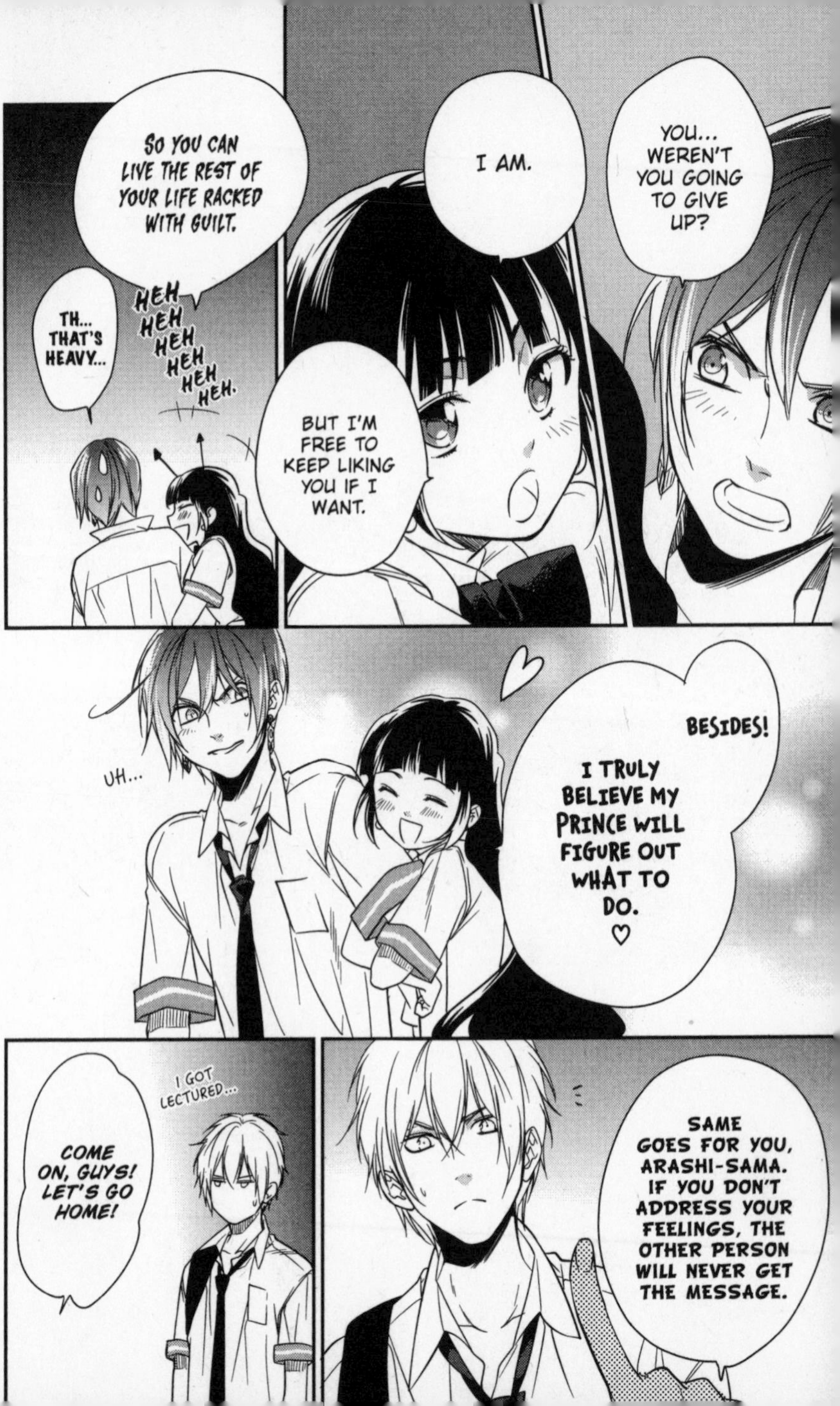
YOU... WEREN'T YOU GOING TO GIVE UP?
I AM.
BUT I'M FREE TO KEEP LIKING YOU IF I WANT.
SO YOU CAN LIVE THE REST OF YOUR LIFE RACKED WITH GUILT.
HEH HEH HEH HEH HEH HEH.
TH... THAT'S HEAVY...
BESIDES!
I TRULY BELIEVE MY PRINCE WILL FIGURE OUT WHAT TO DO. ♡
UH...
SAME GOES FOR YOU, ARASHI-SAMA. IF YOU DON'T ADDRESS YOUR FEELINGS, THE OTHER PERSON WILL NEVER GET THE MESSAGE.
I GOT LECTURED...
COME ON, GUYS! LET'S GO HOME!

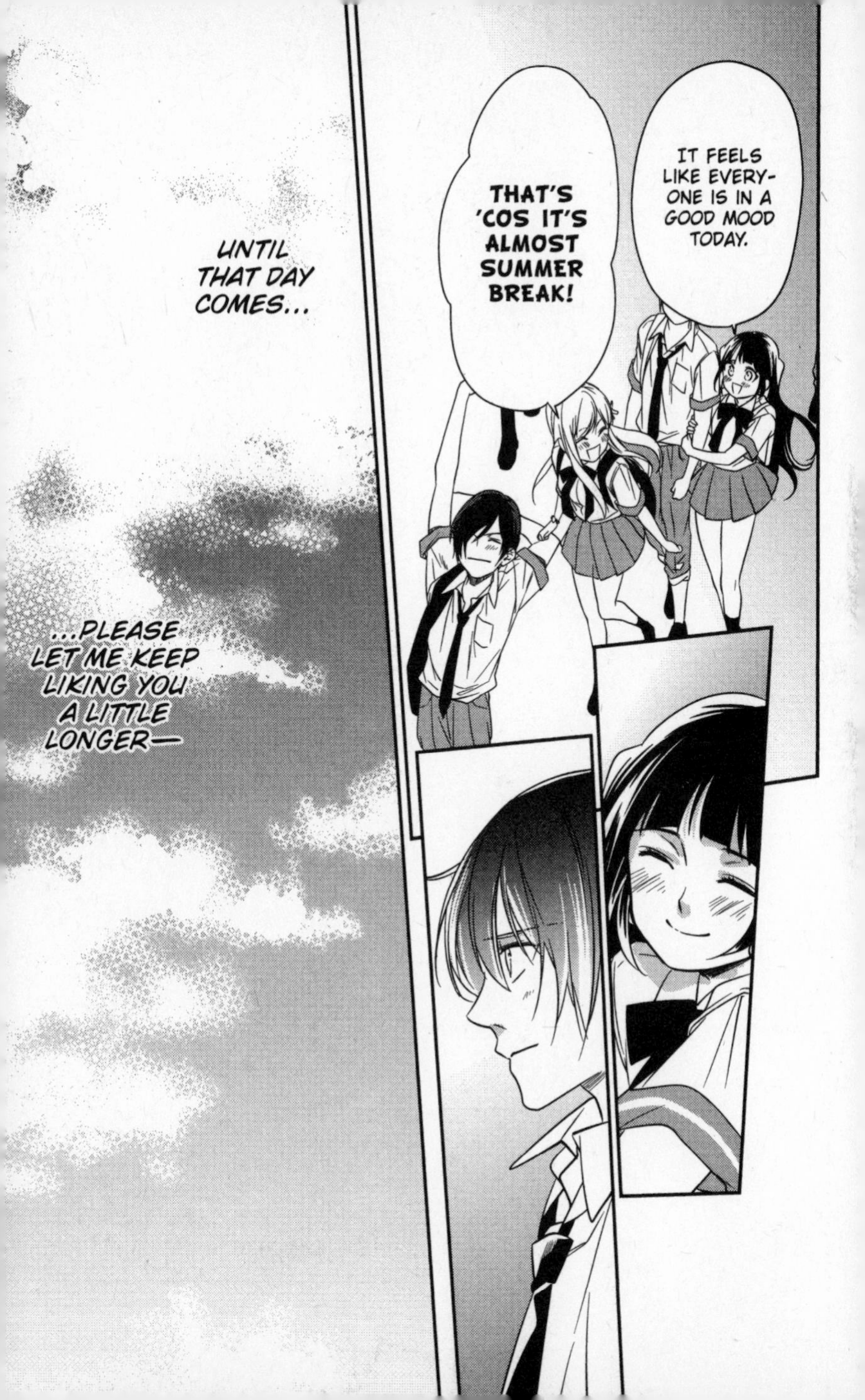
IT FEELS LIKE EVERY-ONE IS IN A GOOD MOOD TODAY.
THAT'S 'COS IT'S ALMOST SUMMER BREAK!
UNTIL THAT DAY COMES...
...PLEASE LET ME KEEP LIKING YOU A LITTLE LONGER—

MERMAID BOYS

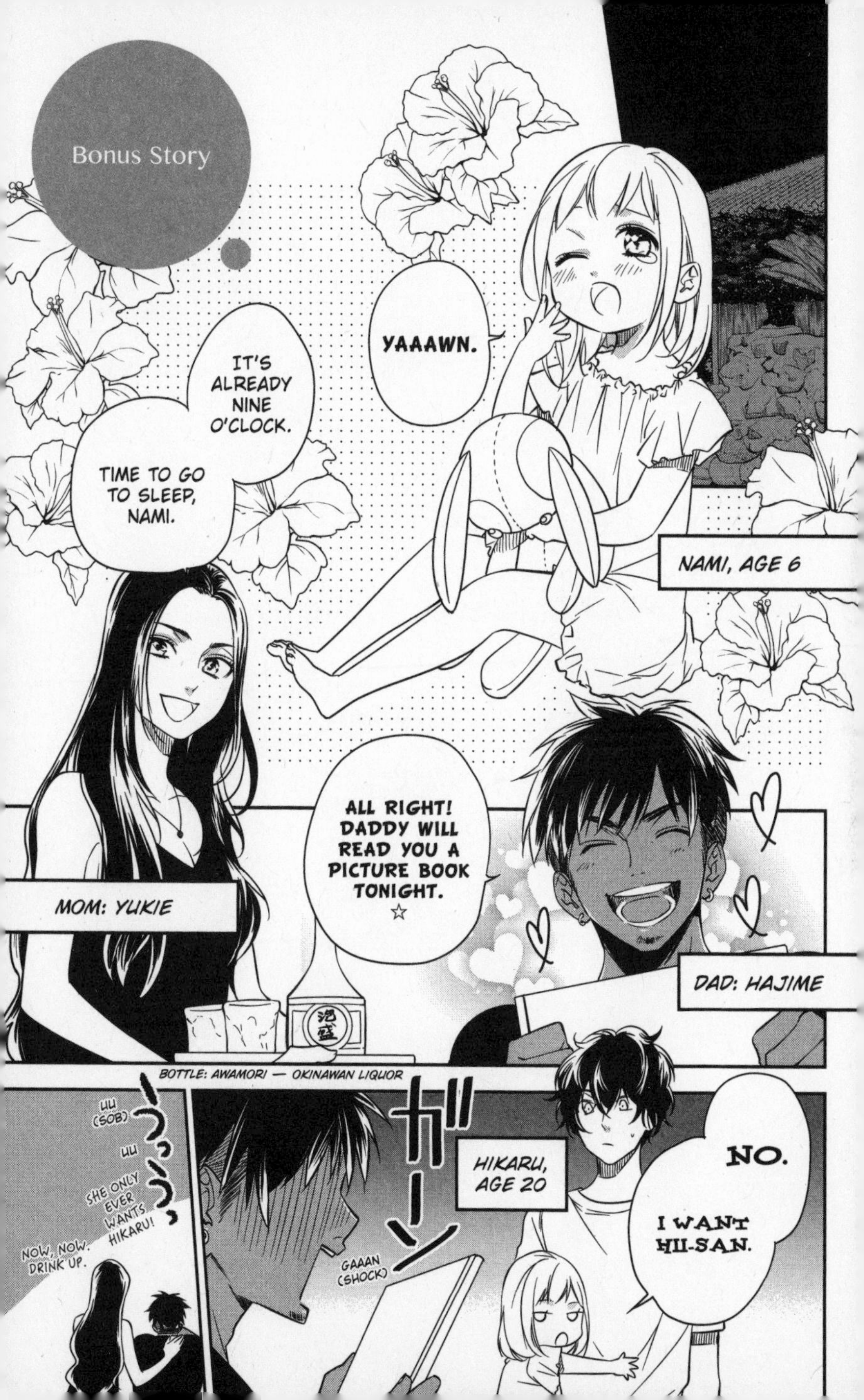
Bonus Story
YAAAWN.
NAMI, AGE 6
IT'S ALREADY NINE O'CLOCK.
TIME TO GO TO SLEEP, NAMI.
DAD: HAJIME
ALL RIGHT! DADDY WILL READ YOU A PICTURE BOOK TONIGHT. ☆
MOM: YUKIE
BOTTLE: AWAMORI — OKINAWAN LIQUOR
NO.
HIKARU, AGE 20
I WANT HII-SAN.
GAAAN (SHOCK)
UU (SOB)
UU
SHE ONLY EVER WANTS HIKARU!
NOW, NOW. DRINK UP.

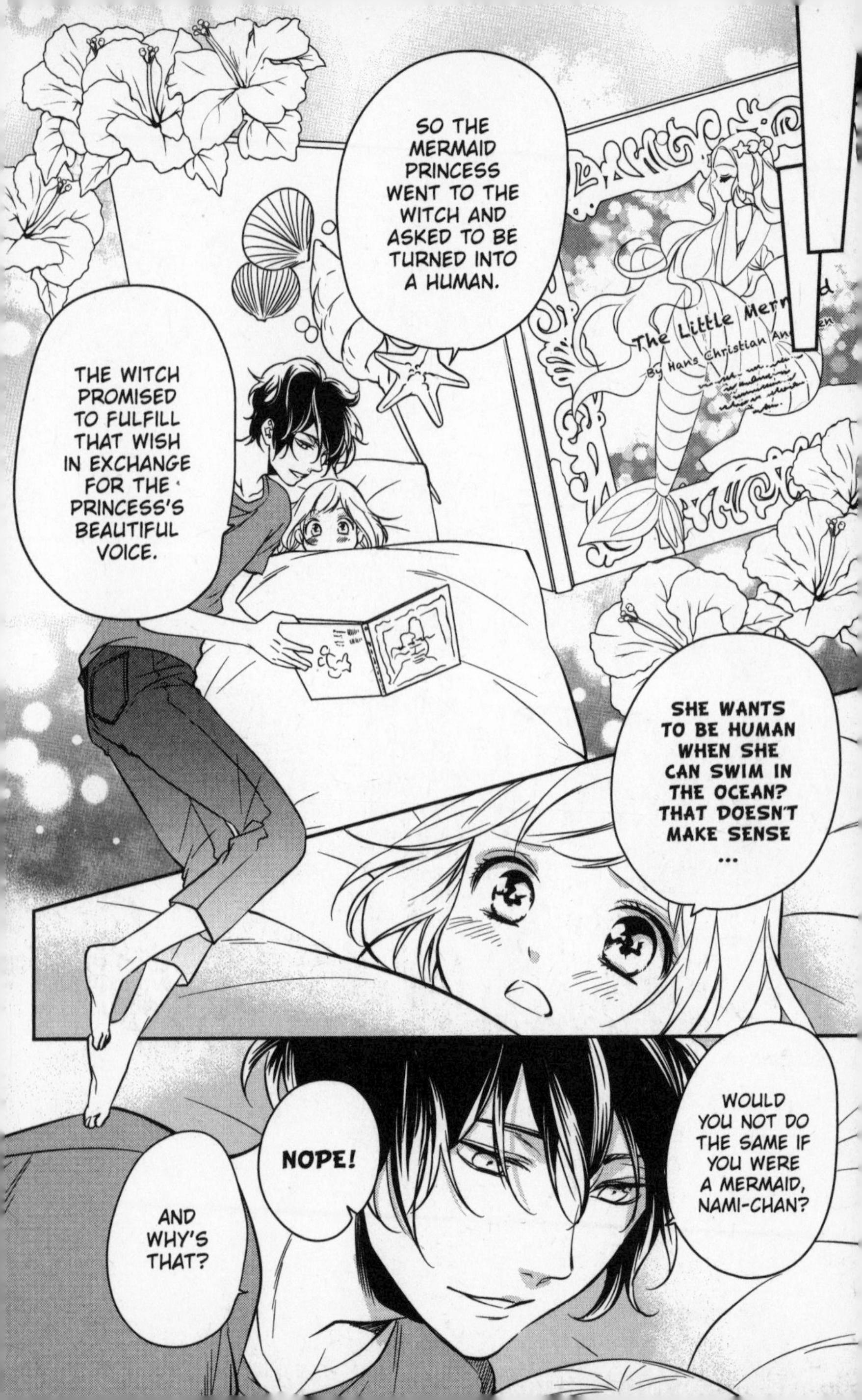
SO THE MERMAID PRINCESS WENT TO THE WITCH AND ASKED TO BE TURNED INTO A HUMAN.
THE WITCH PROMISED TO FULFILL THAT WISH IN EXCHANGE FOR THE PRINCESS'S BEAUTIFUL VOICE.
The Little Mer
By Hans Christian An
SHE WANTS TO BE HUMAN WHEN SHE CAN SWIM IN THE OCEAN? THAT DOESN'T MAKE SENSE ...
WOULD YOU NOT DO THE SAME IF YOU WERE A MERMAID, NAMI-CHAN?
NOPE!
AND WHY'S THAT?

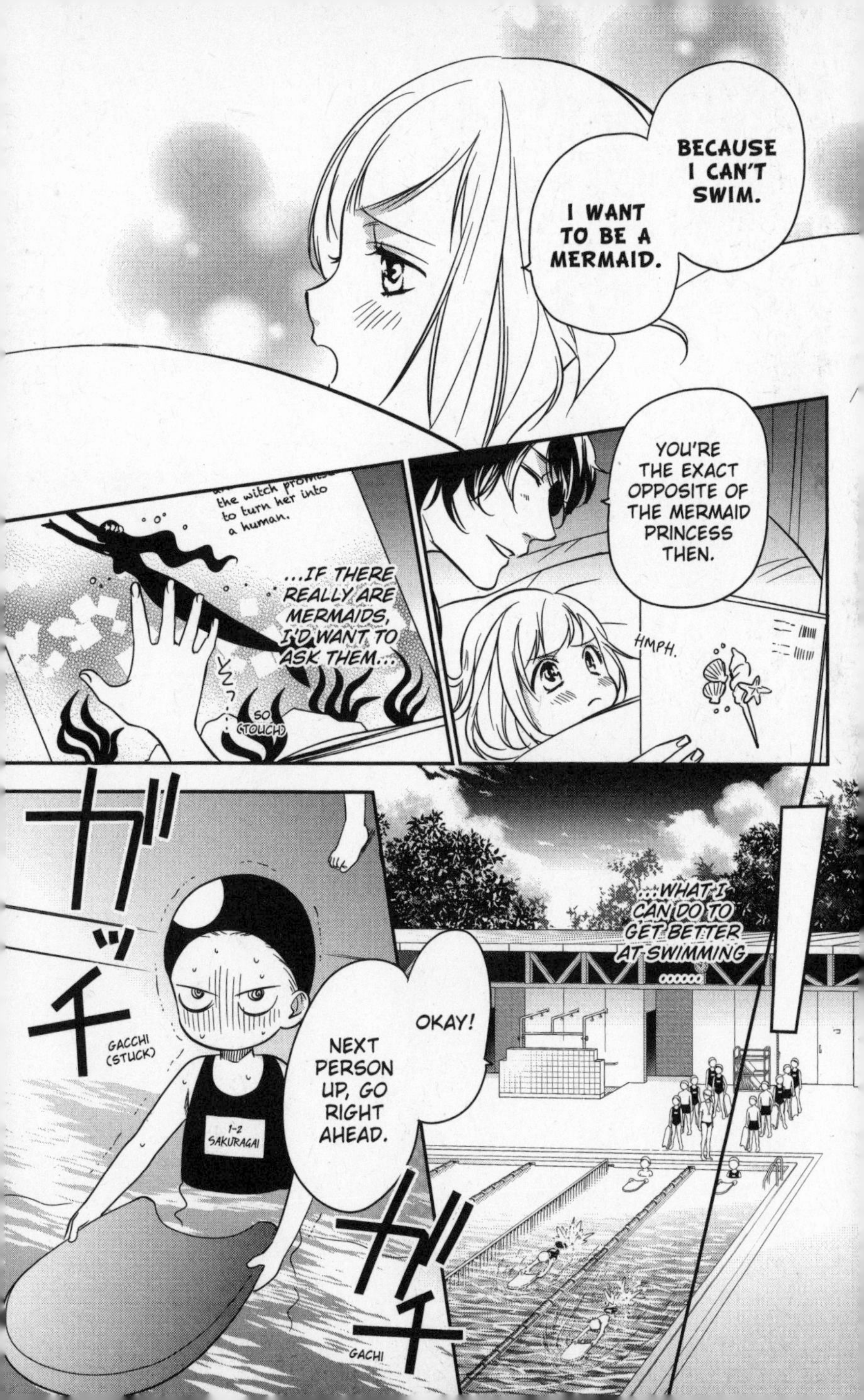
BECAUSE I CAN'T SWIM.
I WANT TO BE A MERMAID.
YOU'RE THE EXACT OPPOSITE OF THE MERMAID PRINCESS THEN.
HMPH.
the witch promise to turn her into a human.
...IF THERE REALLY ARE MERMAIDS, I'D WANT TO ASK THEM...
SO (TOUCH)
...WHAT I CAN DO TO GET BETTER AT SWIMMING ......
OKAY!
NEXT PERSON UP, GO RIGHT AHEAD.
GACCHI (STUCK)
1-2 SAKURAGAI
GACHI

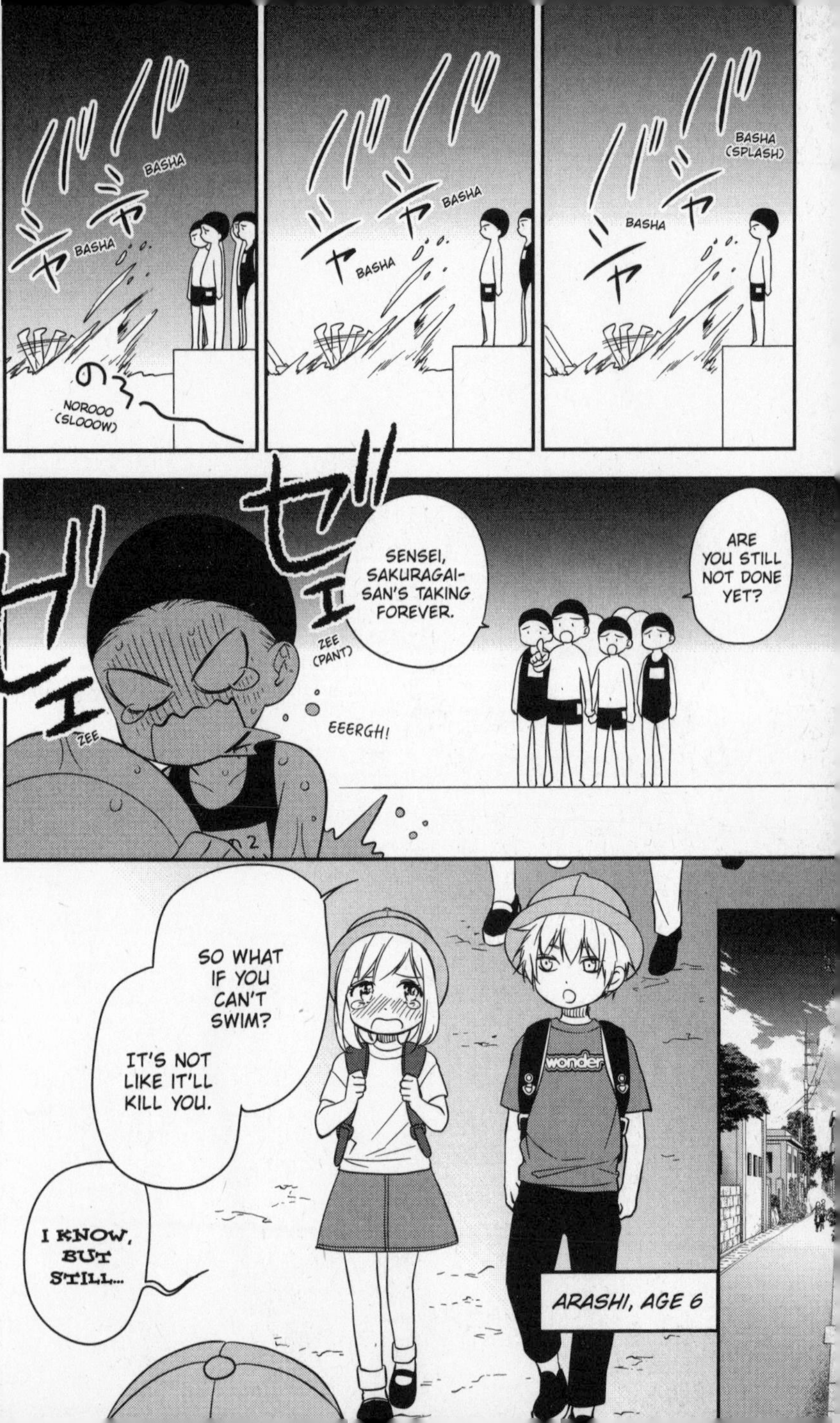
BASHA (SPLASH)
BASHA
BASHA
BASHA
BASHA
BASHA
NOROOO (SLOOOW)
ARE YOU STILL NOT DONE YET?
SENSEI, SAKURAGAI-SAN'S TAKING FOREVER.
ZEE (PANT)
EEERGH!
ZEE
SO WHAT IF YOU CAN'T SWIM?
IT'S NOT LIKE IT'LL KILL YOU.
wonder
I KNOW, BUT STILL...
ARASHI, AGE 6

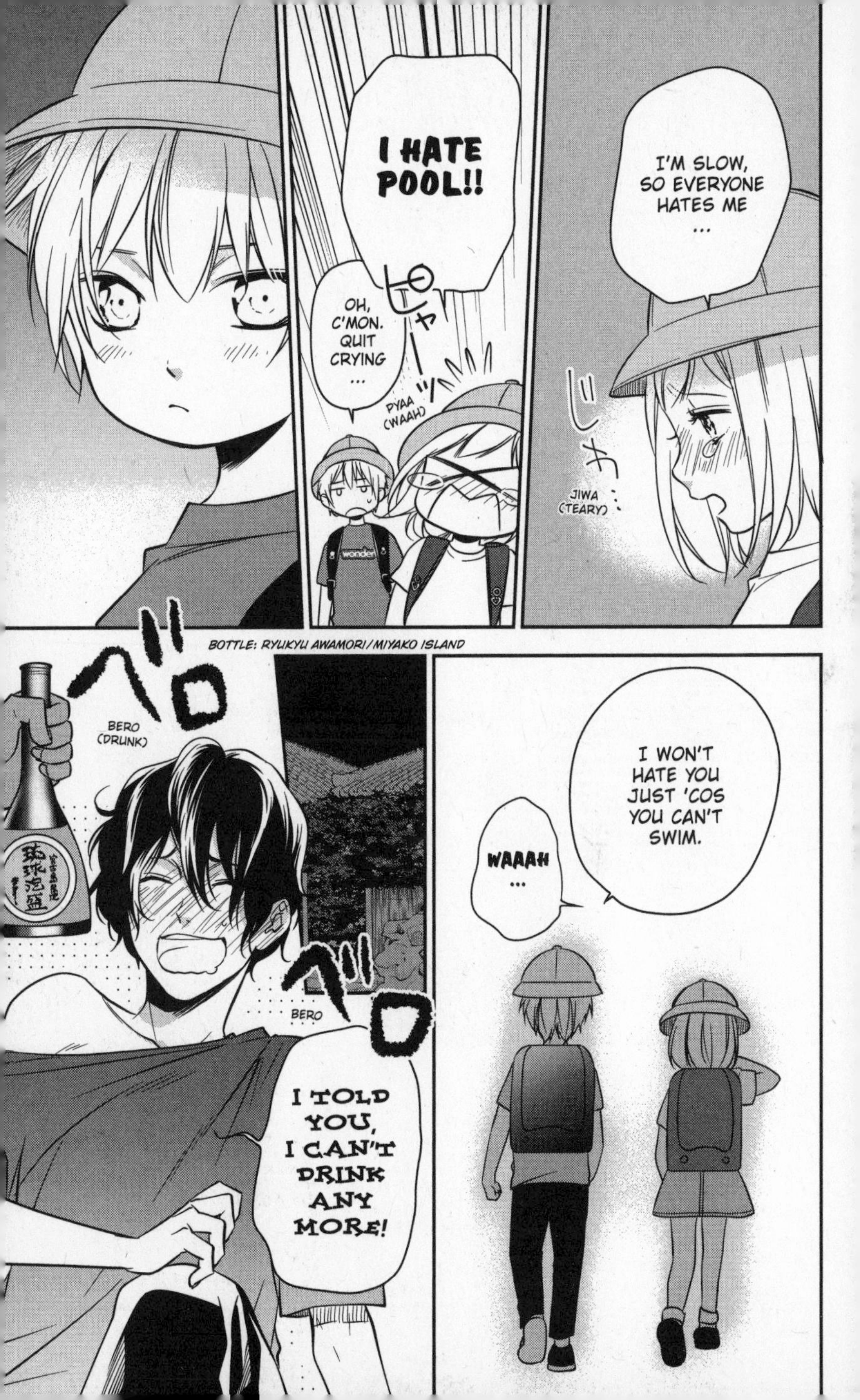
I'M SLOW, SO EVERYONE HATES ME ...
JIWA (TEARY)
I HATE POOL!!
OH, C'MON. QUIT CRYING ...
PYAA (WAAH)
BOTTLE: RYUKYU AWAMORI/MIYAKO ISLAND
I WON'T HATE YOU JUST 'COS YOU CAN'T SWIM.
WAAAH ...
BERO (DRUNK)
琉球泡盛
BERO
I TOLD YOU, I CAN'T DRINK ANY MORE!

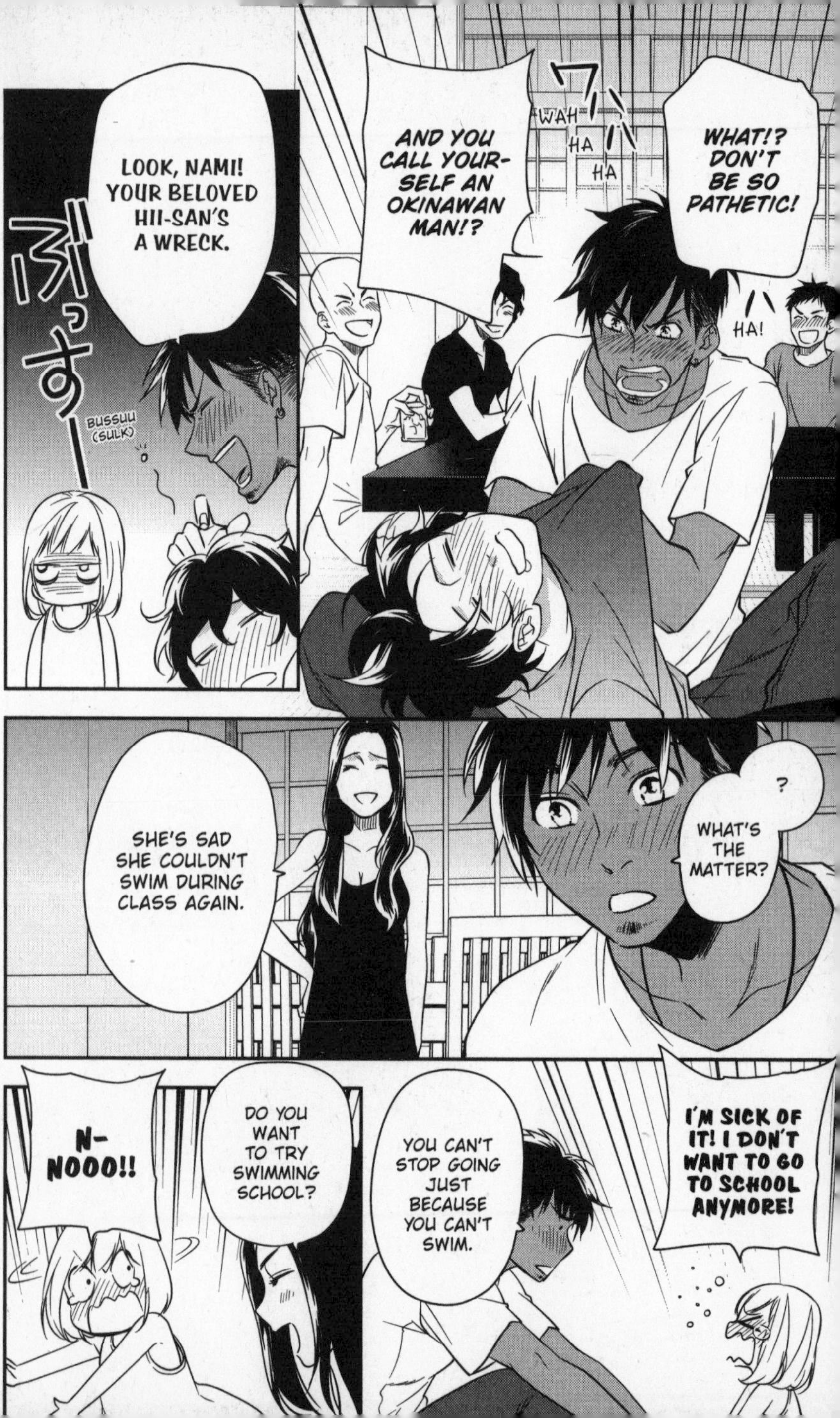
WHAT!? DON'T BE SO PATHETIC!
WAH HA HA
AND YOU CALL YOUR-SELF AN OKINAWAN MAN!?
HA!
LOOK, NAMI! YOUR BELOVED HII-SAN'S A WRECK.
BUSSUU (SULK)
?
WHAT'S THE MATTER?
SHE'S SAD SHE COULDN'T SWIM DURING CLASS AGAIN.
I'M SICK OF IT! I DON'T WANT TO GO TO SCHOOL ANYMORE!
YOU CAN'T STOP GOING JUST BECAUSE YOU CAN'T SWIM.
DO YOU WANT TO TRY SWIMMING SCHOOL?
N-NOOO!!

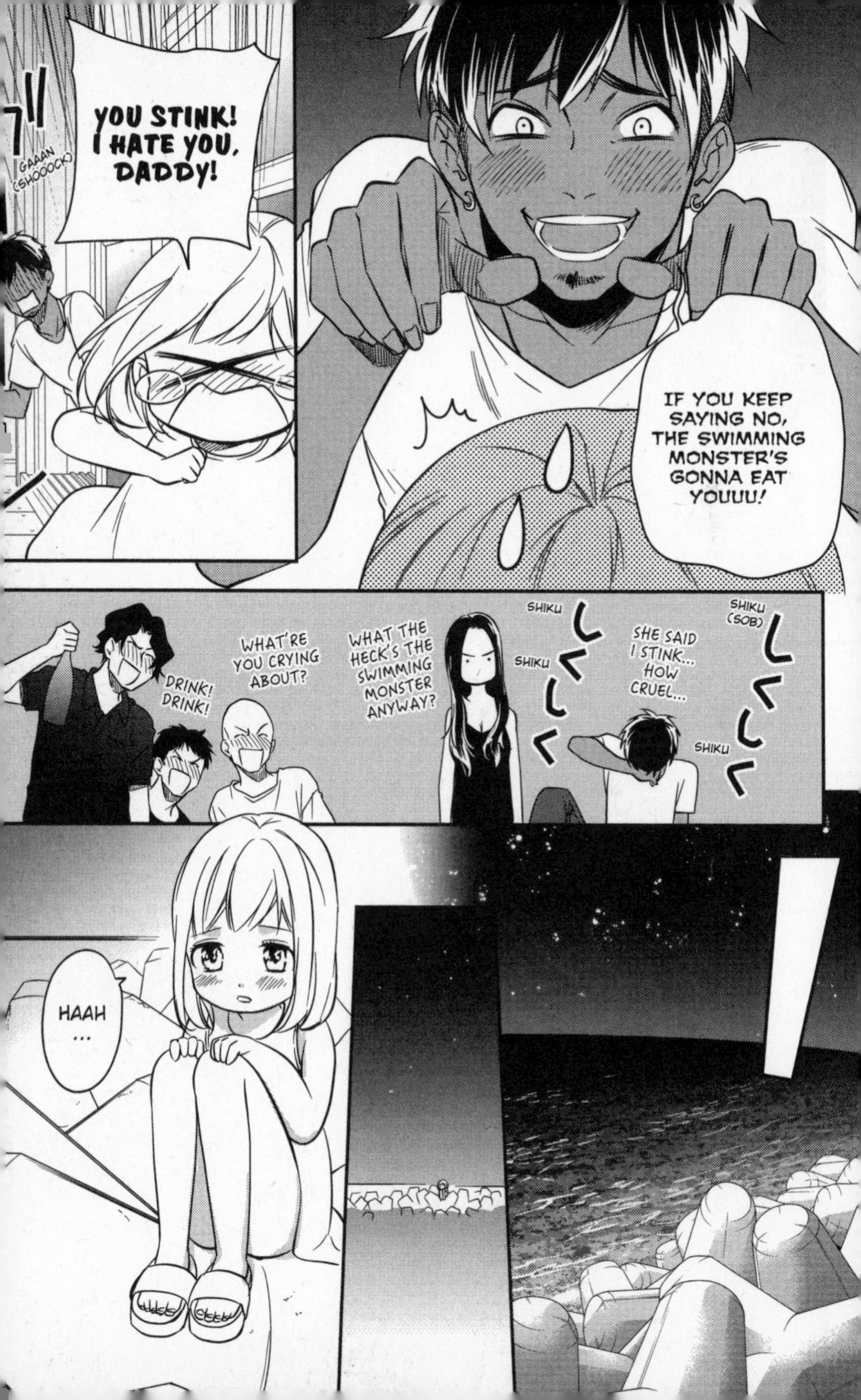
IF YOU KEEP SAYING NO, THE SWIMMING MONSTER'S GONNA EAT YOUUU!
YOU STINK! I HATE YOU, DADDY!
GAAAN (SHOOOCK)
SHIKU (SOB)
SHE SAID I STINK... HOW CRUEL...
SHIKU
SHIKU
SHIKU
WHAT THE HECK'S THE SWIMMING MONSTER ANYWAY?
WHAT'RE YOU CRYING ABOUT?
DRINK! DRINK!
HAAH ...

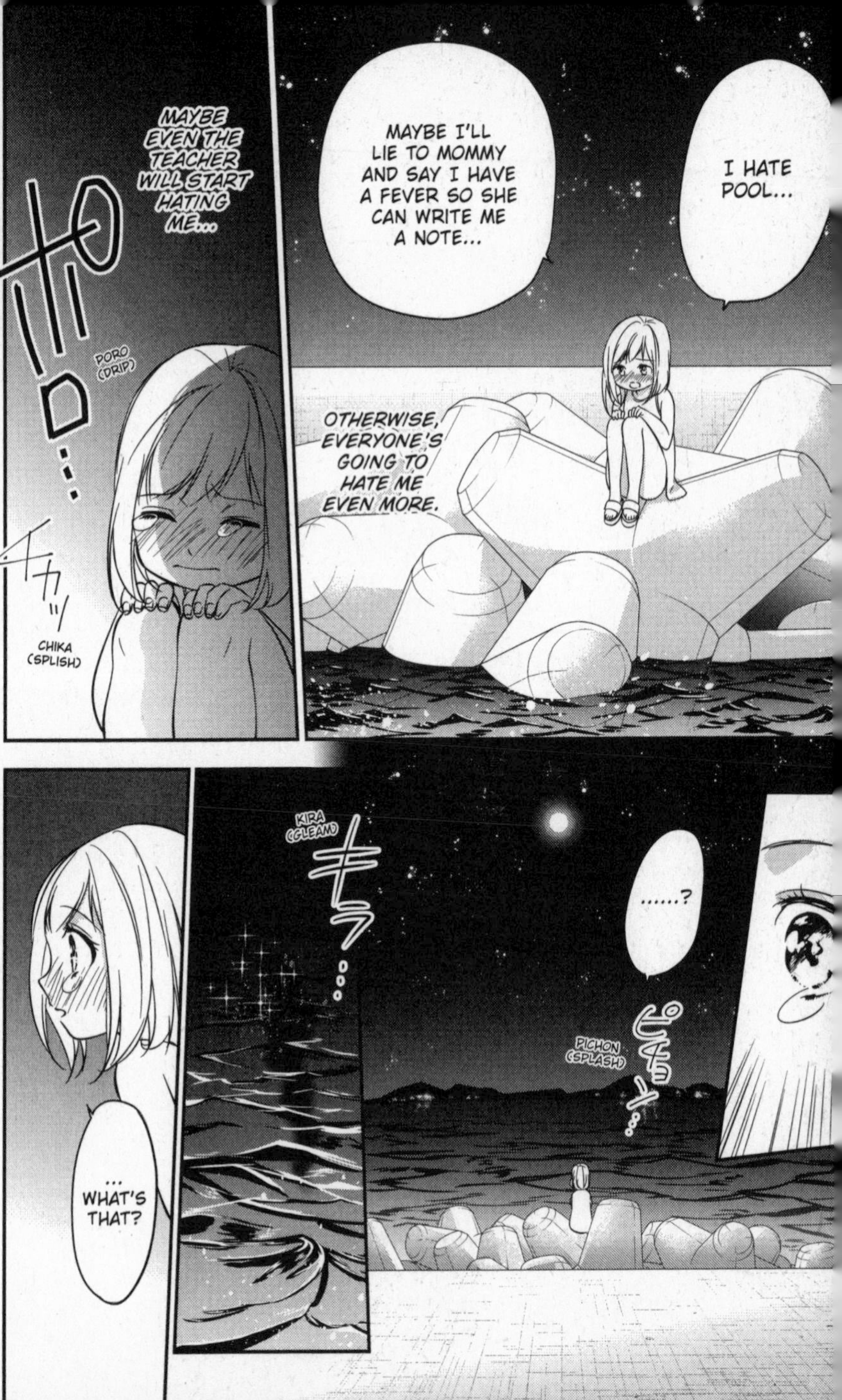
I HATE POOL...
MAYBE I'LL LIE TO MOMMY AND SAY I HAVE A FEVER SO SHE CAN WRITE ME A NOTE...
OTHERWISE, EVERYONE'S GOING TO HATE ME EVEN MORE.
MAYBE EVEN THE TEACHER WILL START HATING ME...
PORO (DRIP)
CHIKA (SPLISH)
......?
KIRA (GLEAM)
PICHON (SPLASH)
... WHAT'S THAT?

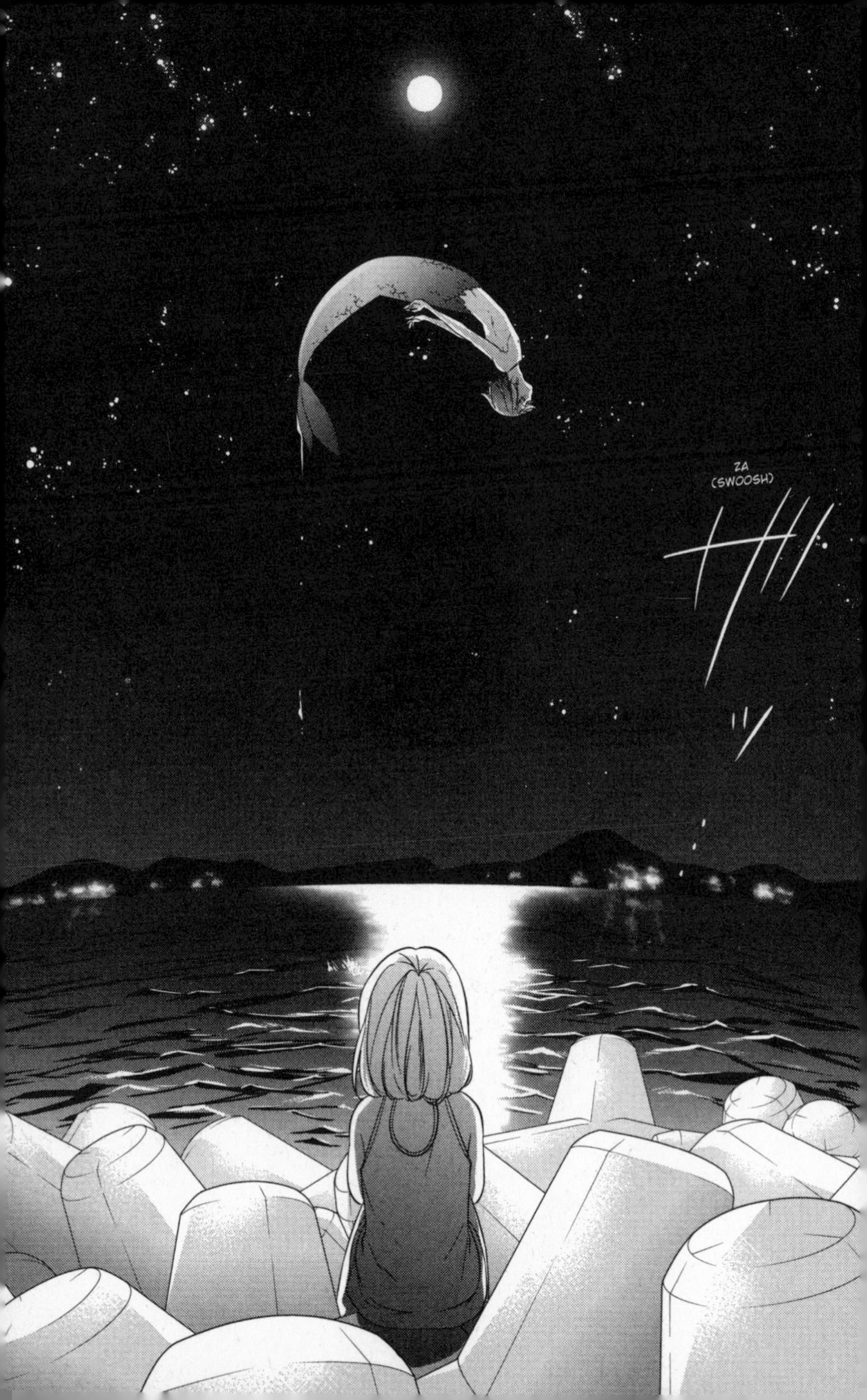
ZA
(SWOOSH)

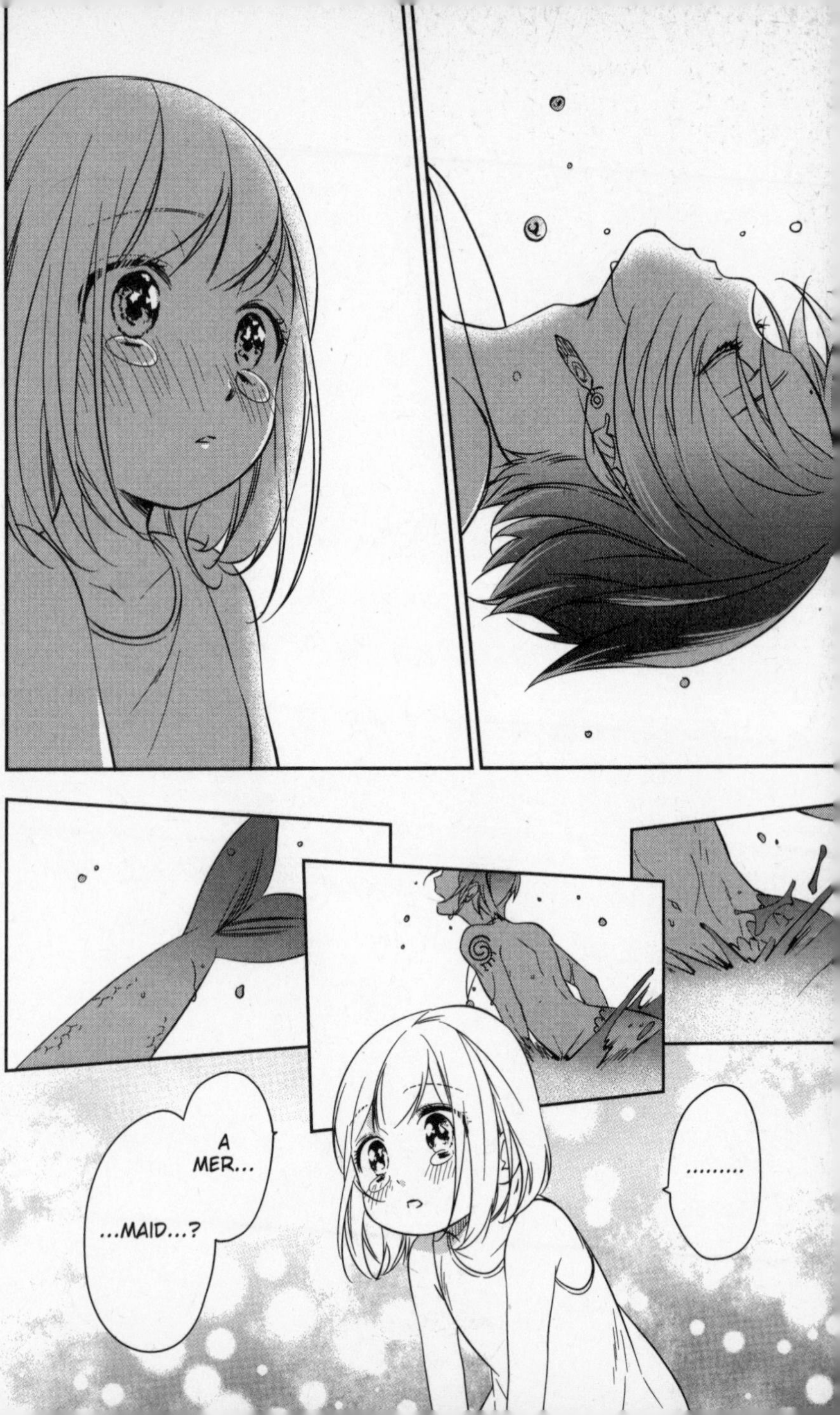
....
A MER...
...MAID...?

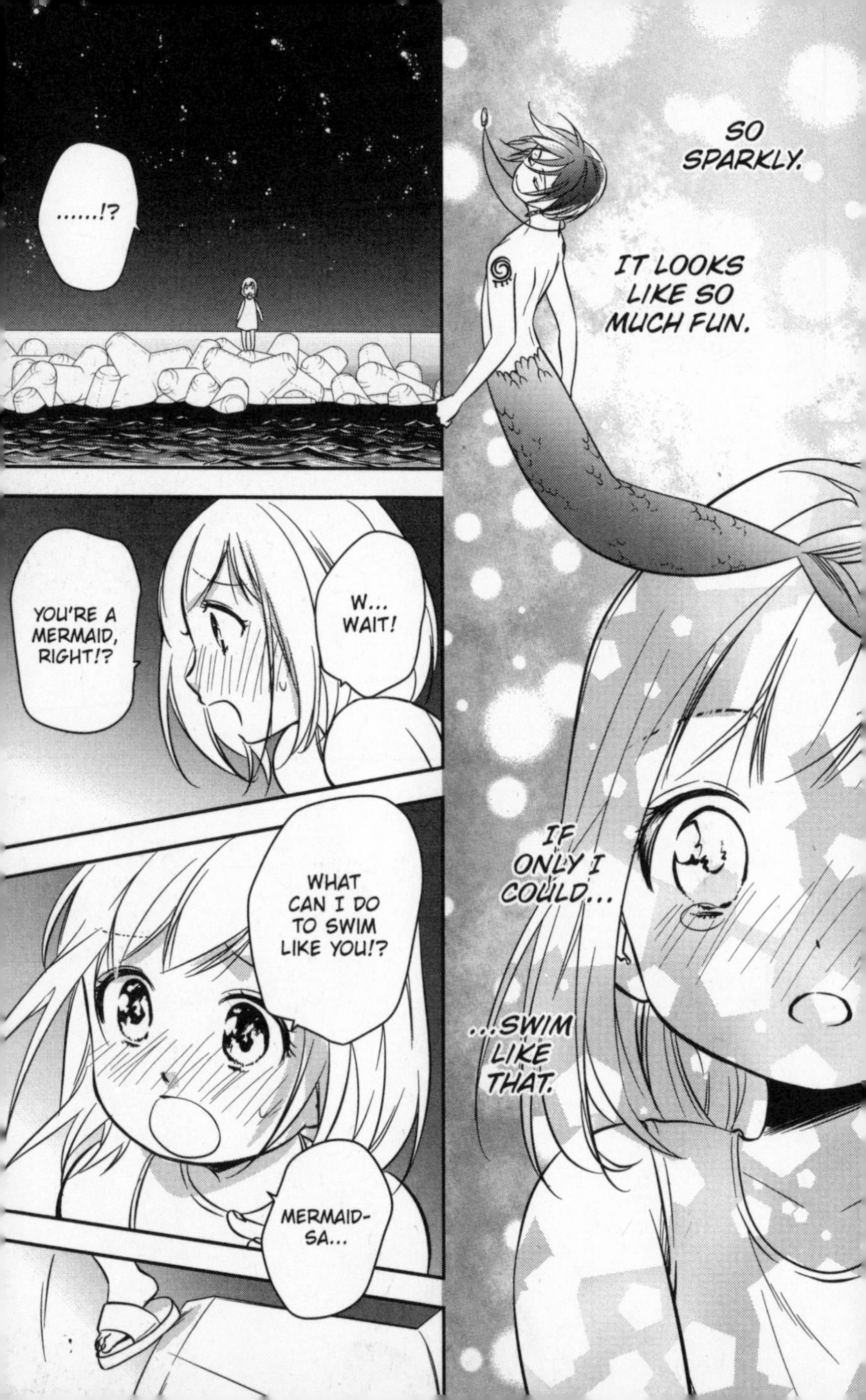
SO SPARKLY.
IT LOOKS LIKE SO MUCH FUN.
IF ONLY I COULD...
...SWIM LIKE THAT.
......!?
W... WAIT!
YOU'RE A MERMAID, RIGHT!?
WHAT CAN I DO TO SWIM LIKE YOU!?
MERMAID-SA...

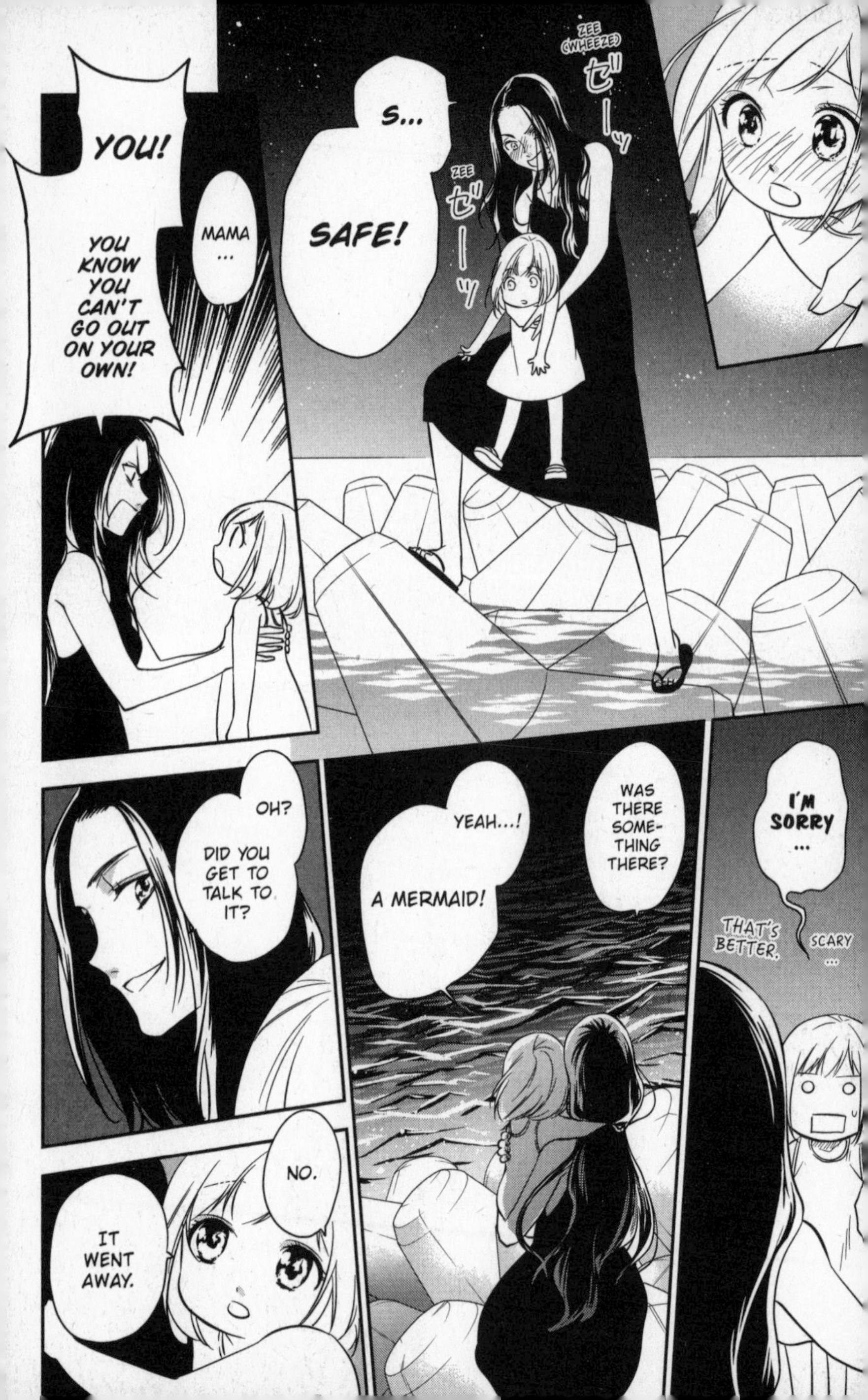
ZEE (WHEEZE)
ZEE
S...
SAFE!
MAMA...
YOU!
YOU KNOW YOU CAN'T GO OUT ON YOUR OWN!
I'M SORRY...
SCARY...
THAT'S BETTER.
WAS THERE SOMETHING THERE?
YEAH...!
A MERMAID!
OH?
DID YOU GET TO TALK TO IT?
NO.
IT WENT AWAY.

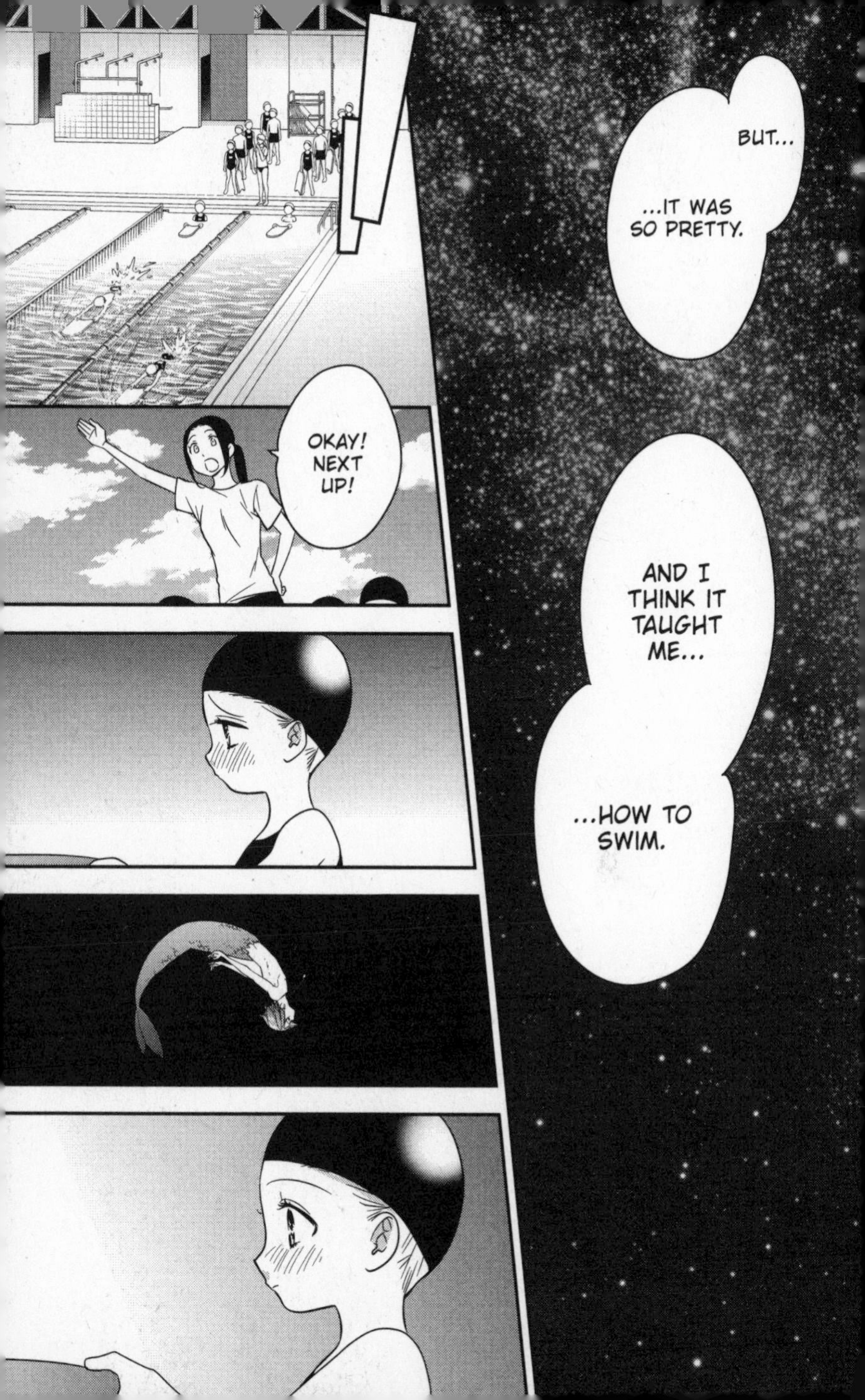
BUT...
...IT WAS SO PRETTY.
AND I THINK IT TAUGHT ME...
...HOW TO SWIM.
OKAY! NEXT UP!

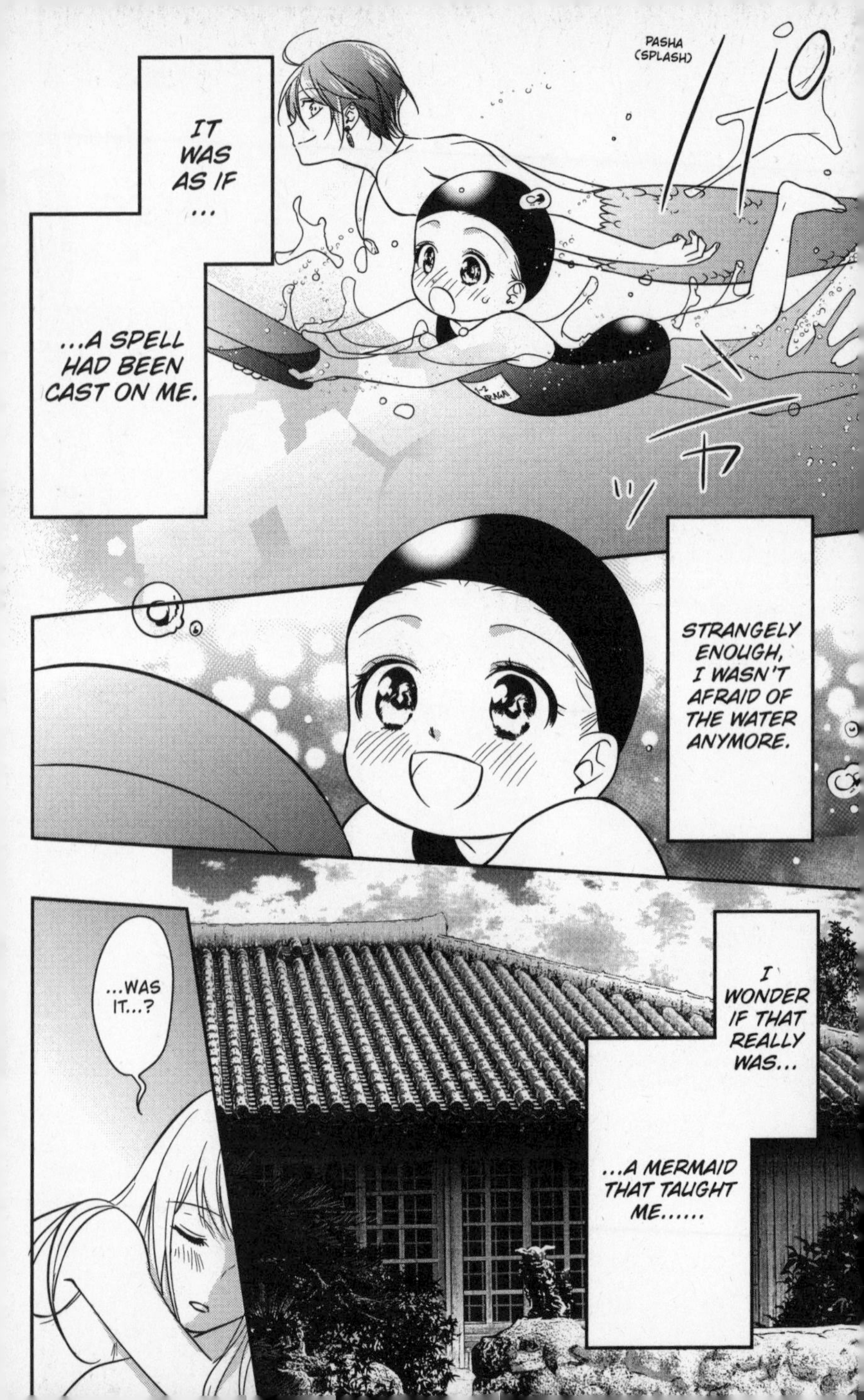
PASHA (SPLASH)
IT WAS AS IF ...
...A SPELL HAD BEEN CAST ON ME.
STRANGELY ENOUGH, I WASN'T AFRAID OF THE WATER ANYMORE.
I WONDER IF THAT REALLY WAS...
...A MERMAID THAT TAUGHT ME......
...WAS IT...?

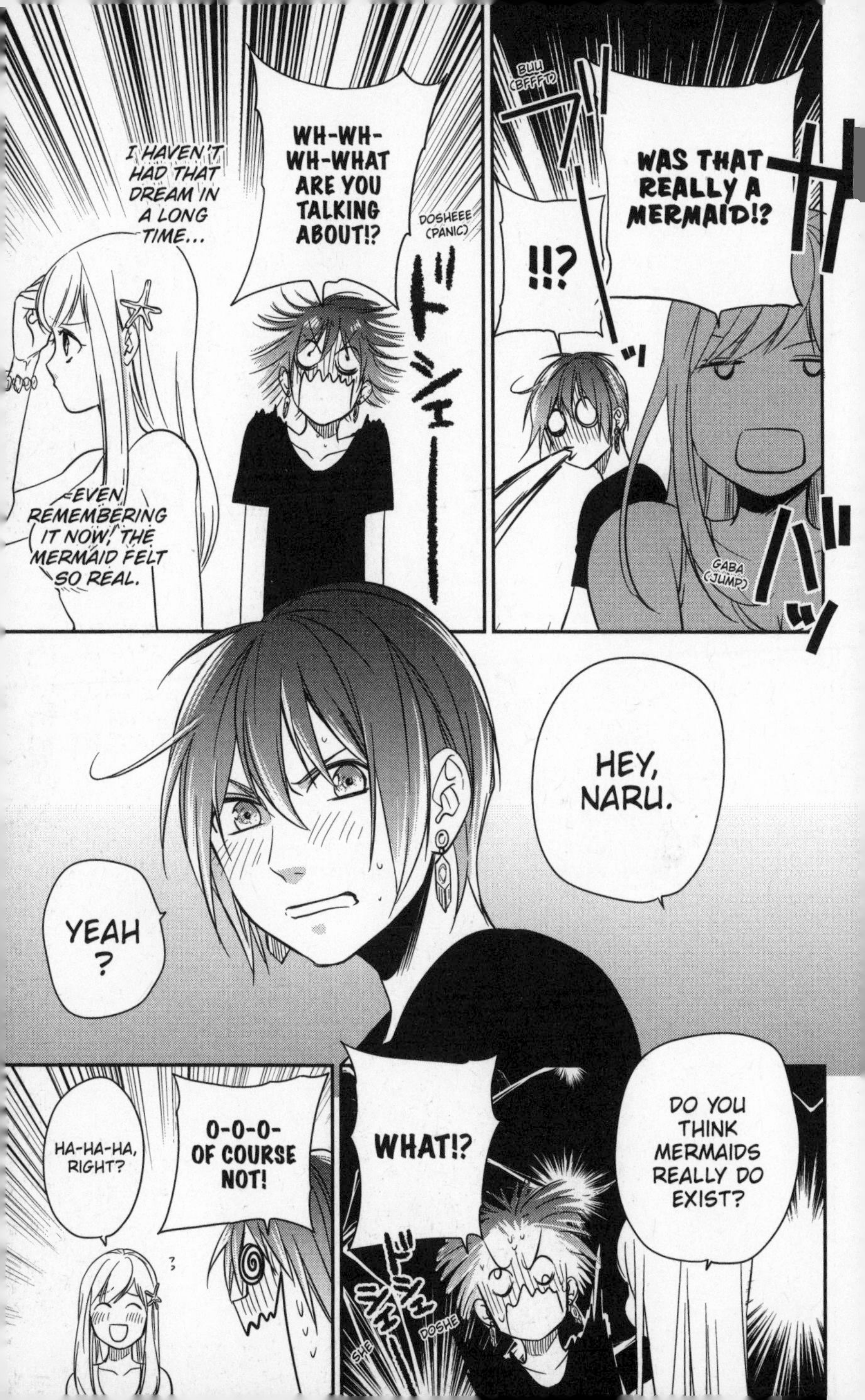
BUU (BFFFT)
WAS THAT REALLY A MERMAID!?
!!?
GABA (JUMP)
WH-WH-WH-WHAT ARE YOU TALKING ABOUT!?
DOSHEEE (PANIC)
I HAVEN'T HAD THAT DREAM IN A LONG TIME...
EVEN REMEMBERING IT NOW, THE MERMAID FELT SO REAL.
HEY, NARU.
YEAH?
DO YOU THINK MERMAIDS REALLY DO EXIST?
WHAT!?
DOSHE
SHE
O-O-O-OF COURSE NOT!
HA-HA-HA, RIGHT?

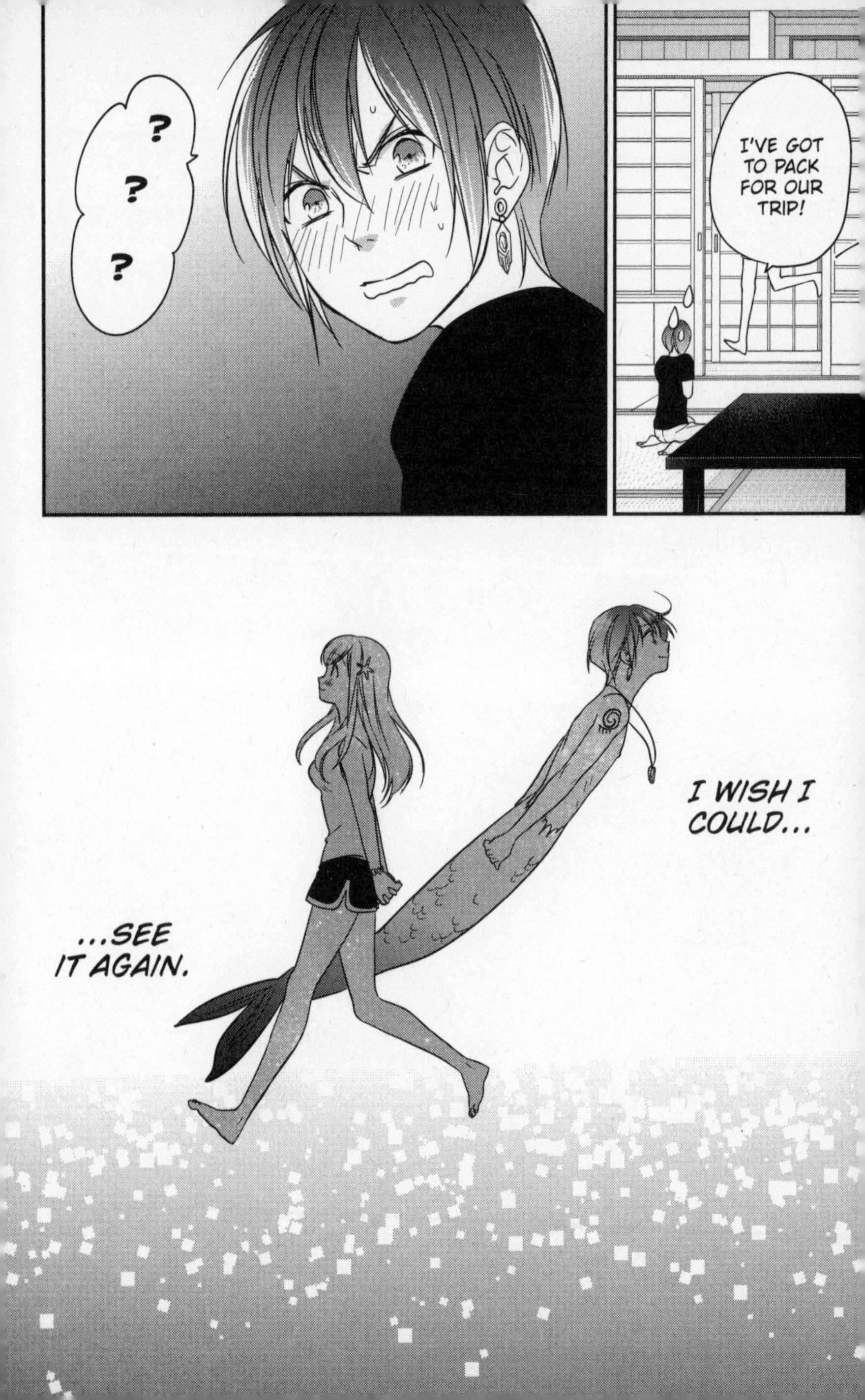
I'VE GOT TO PACK FOR OUR TRIP!
? ? ?
I WISH I COULD...
...SEE IT AGAIN.

MERMAID BOYS

MERMAID BOYS

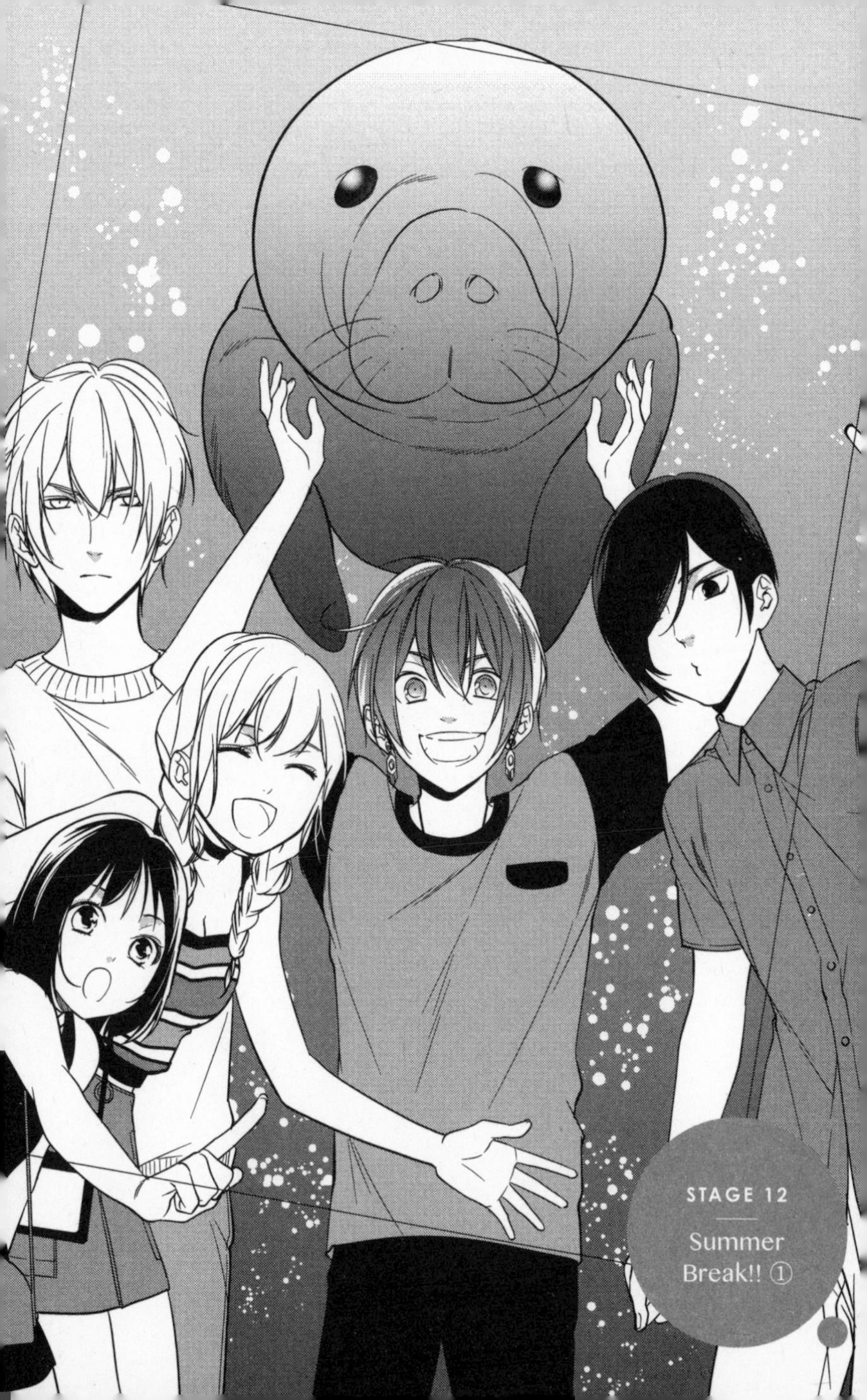
STAGE 12
Summer Break!! ①

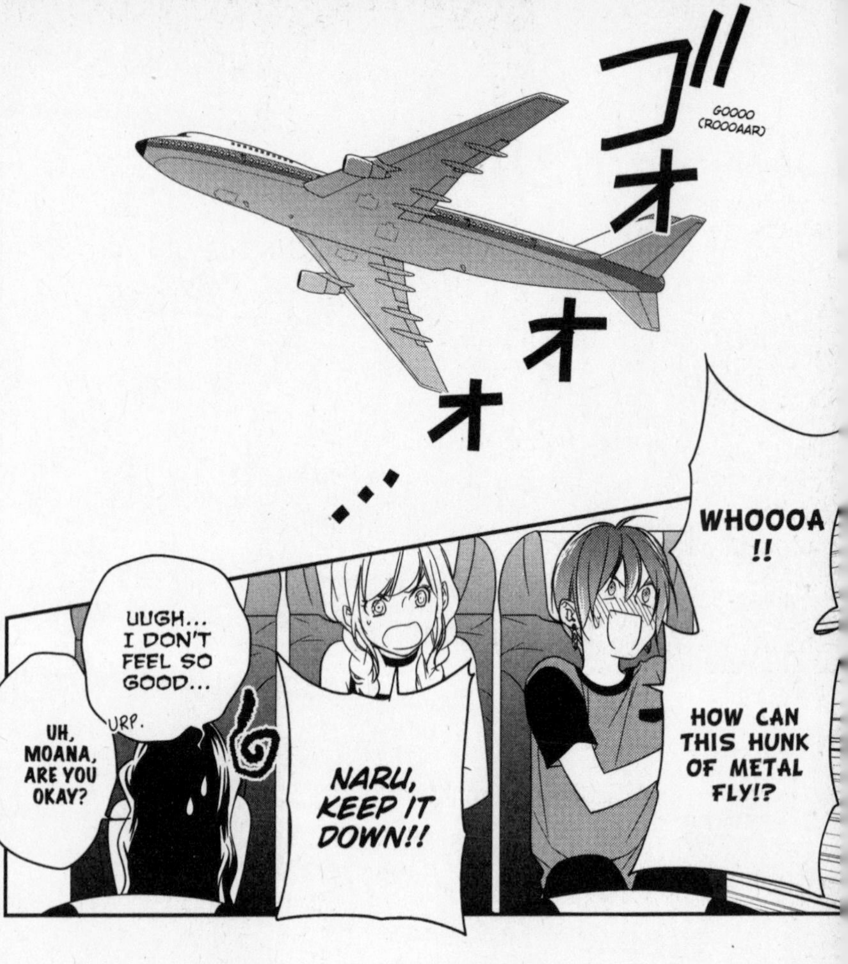
ゴオオオ…
GOOOO (ROOOAAR)
WHOOOA!!
HOW CAN THIS HUNK OF METAL FLY!?
NARU, KEEP IT DOWN!!
UUGH... I DON'T FEEL SO GOOD...
URP.
UH, MOANA, ARE YOU OKAY?

MERMAID BOYS

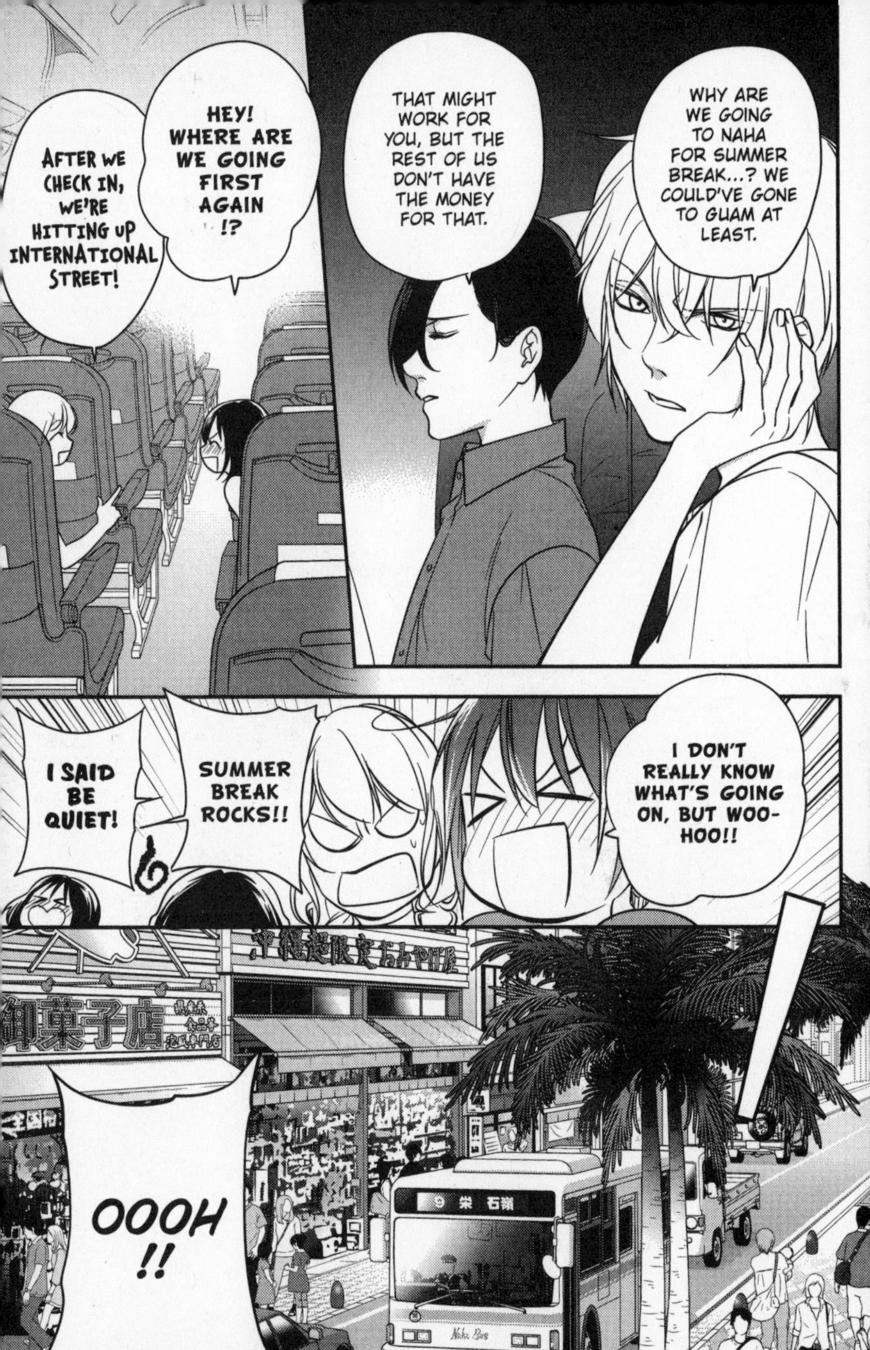
WHY ARE WE GOING TO NAHA FOR SUMMER BREAK...? WE COULD'VE GONE TO GUAM AT LEAST.
THAT MIGHT WORK FOR YOU, BUT THE REST OF US DON'T HAVE THE MONEY FOR THAT.
HEY! WHERE ARE WE GOING FIRST AGAIN !?
AFTER WE CHECK IN, WE'RE HITTING UP INTERNATIONAL STREET!
I DON'T REALLY KNOW WHAT'S GOING ON, BUT WOO-HOO!!
SUMMER BREAK ROCKS!!
I SAID BE QUIET!
OOOH !!

SNACK SHOP — LOCAL GOODS, FOOD, AWAMORI / LIMITED EDITION OKINAWA SOUVENIR SHOP / #9 SHIMANE-BOUND

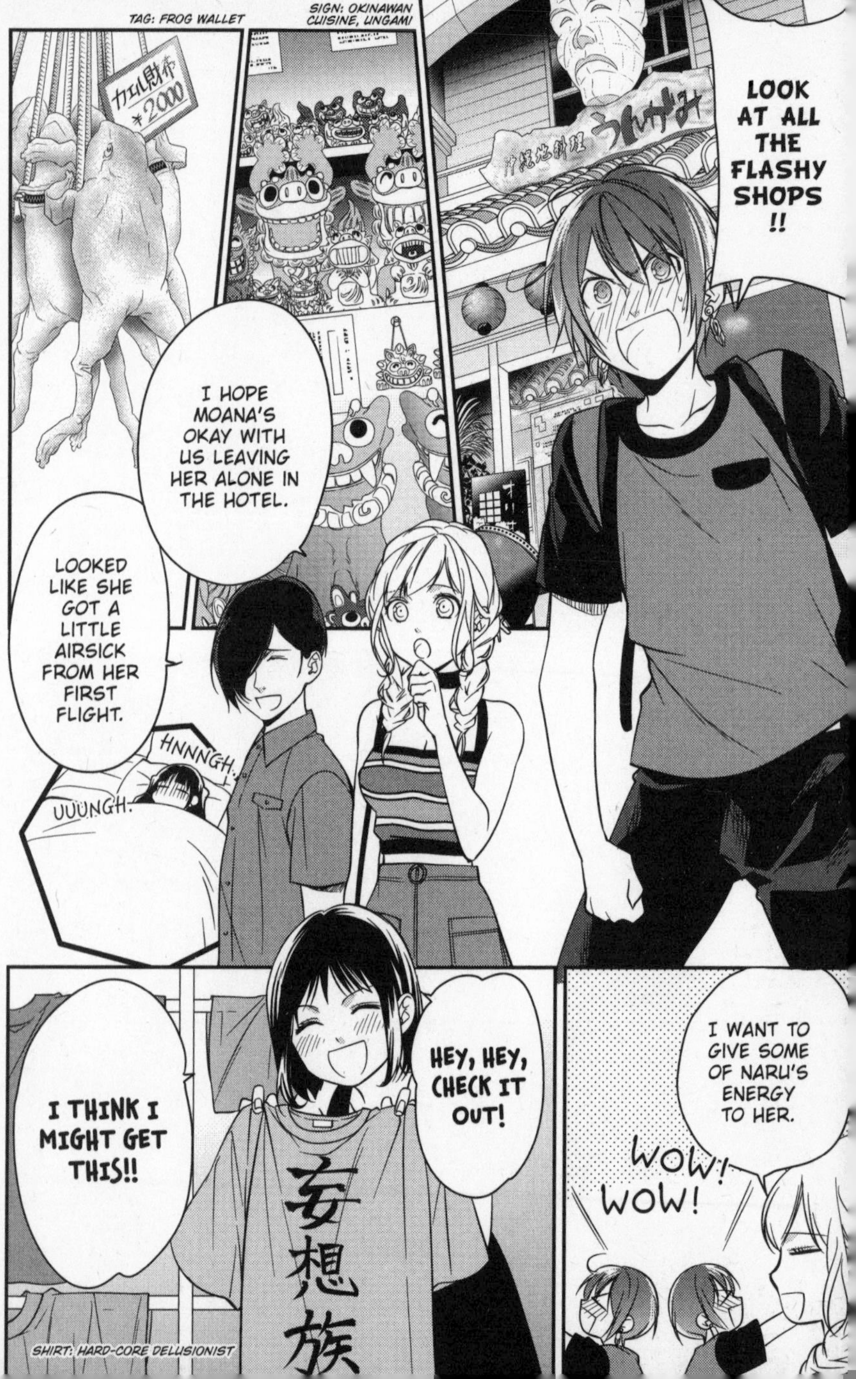
SIGN: OKINAWAN CUISINE, UNGAMI
LOOK AT ALL THE FLASHY SHOPS !!
TAG: FROG WALLET
カエル財布 ¥2000
I HOPE MOANA'S OKAY WITH US LEAVING HER ALONE IN THE HOTEL.
LOOKED LIKE SHE GOT A LITTLE AIRSICK FROM HER FIRST FLIGHT.
HNNNGH.
UUUNGH.
I WANT TO GIVE SOME OF NARU'S ENERGY TO HER.
WOW! WOW!
HEY, HEY, CHECK IT OUT!
I THINK I MIGHT GET THIS!!
妄想族
SHIRT: HARD-CORE DELUSIONIST

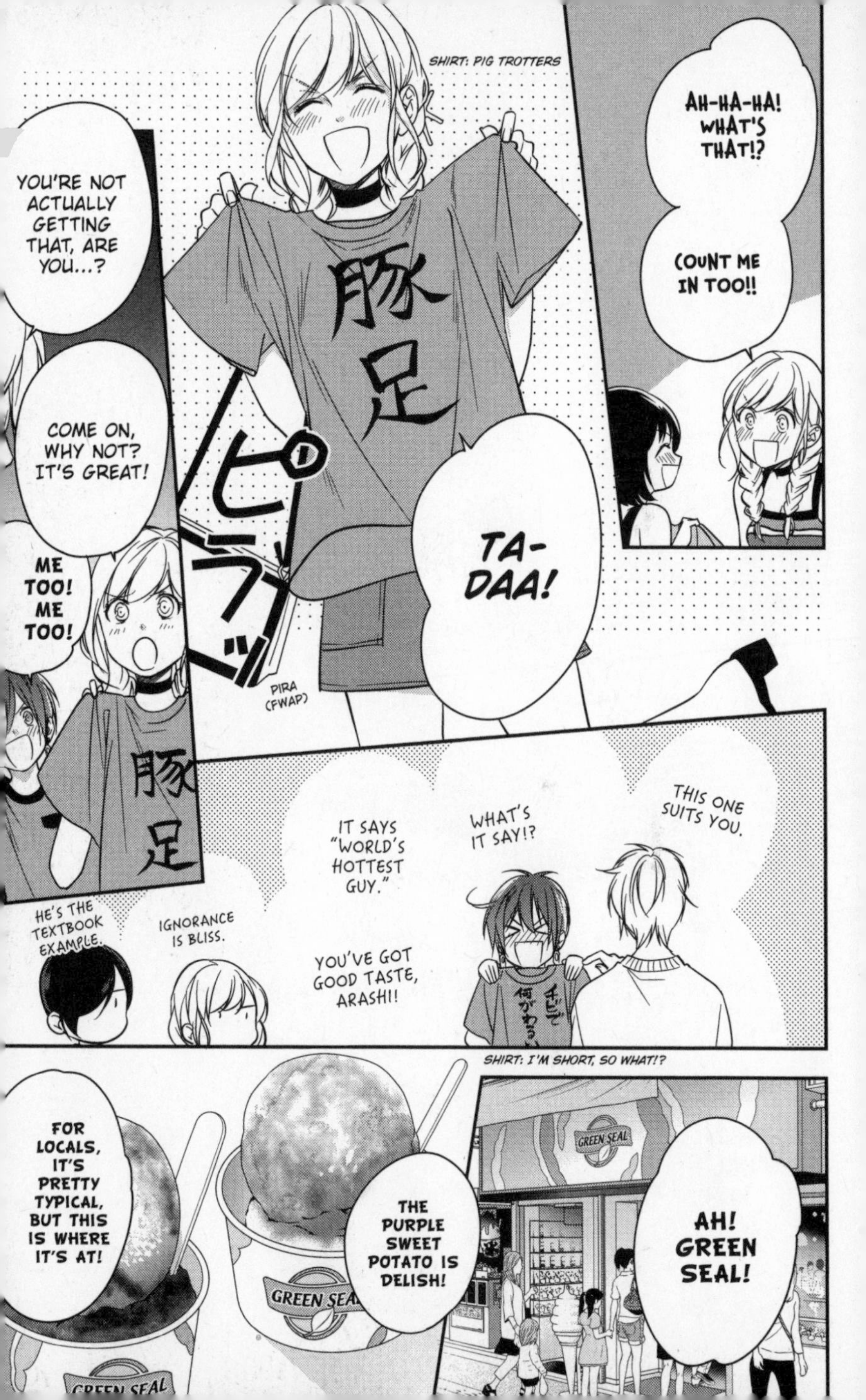
AH-HA-HA! WHAT'S THAT!?
COUNT ME IN TOO!!
SHIRT: PIG TROTTERS
TA-DAA!
PIRA (FWAP)
YOU'RE NOT ACTUALLY GETTING THAT, ARE YOU...?
COME ON, WHY NOT? IT'S GREAT!
ME TOO! ME TOO!
THIS ONE SUITS YOU.
WHAT'S IT SAY!?
IT SAYS "WORLD'S HOTTEST GUY."
YOU'VE GOT GOOD TASTE, ARASHI!
IGNORANCE IS BLISS.
HE'S THE TEXTBOOK EXAMPLE.
SHIRT: I'M SHORT, SO WHAT!?
GREEN SEAL
AH! GREEN SEAL!
THE PURPLE SWEET POTATO IS DELISH!
FOR LOCALS, IT'S PRETTY TYPICAL, BUT THIS IS WHERE IT'S AT!
GREEN SEAL
GREEN SEAL

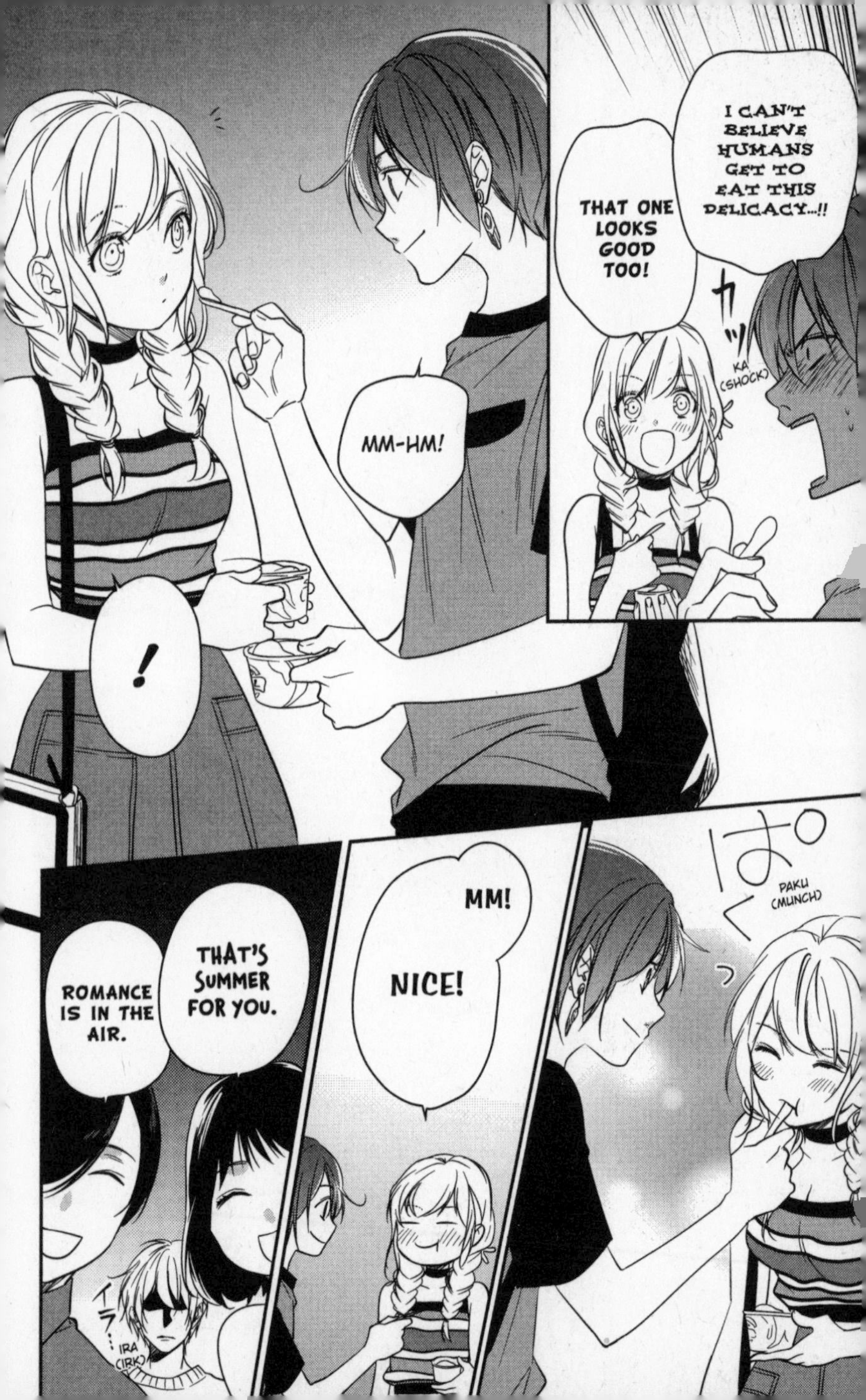
I CAN'T BELIEVE HUMANS GET TO EAT THIS DELICACY...!!
THAT ONE LOOKS GOOD TOO!
カッ
KA (SHOCK)
MM-HM!
!
ぱく
PAKU (MUNCH)
MM!
NICE!
THAT'S SUMMER FOR YOU.
ROMANCE IS IN THE AIR.
イラ...
IRA (IRK)

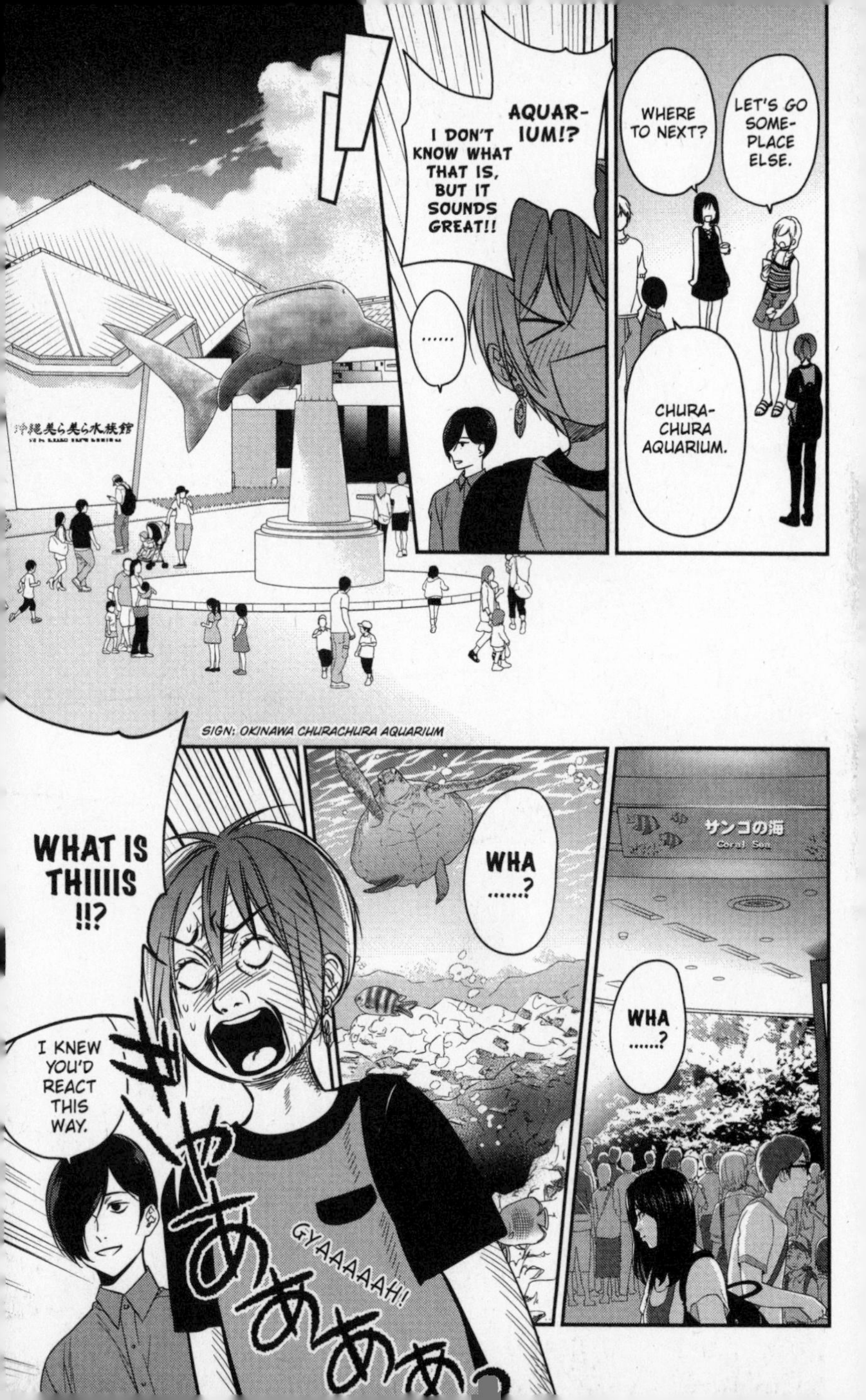
LET'S GO SOME-PLACE ELSE.
WHERE TO NEXT?
CHURA-CHURA AQUARIUM.
AQUAR-IUM!?
I DON'T KNOW WHAT THAT IS, BUT IT SOUNDS GREAT!!
......
沖縄美ら美ら水族館
SIGN: OKINAWA CHURACHURA AQUARIUM
サンゴの海
Coral Sea
WHA ......?
WHA ......?
WHAT IS THIIIIIS !!?
GYAAAAAAH!
I KNEW YOU'D REACT THIS WAY.

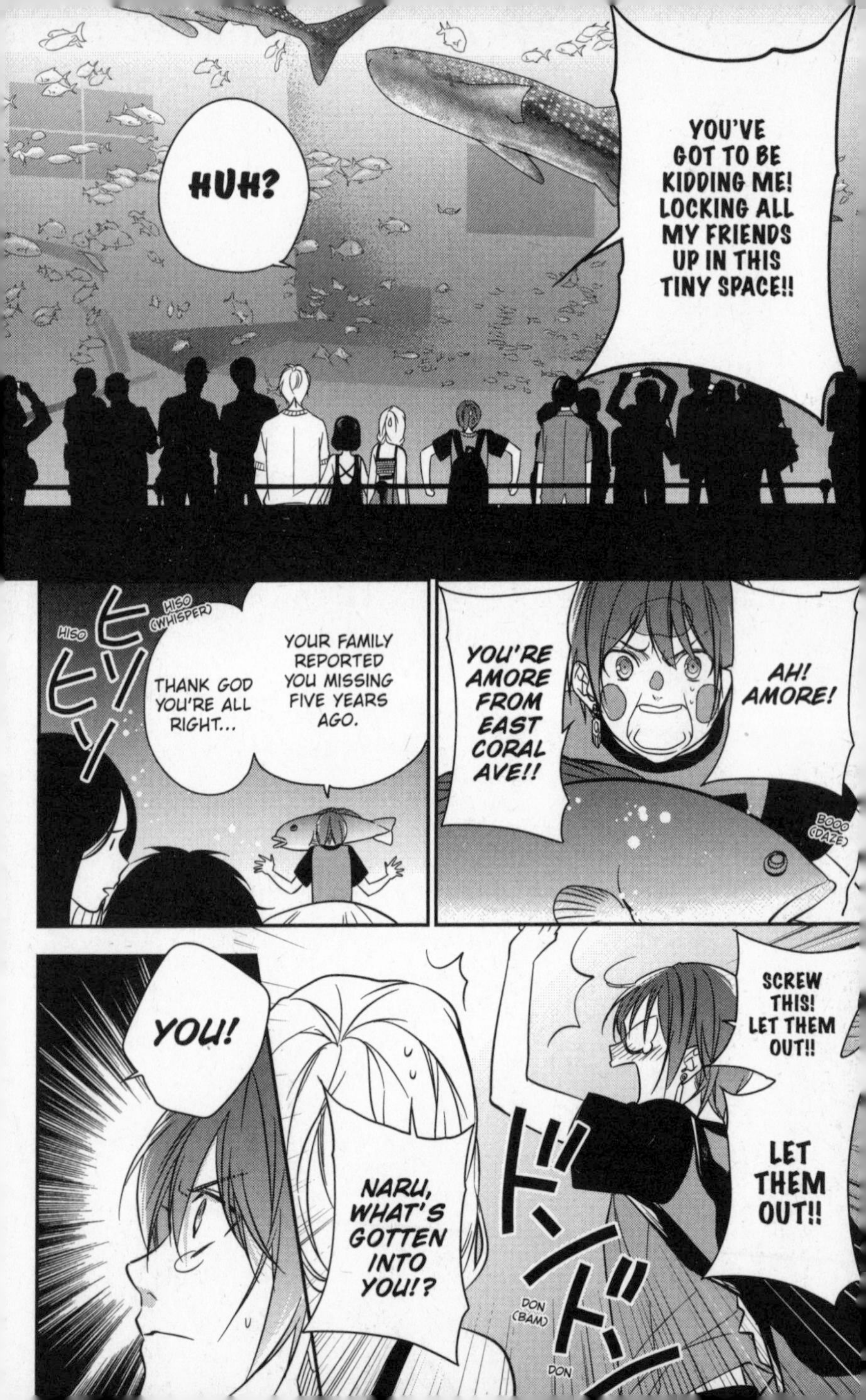
YOU'VE GOT TO BE KIDDING ME! LOCKING ALL MY FRIENDS UP IN THIS TINY SPACE!!
HUH?
AH! AMORE!
YOU'RE AMORE FROM EAST CORAL AVE!!
BOOO (DAZE)
YOUR FAMILY REPORTED YOU MISSING FIVE YEARS AGO.
THANK GOD YOU'RE ALL RIGHT...
HISO (WHISPER)
HISO
SCREW THIS! LET THEM OUT!!
LET THEM OUT!!
DON (BAM)
DON
NARU, WHAT'S GOTTEN INTO YOU!?
YOU!

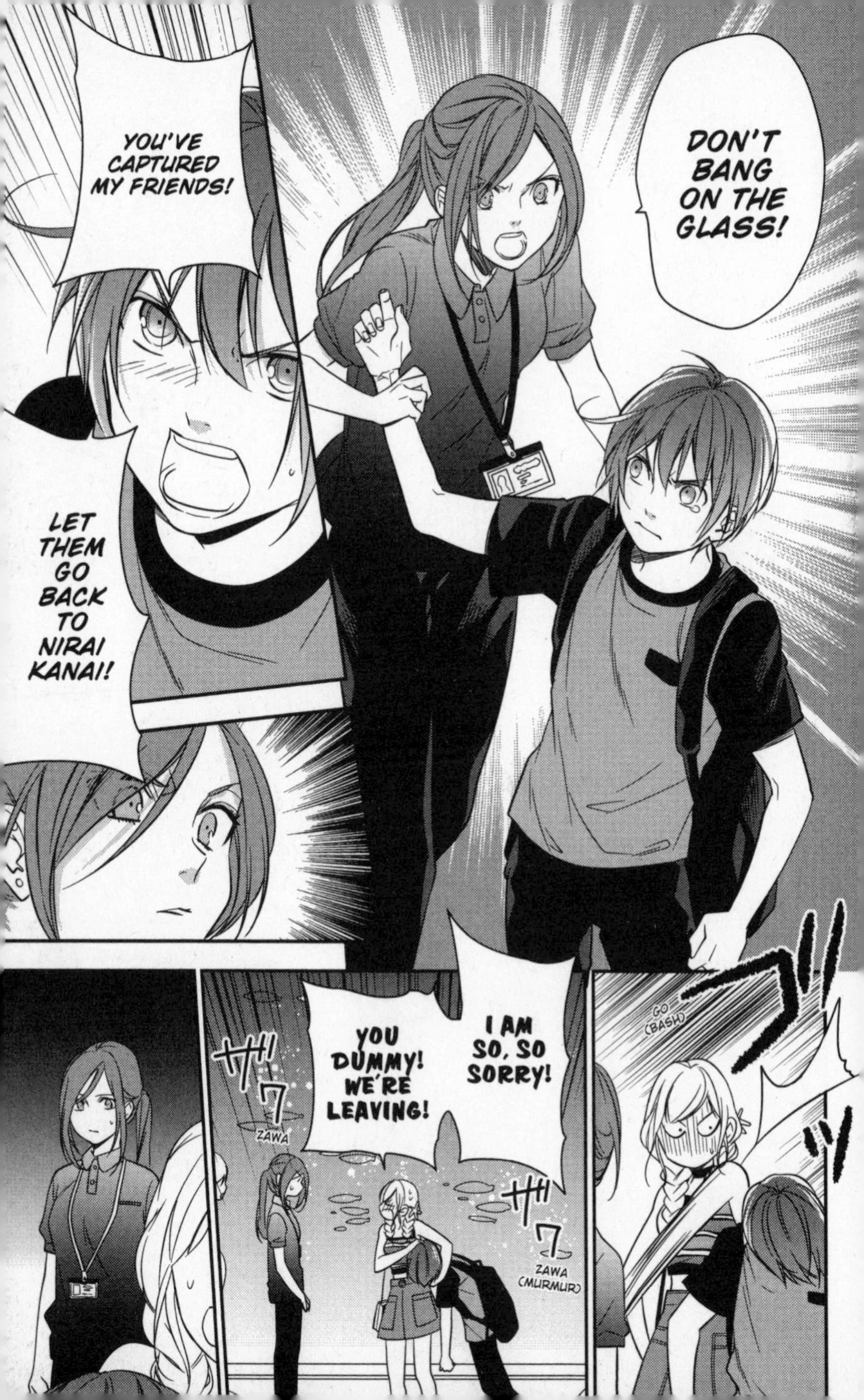
DON'T BANG ON THE GLASS!
YOU'VE CAPTURED MY FRIENDS!
LET THEM GO BACK TO NIRAI KANAI!
GO (BASH)
I AM SO, SO SORRY!
YOU DUMMY! WE'RE LEAVING!
ZAWA
ZAWA (MURMUR)

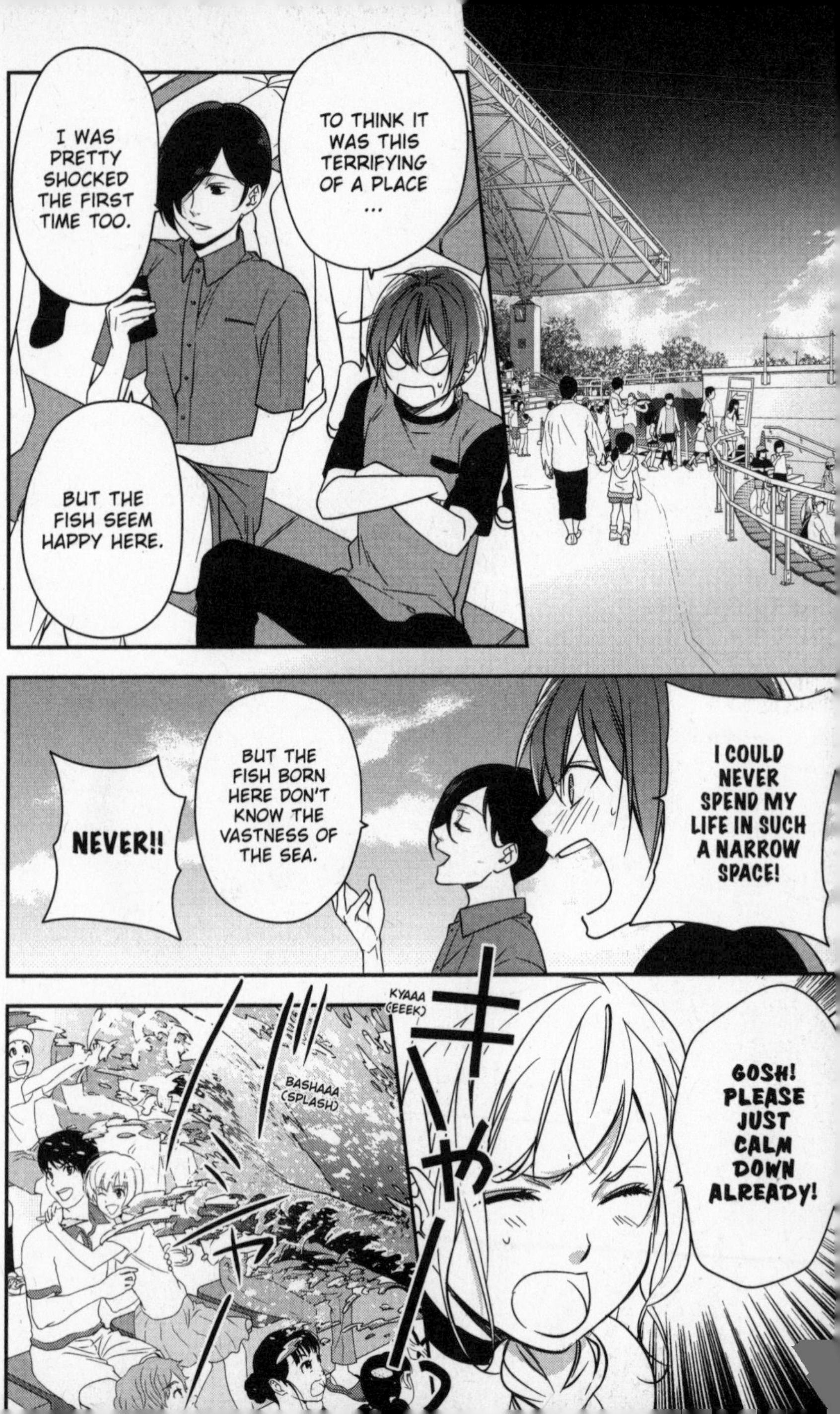
TO THINK IT WAS THIS TERRIFYING OF A PLACE ...
I WAS PRETTY SHOCKED THE FIRST TIME TOO.
BUT THE FISH SEEM HAPPY HERE.
I COULD NEVER SPEND MY LIFE IN SUCH A NARROW SPACE!
BUT THE FISH BORN HERE DON'T KNOW THE VASTNESS OF THE SEA.
NEVER!!
GOSH! PLEASE JUST CALM DOWN ALREADY!
KYAAA (EEEK)
BASHAAA (SPLASH)

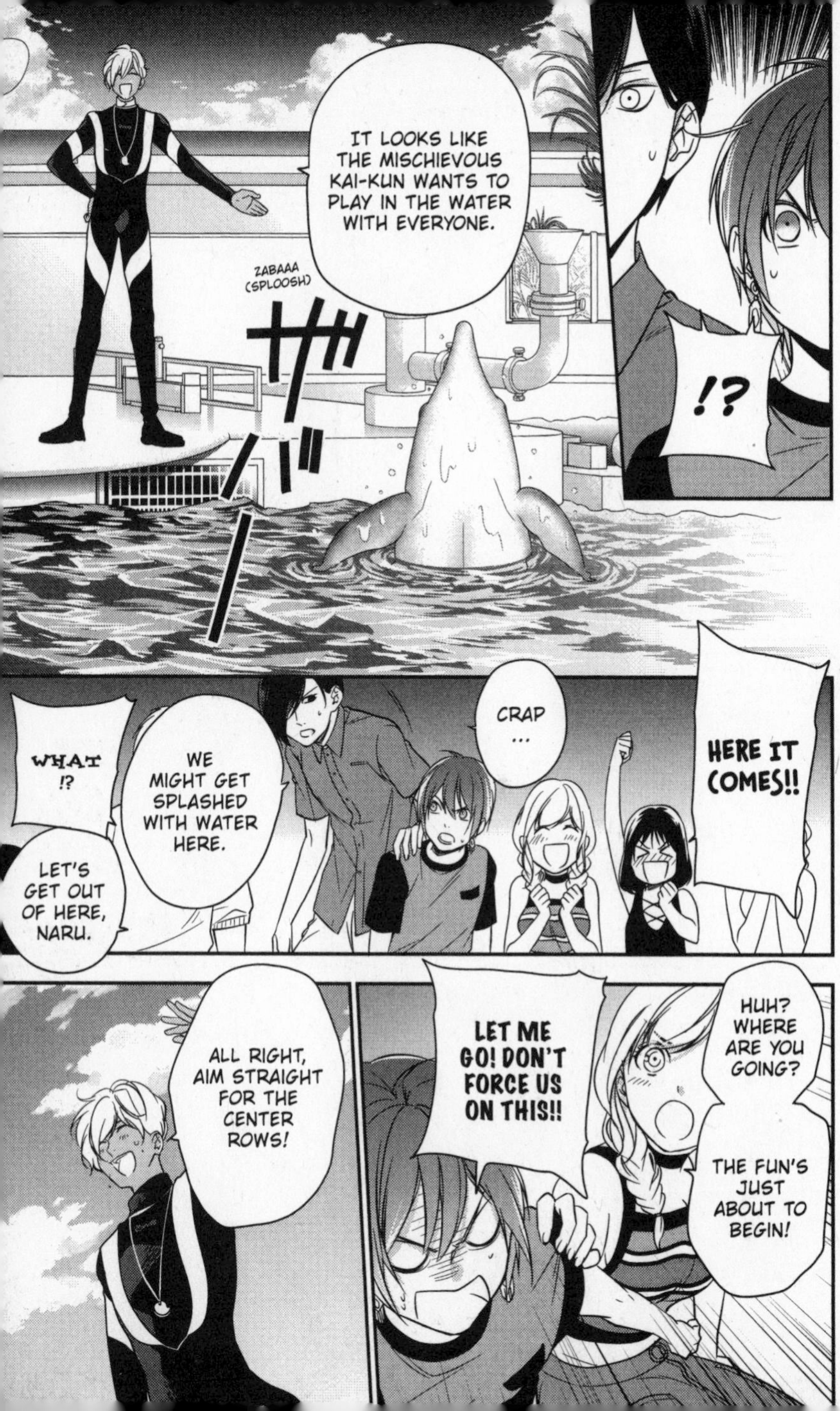
!?
IT LOOKS LIKE THE MISCHIEVOUS KAI-KUN WANTS TO PLAY IN THE WATER WITH EVERYONE.
ZABAAA (SPLOOSH)
HERE IT COMES!!
CRAP ...
WE MIGHT GET SPLASHED WITH WATER HERE.
WHAT !?
LET'S GET OUT OF HERE, NARU.
HUH? WHERE ARE YOU GOING?
LET ME GO! DON'T FORCE US ON THIS!!
THE FUN'S JUST ABOUT TO BEGIN!
ALL RIGHT, AIM STRAIGHT FOR THE CENTER ROWS!

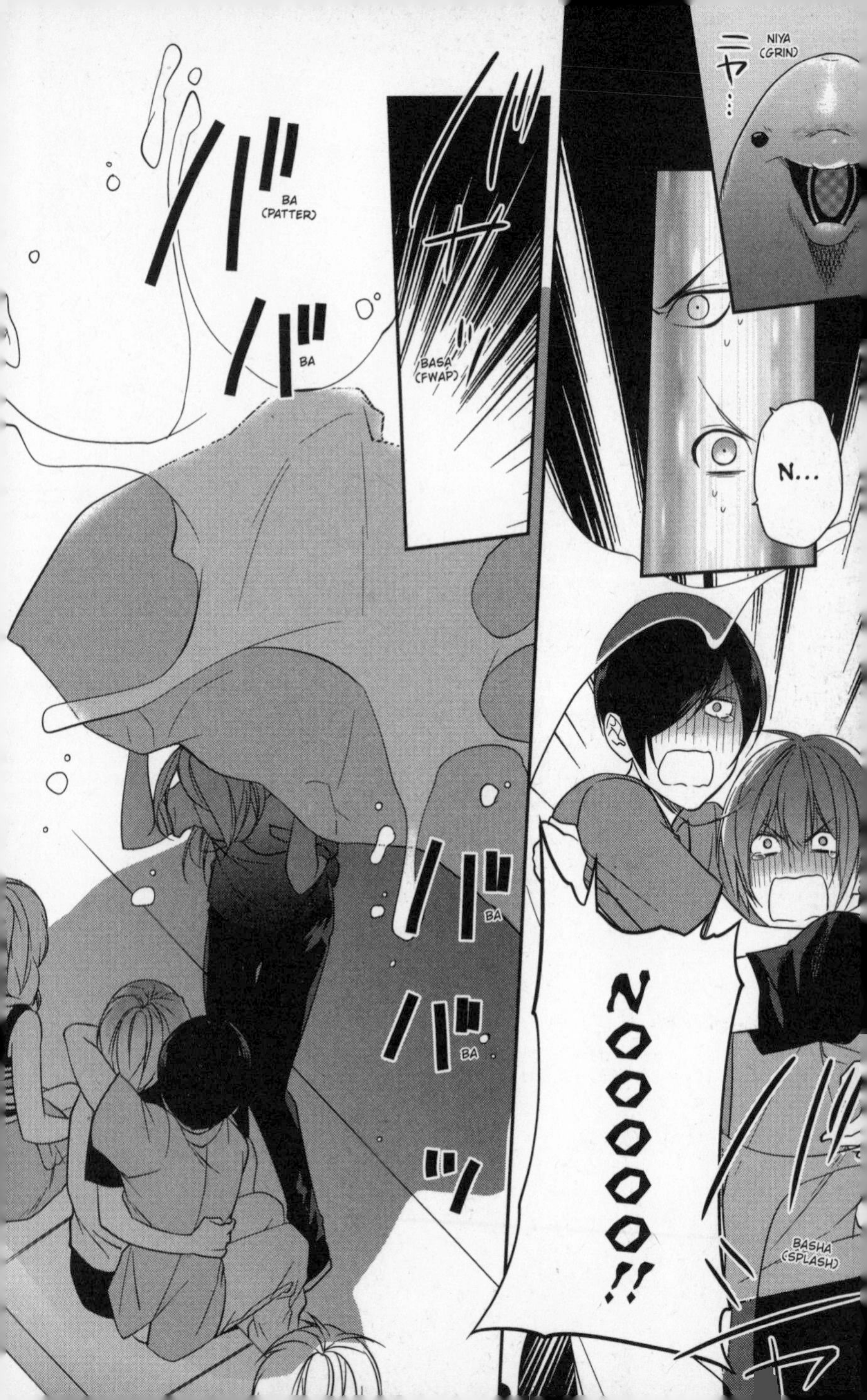
ニヤ…
NIYA (GRIN)
N...
NOOOOOO!!
BASHA (SPLASH)
BASA (FWAP)
BA (PATTER)
BA
BA
BA

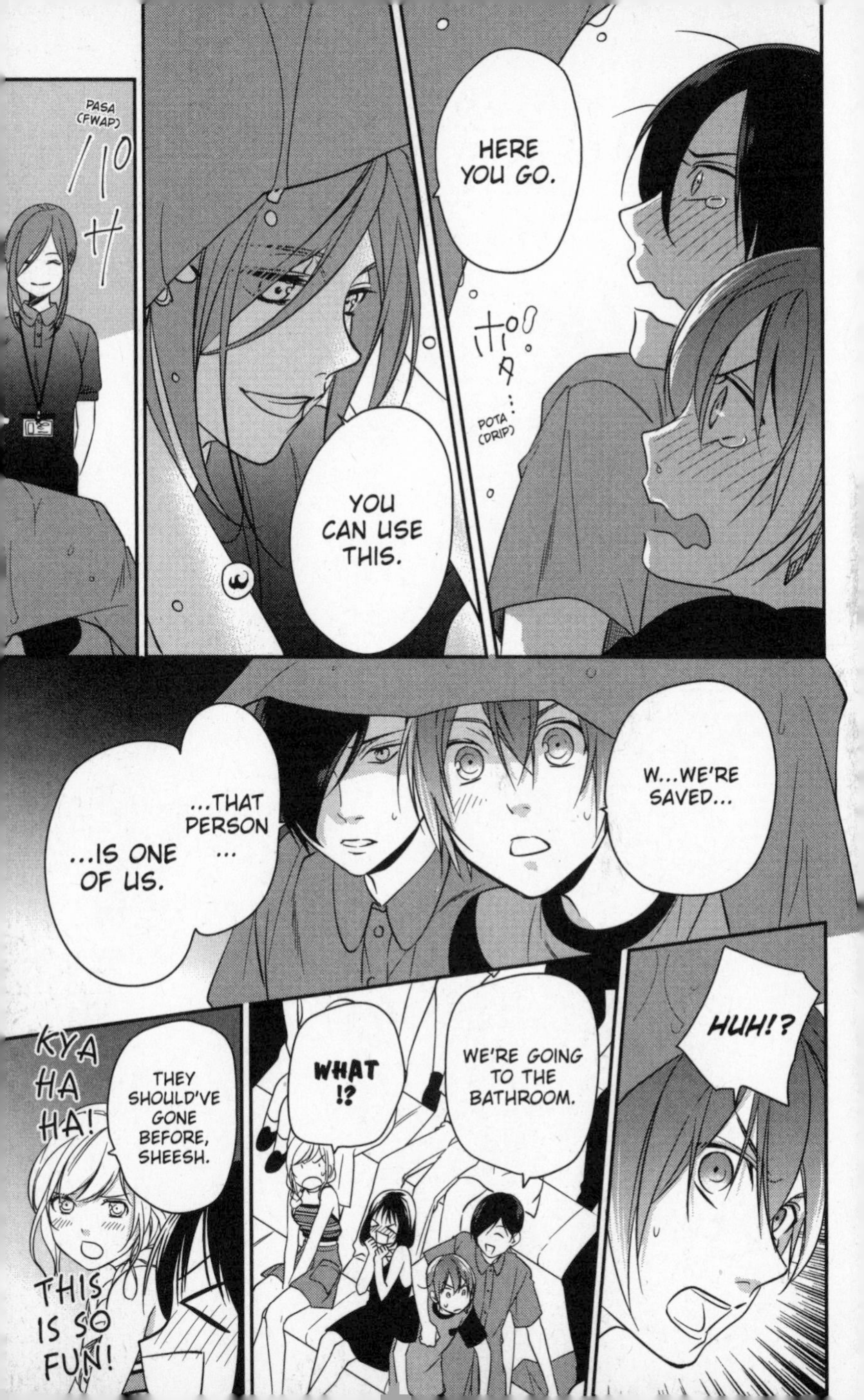
HERE YOU GO.
POTA (DRIP)
YOU CAN USE THIS.
PASA (FWAP)
W...WE'RE SAVED...
...THAT PERSON...
...IS ONE OF US.
HUH!?
WE'RE GOING TO THE BATHROOM.
WHAT!?
KYA HA HA!
THEY SHOULD'VE GONE BEFORE, SHEESH.
THIS IS SO FUN!

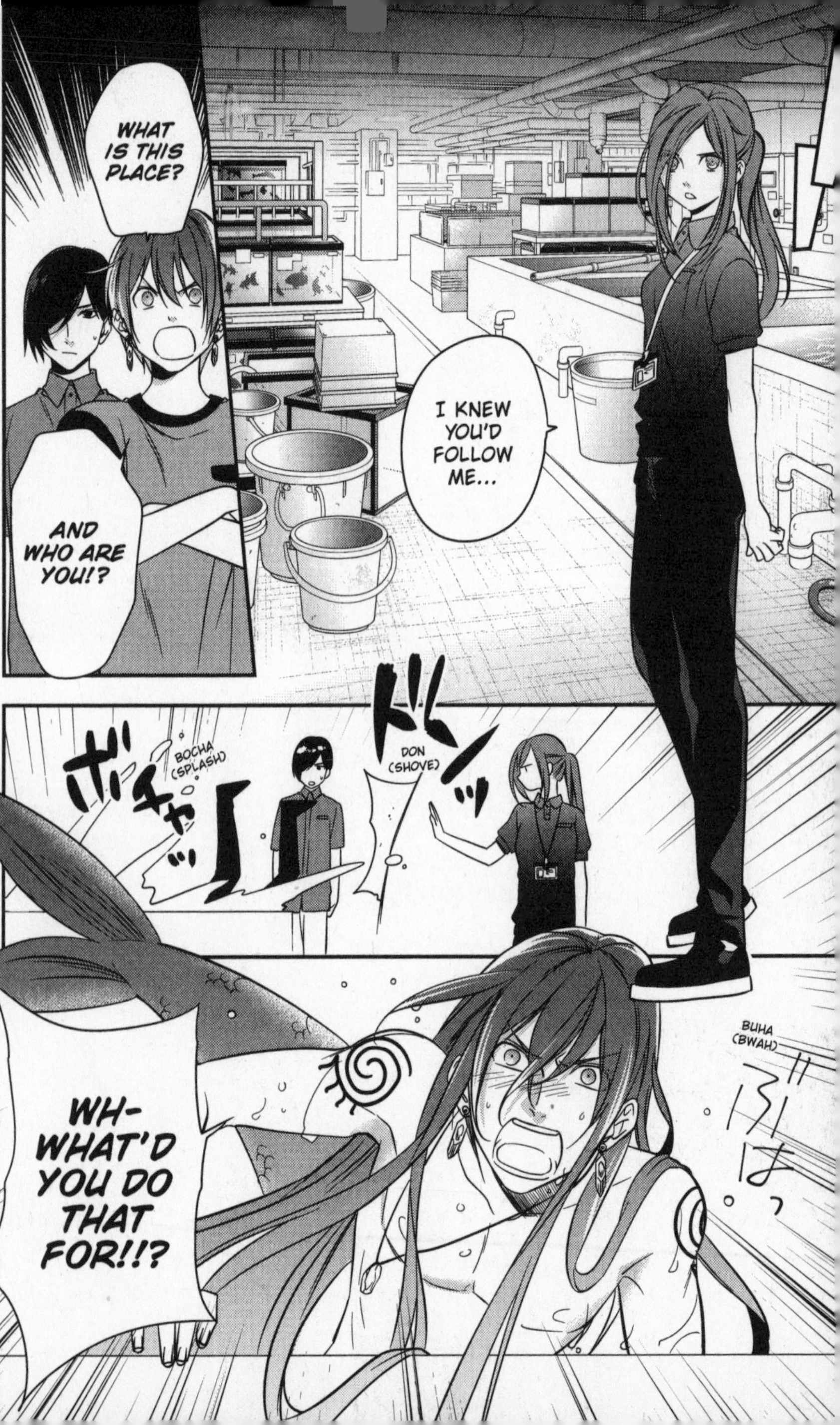
I KNEW YOU'D FOLLOW ME...
WHAT IS THIS PLACE?
AND WHO ARE YOU!?
DON (SHOVE)
BOCHA (SPLASH)
BUHA (BWAH)
WH-WHAT'D YOU DO THAT FOR!!?

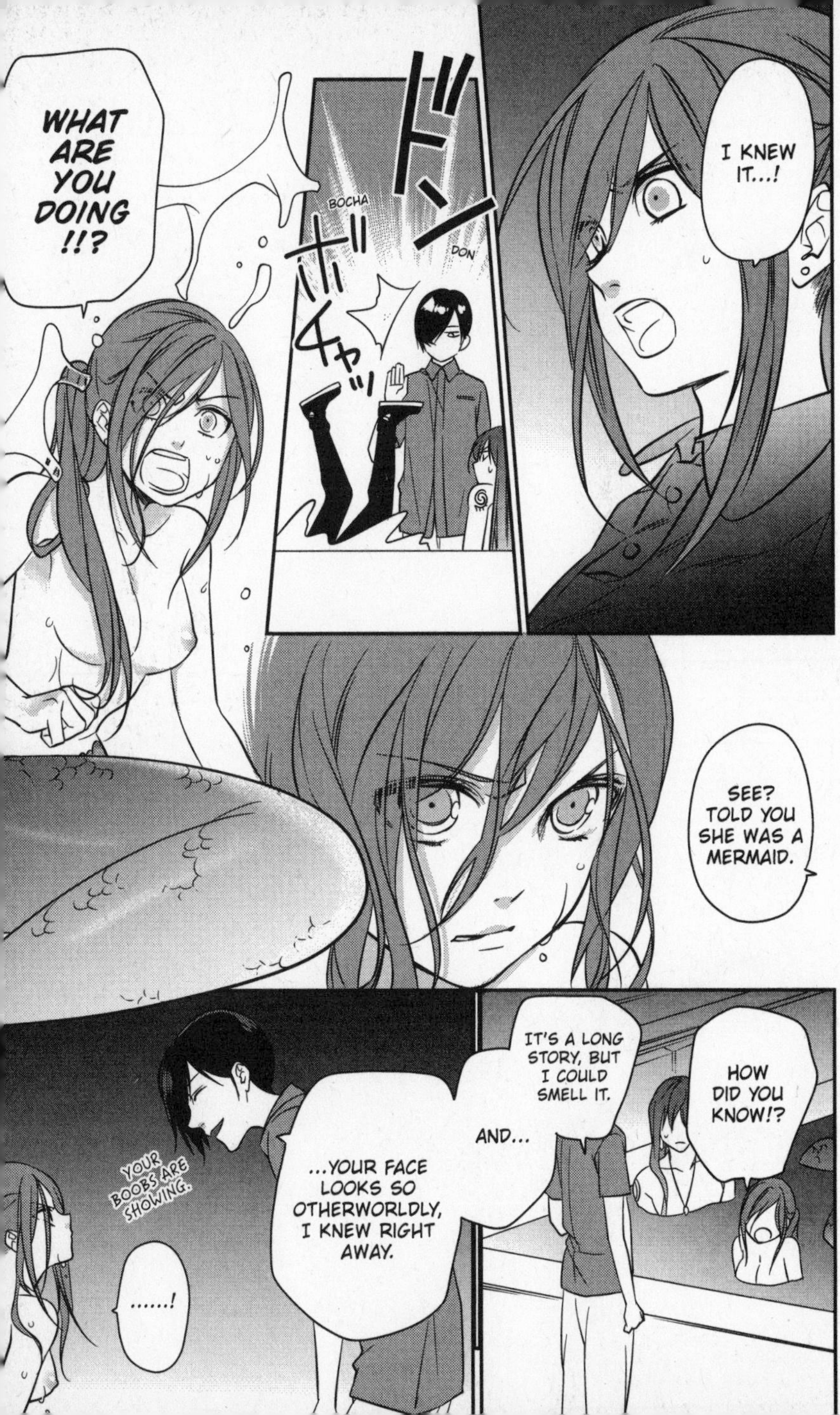
I KNEW IT...!
ドン
DON
ボチャッ
BOCHA
WHAT ARE YOU DOING!!?
SEE? TOLD YOU SHE WAS A MERMAID.
HOW DID YOU KNOW!?
IT'S A LONG STORY, BUT I COULD SMELL IT.
AND...
...YOUR FACE LOOKS SO OTHERWORLDLY, I KNEW RIGHT AWAY.
YOUR BOOBS ARE SHOWING.
......!

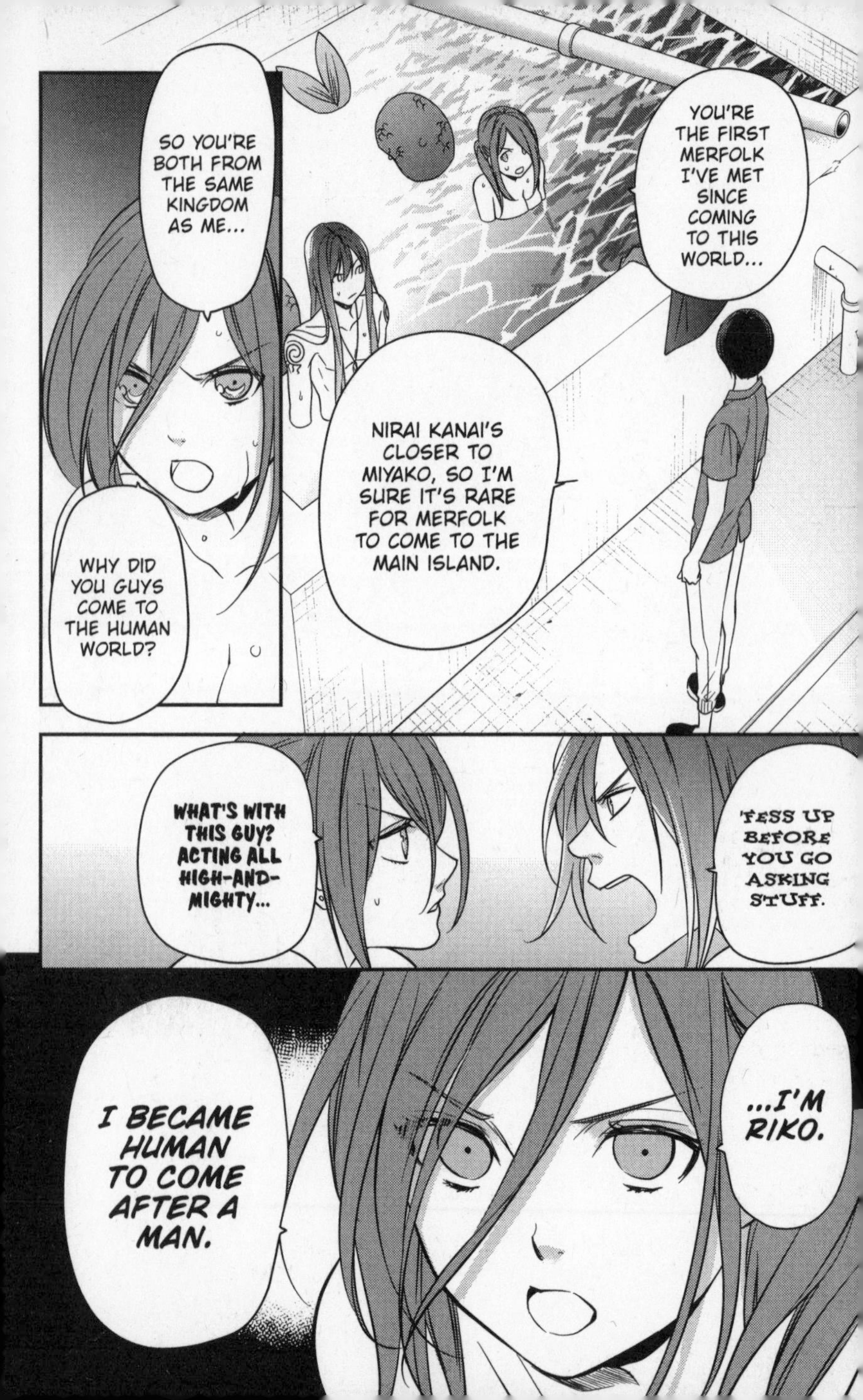
YOU'RE THE FIRST MERFOLK I'VE MET SINCE COMING TO THIS WORLD...
NIRAI KANAI'S CLOSER TO MIYAKO, SO I'M SURE IT'S RARE FOR MERFOLK TO COME TO THE MAIN ISLAND.
SO YOU'RE BOTH FROM THE SAME KINGDOM AS ME...
WHY DID YOU GUYS COME TO THE HUMAN WORLD?
'FESS UP BEFORE YOU GO ASKING STUFF.
WHAT'S WITH THIS GUY? ACTING ALL HIGH-AND-MIGHTY...
...I'M RIKO.
I BECAME HUMAN TO COME AFTER A MAN.

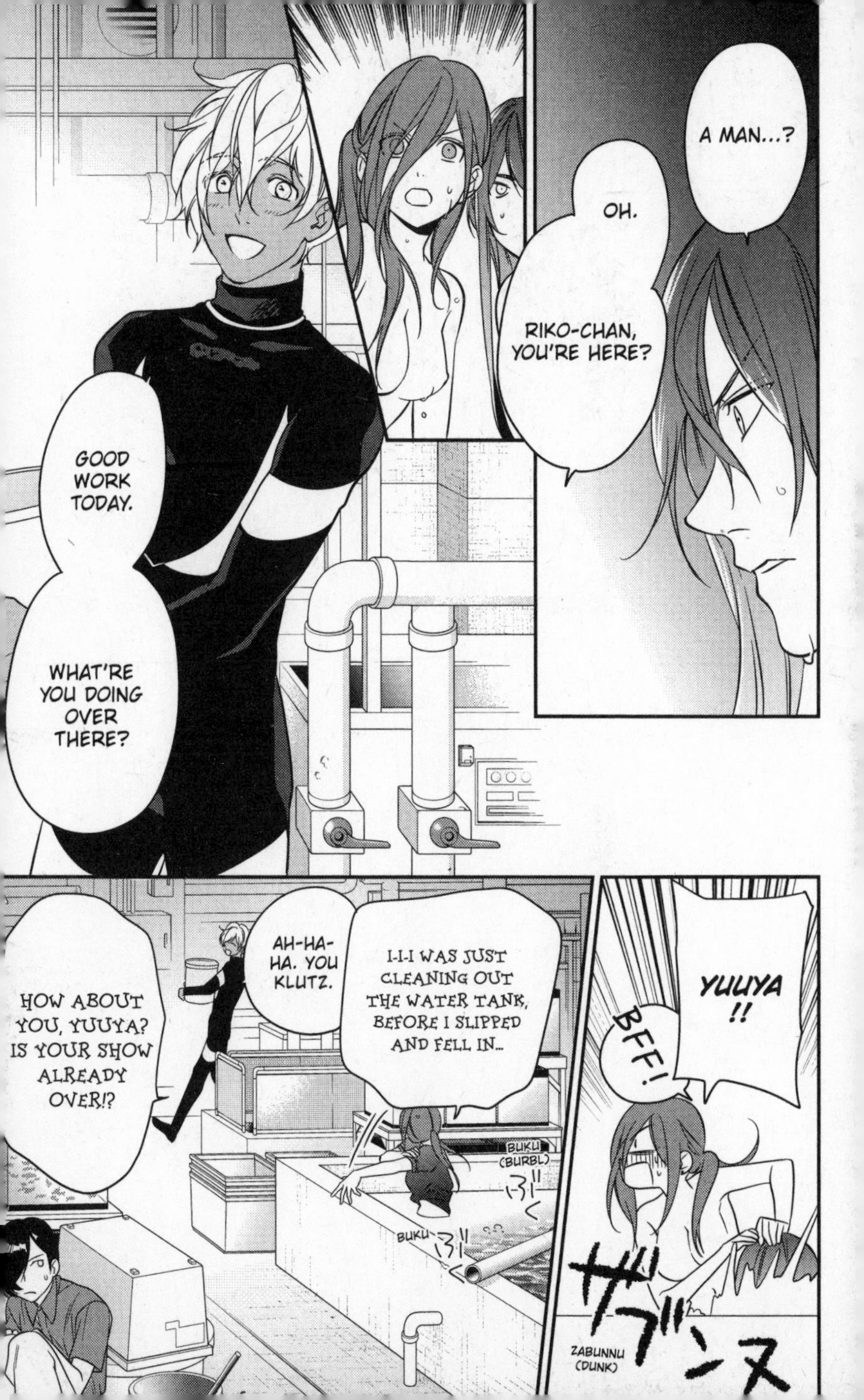
A MAN...?
OH.
RIKO-CHAN, YOU'RE HERE?
GOOD WORK TODAY.
WHAT'RE YOU DOING OVER THERE?
YUUYA !!
BFF!
ザブンヌ
ZABUNNU (DUNK)
I-I-I WAS JUST CLEANING OUT THE WATER TANK, BEFORE I SLIPPED AND FELL IN...
AH-HA-HA. YOU KLUTZ.
HOW ABOUT YOU, YUUYA? IS YOUR SHOW ALREADY OVER!?
ぶく
BUKU (BURBL)
ぶく
BUKU

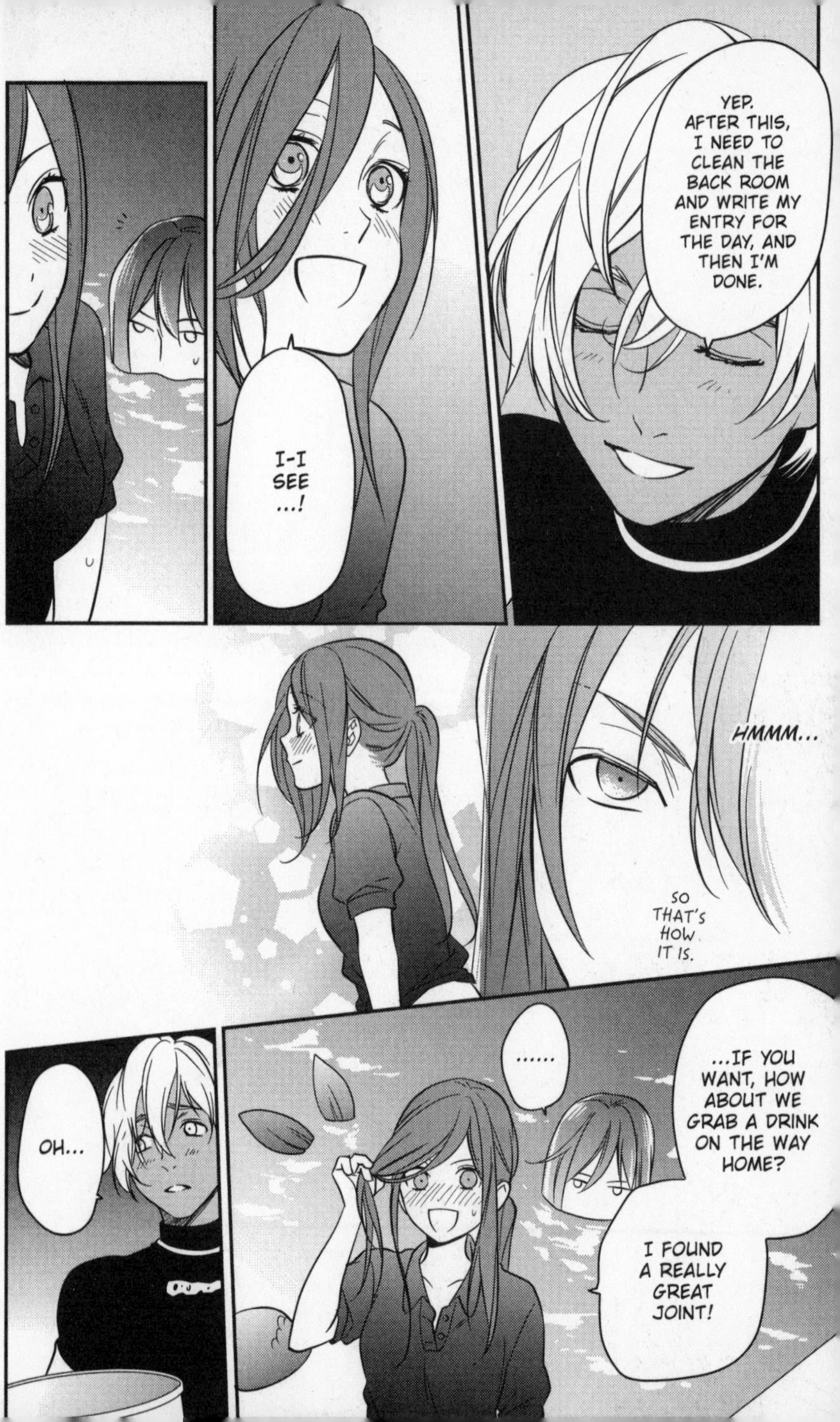
YEP. AFTER THIS, I NEED TO CLEAN THE BACK ROOM AND WRITE MY ENTRY FOR THE DAY, AND THEN I'M DONE.
I-I SEE ...!
HMMM...
SO THAT'S HOW IT IS.
......
...IF YOU WANT, HOW ABOUT WE GRAB A DRINK ON THE WAY HOME?
I FOUND A REALLY GREAT JOINT!
OH...

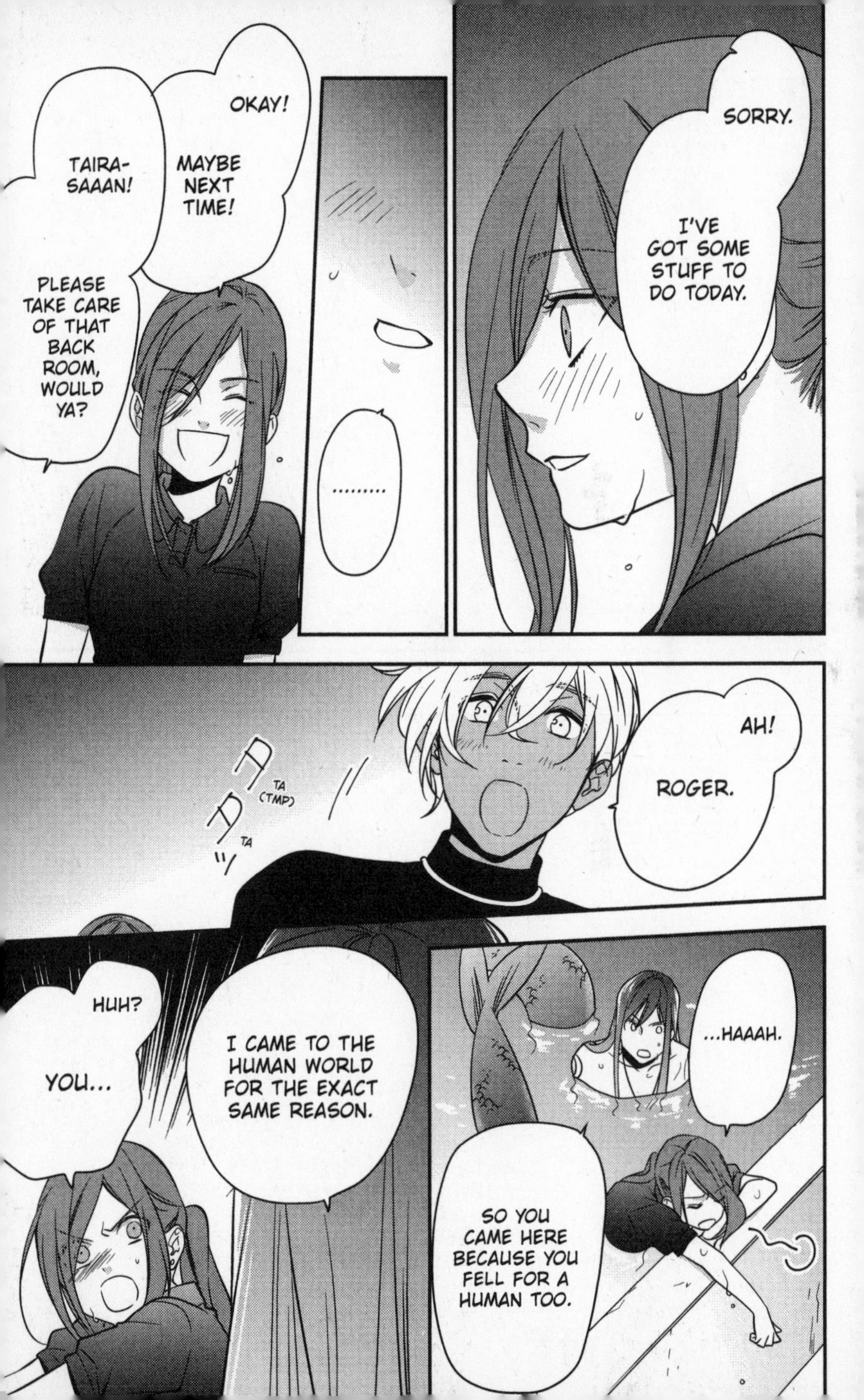

SORRY.
I'VE GOT SOME STUFF TO DO TODAY.
....
OKAY!
MAYBE NEXT TIME!
TAIRA-SAAAN!
PLEASE TAKE CARE OF THAT BACK ROOM, WOULD YA?
AH!
ROGER.
TA (TMP)
TA
...HAAAH.
SO YOU CAME HERE BECAUSE YOU FELL FOR A HUMAN TOO.
I CAME TO THE HUMAN WORLD FOR THE EXACT SAME REASON.
HUH?
YOU...

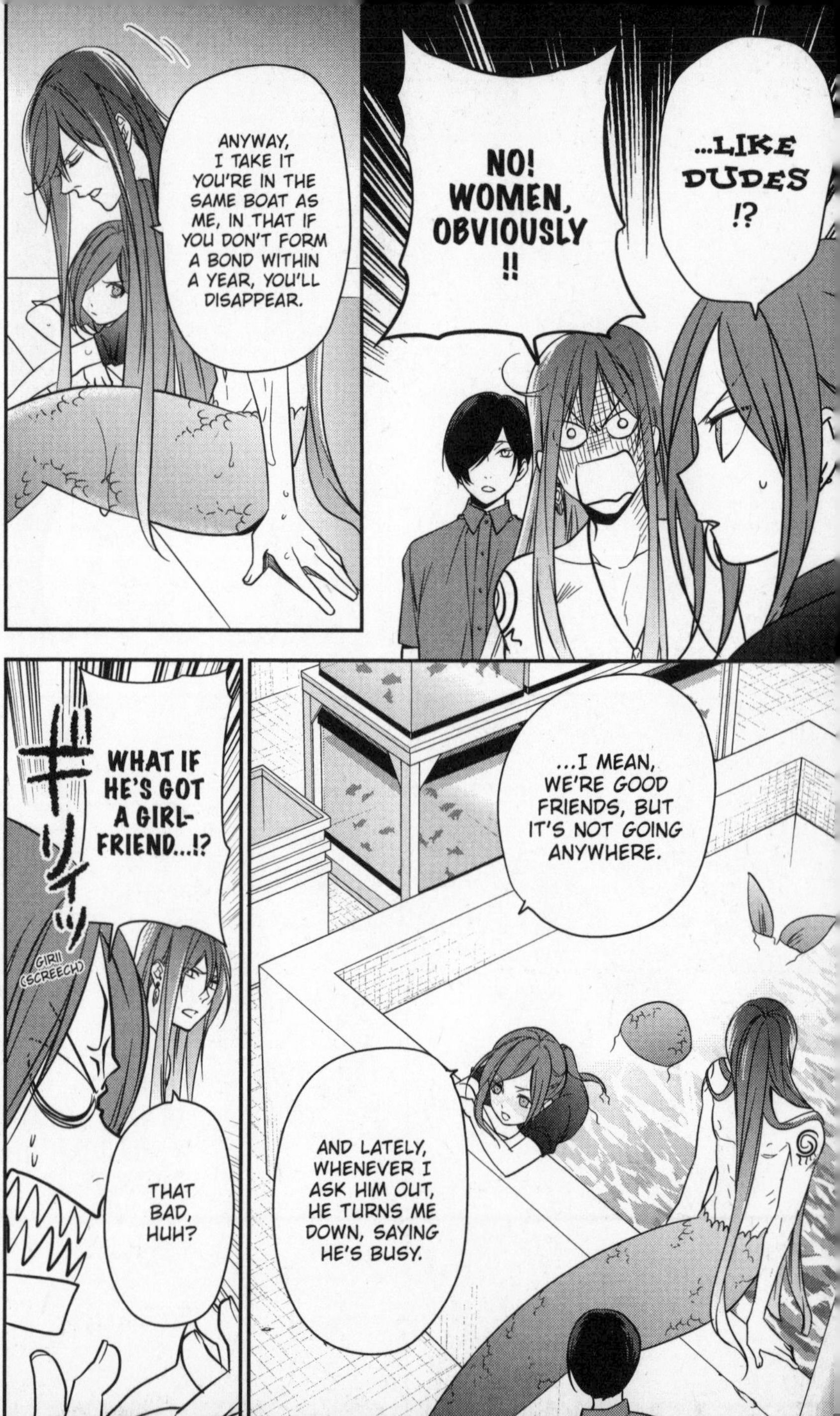
...LIKE DUDES !?
NO! WOMEN, OBVIOUSLY !!
ANYWAY, I TAKE IT YOU'RE IN THE SAME BOAT AS ME, IN THAT IF YOU DON'T FORM A BOND WITHIN A YEAR, YOU'LL DISAPPEAR.
...I MEAN, WE'RE GOOD FRIENDS, BUT IT'S NOT GOING ANYWHERE.
AND LATELY, WHENEVER I ASK HIM OUT, HE TURNS ME DOWN, SAYING HE'S BUSY.
WHAT IF HE'S GOT A GIRL-FRIEND...!?
GIRII (SCREECH)
THAT BAD, HUH?

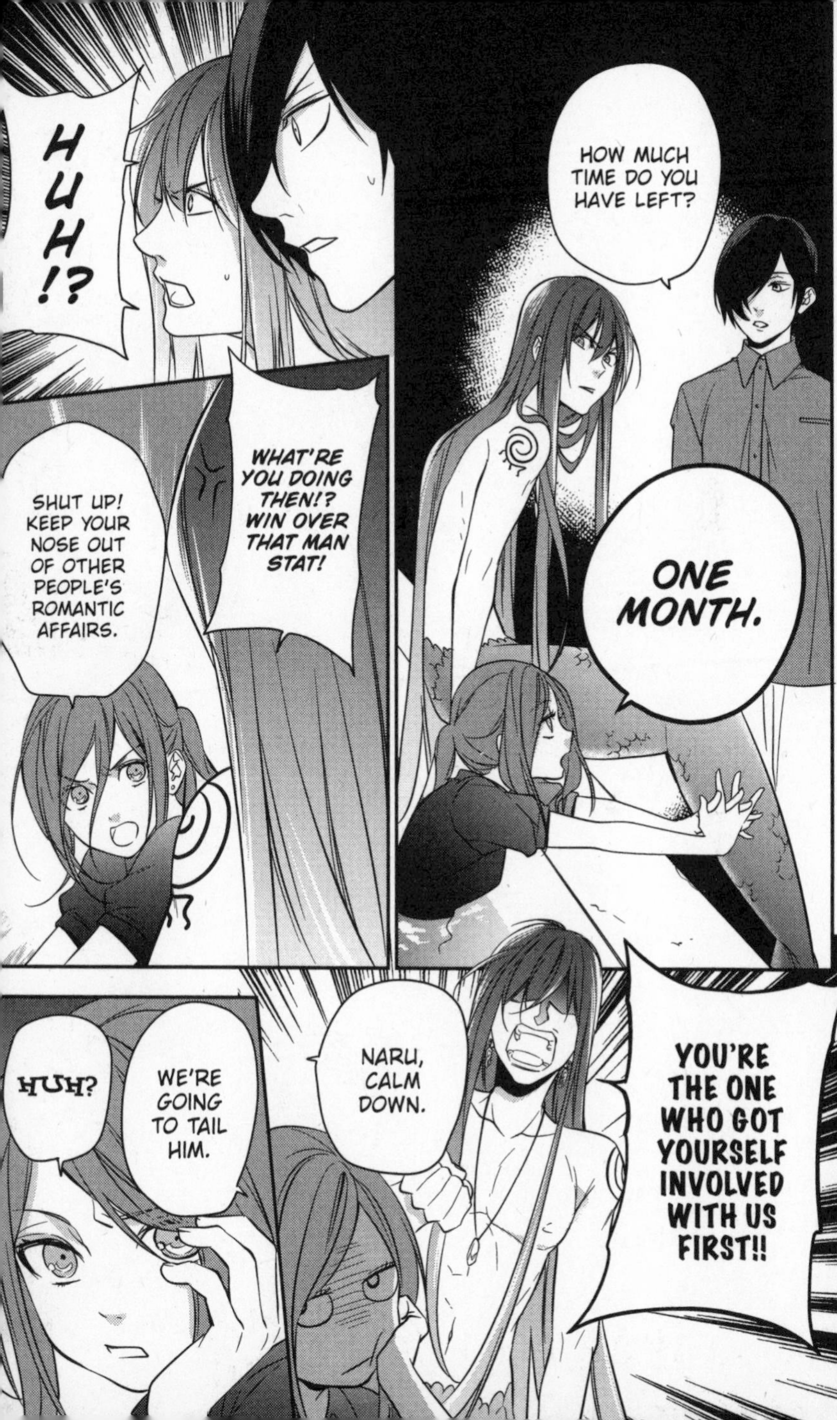
HOW MUCH TIME DO YOU HAVE LEFT?
ONE MONTH.
HUH!?
WHAT'RE YOU DOING THEN!? WIN OVER THAT MAN STAT!
SHUT UP! KEEP YOUR NOSE OUT OF OTHER PEOPLE'S ROMANTIC AFFAIRS.
YOU'RE THE ONE WHO GOT YOURSELF INVOLVED WITH US FIRST!!
NARU, CALM DOWN.
WE'RE GOING TO TAIL HIM.
HUH?

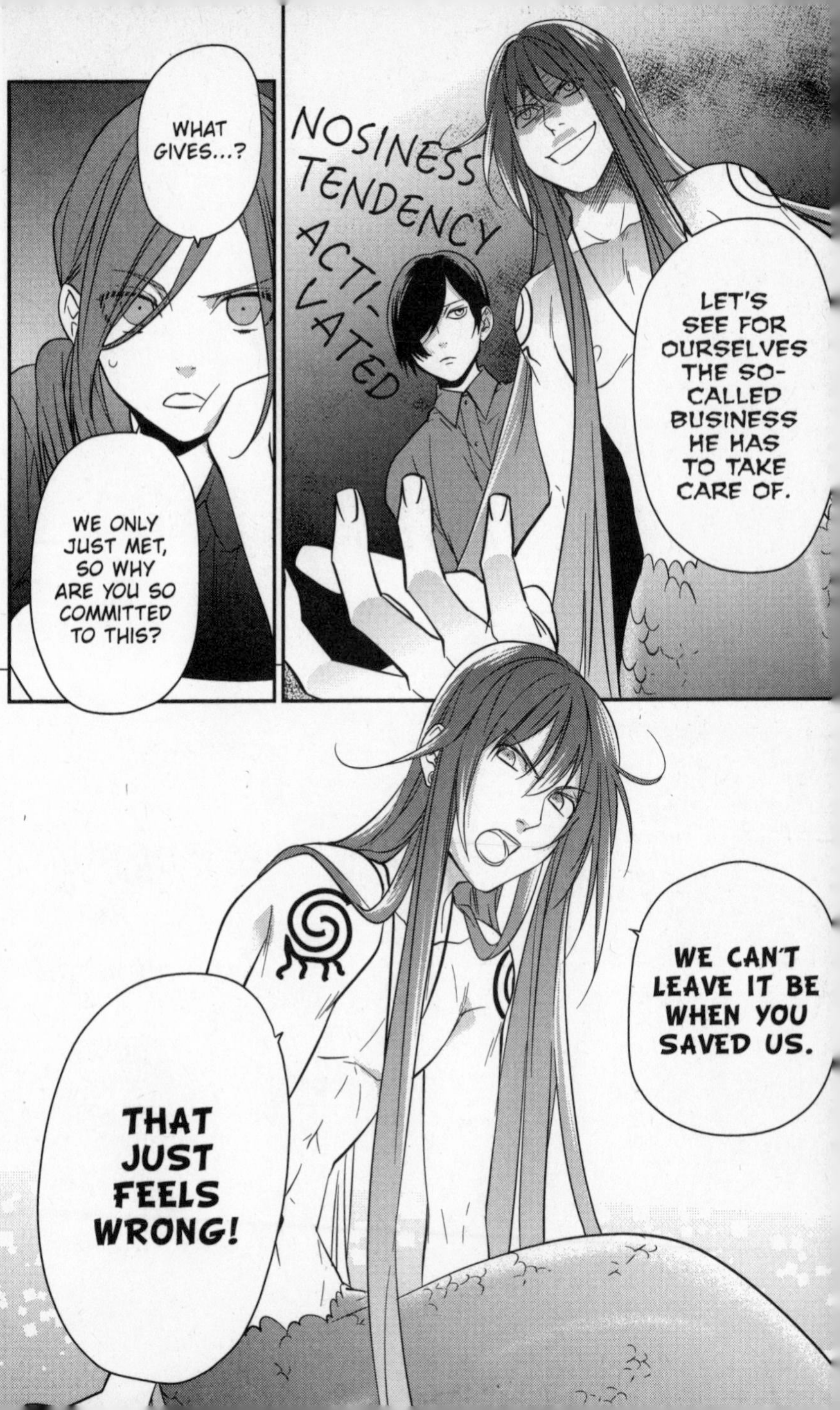
LET'S SEE FOR OURSELVES THE SO-CALLED BUSINESS HE HAS TO TAKE CARE OF.
NOSINESS TENDENCY ACTI-VATED
WHAT GIVES...?
WE ONLY JUST MET, SO WHY ARE YOU SO COMMITTED TO THIS?
WE CAN'T LEAVE IT BE WHEN YOU SAVED US.
THAT JUST FEELS WRONG!

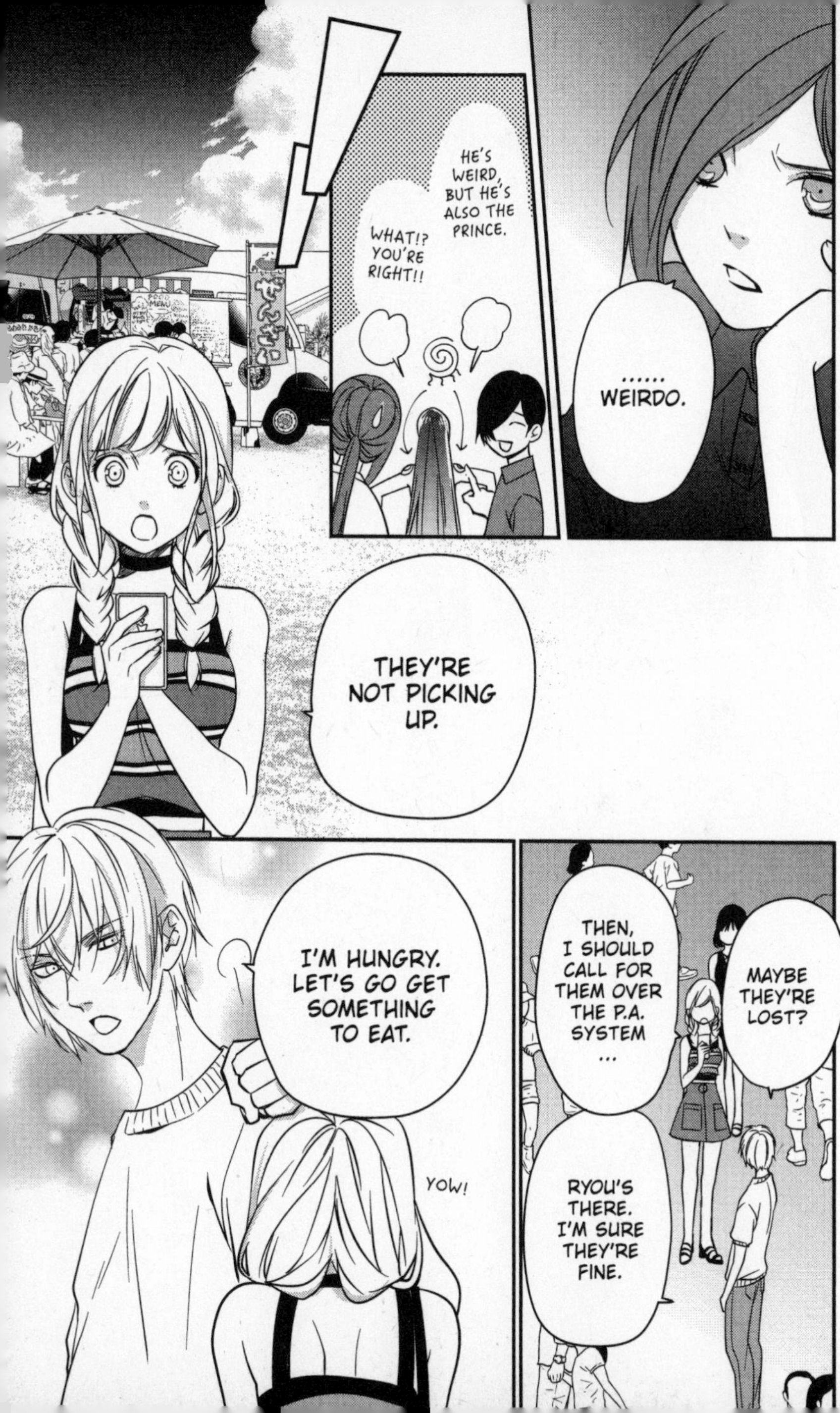
...... WEIRDO.
HE'S WEIRD, BUT HE'S ALSO THE PRINCE.
WHAT!? YOU'RE RIGHT!!
THEY'RE NOT PICKING UP.
MAYBE THEY'RE LOST?
THEN, I SHOULD CALL FOR THEM OVER THE P.A. SYSTEM ...
RYOU'S THERE. I'M SURE THEY'RE FINE.
I'M HUNGRY. LET'S GO GET SOMETHING TO EAT.
YOW!

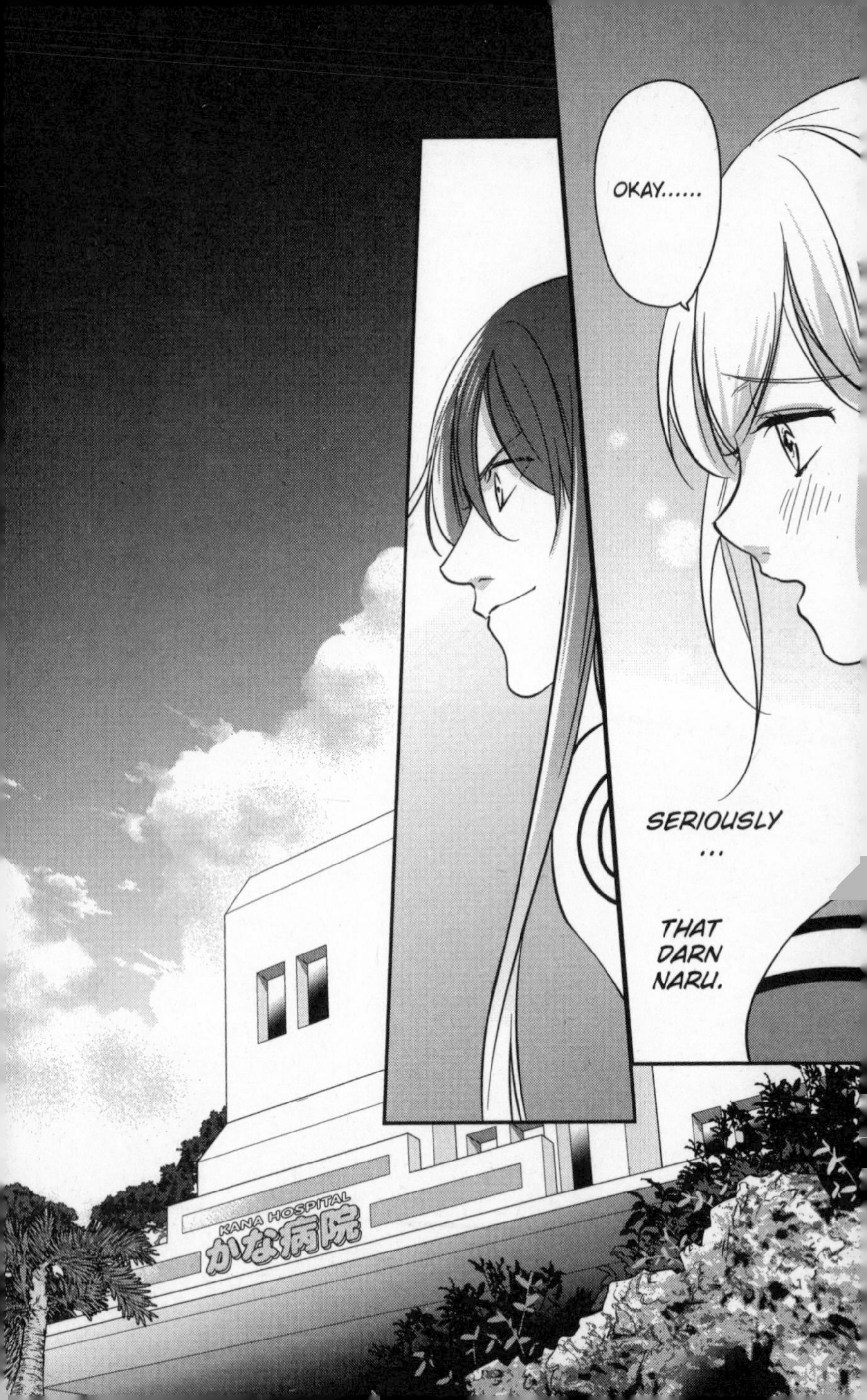
OKAY......
SERIOUSLY ...
THAT DARN NARU.
KANA HOSPITAL
かな病院

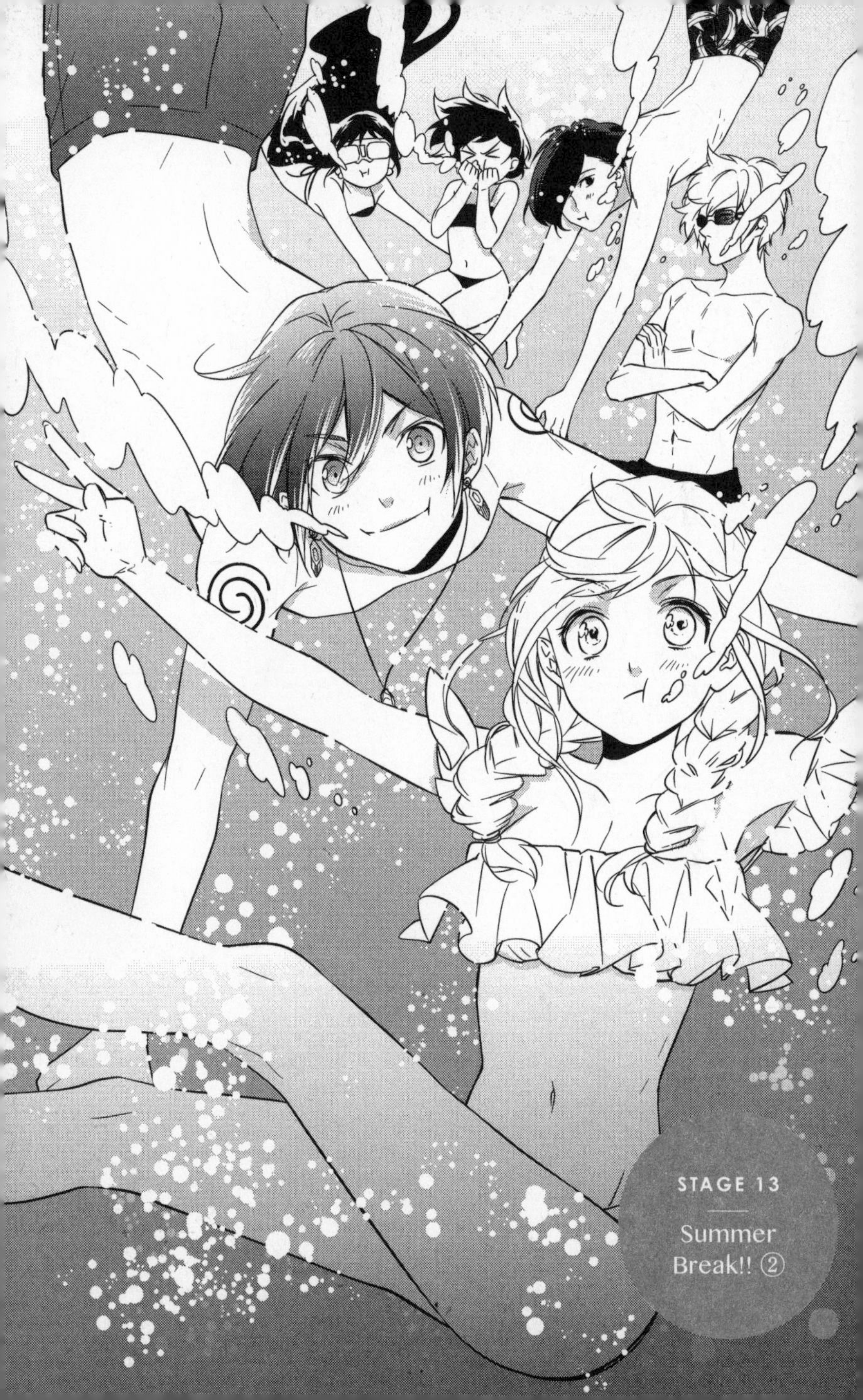
STAGE 13
Summer Break!! ②

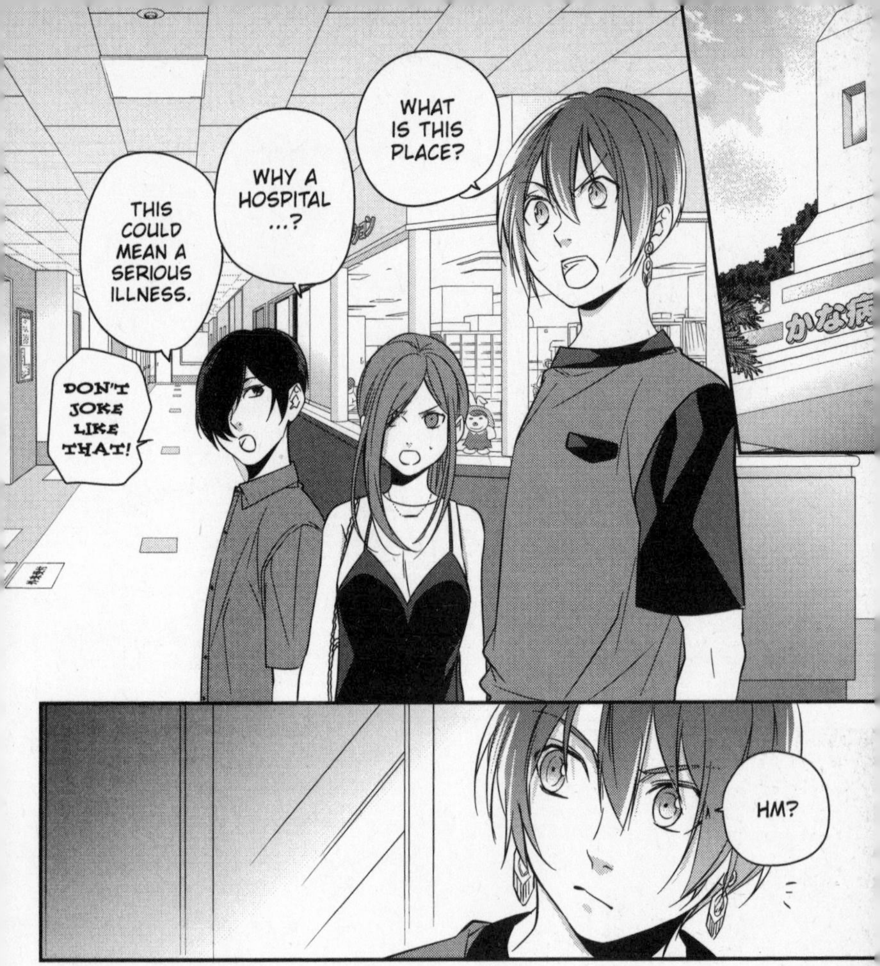
WHAT IS THIS PLACE?
WHY A HOSPITAL ...?
THIS COULD MEAN A SERIOUS ILLNESS.
DON'T JOKE LIKE THAT!
HM?

MERMAID BOYS

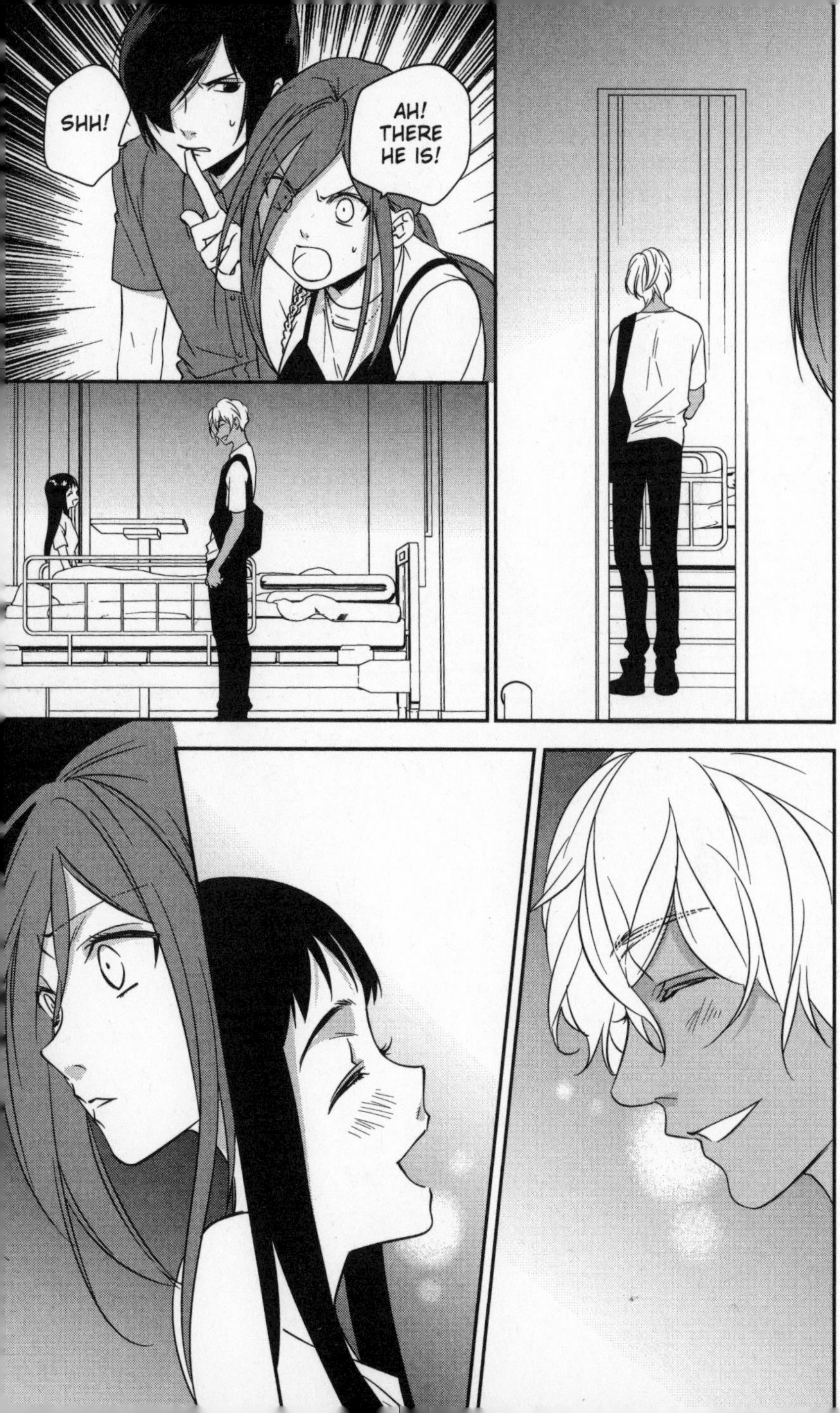
AH! THERE HE IS!
SHH!

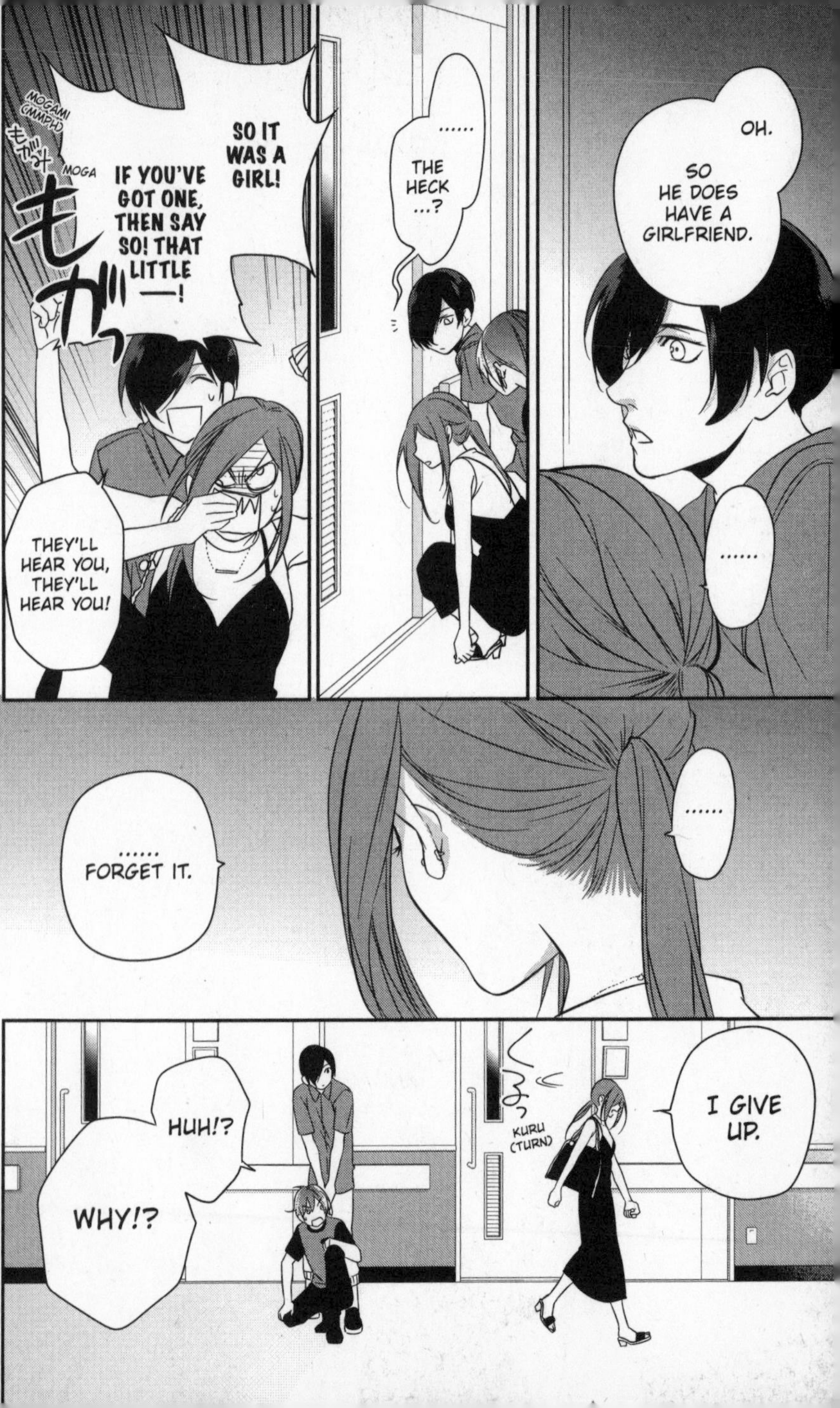
OH.
SO HE DOES HAVE A GIRLFRIEND.
......
......
THE HECK ...?
SO IT WAS A GIRL!
IF YOU'VE GOT ONE, THEN SAY SO! THAT LITTLE—!
MOGAMI (MMPH)
MOGA
THEY'LL HEAR YOU, THEY'LL HEAR YOU!
......
...... FORGET IT.
I GIVE UP.
KURU (TURN)
HUH!?
WHY!?

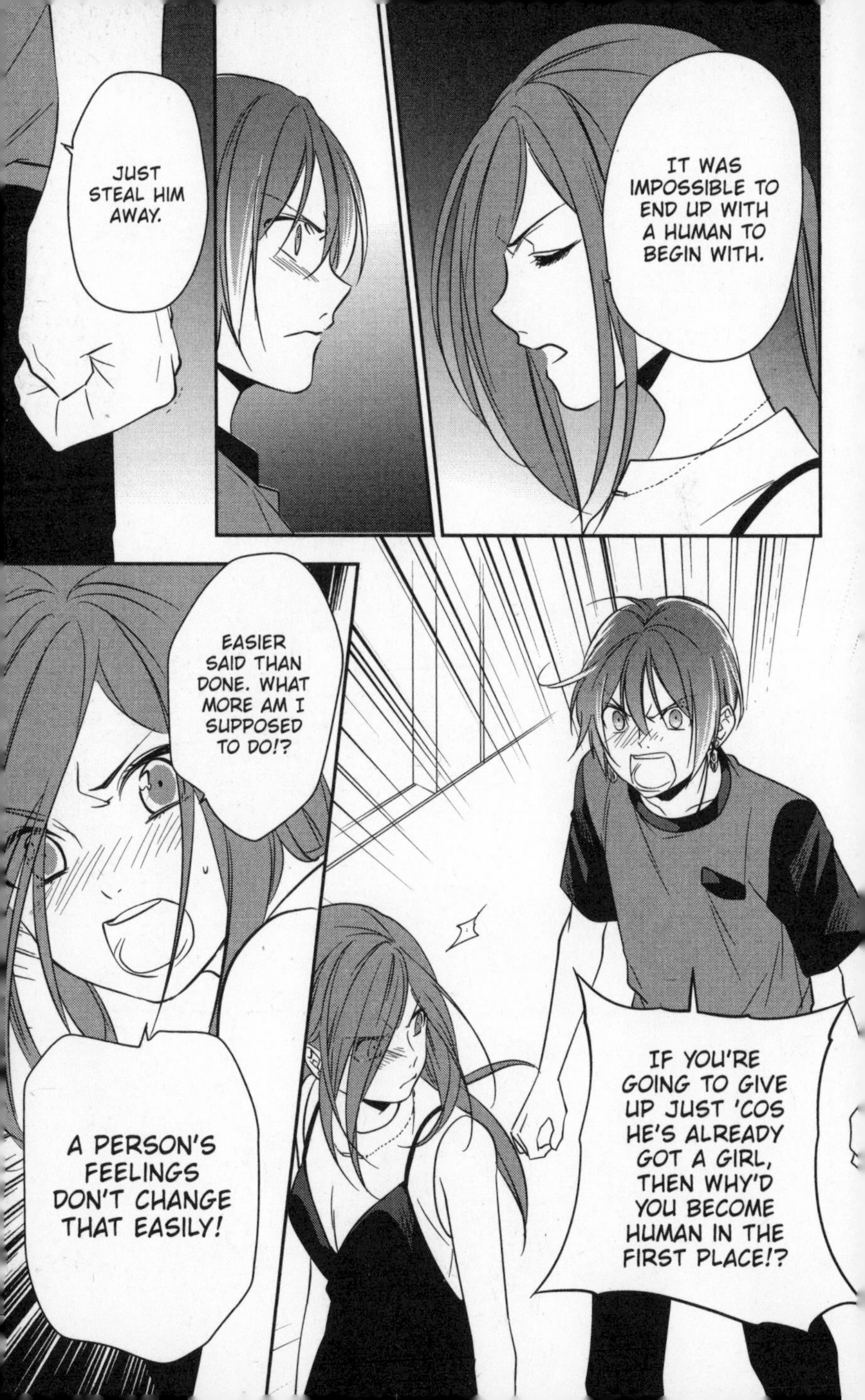
IT WAS IMPOSSIBLE TO END UP WITH A HUMAN TO BEGIN WITH.
JUST STEAL HIM AWAY.
IF YOU'RE GOING TO GIVE UP JUST 'COS HE'S ALREADY GOT A GIRL, THEN WHY'D YOU BECOME HUMAN IN THE FIRST PLACE!?
EASIER SAID THAN DONE. WHAT MORE AM I SUPPOSED TO DO!?
A PERSON'S FEELINGS DON'T CHANGE THAT EASILY!

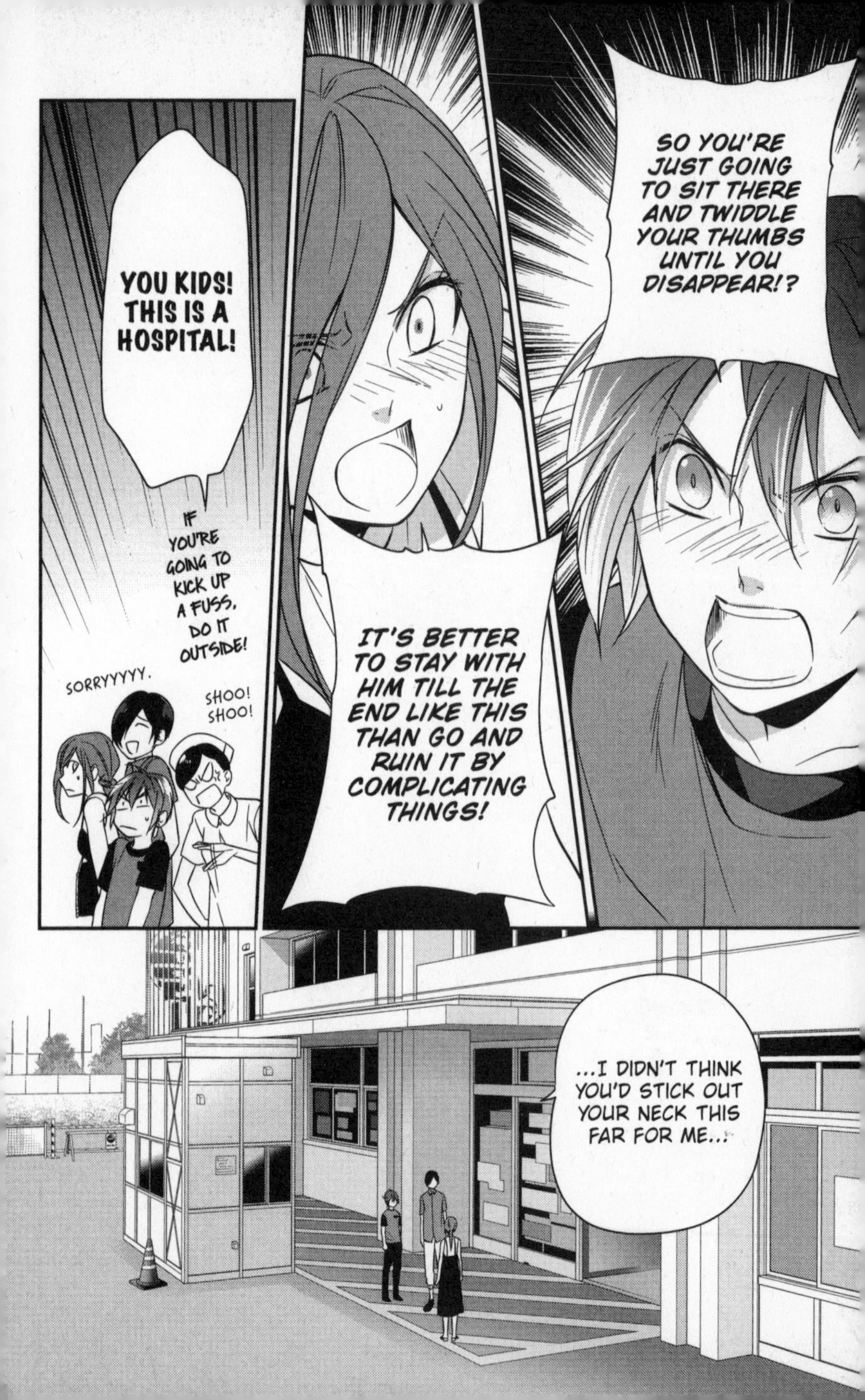
SO YOU'RE JUST GOING TO SIT THERE AND TWIDDLE YOUR THUMBS UNTIL YOU DISAPPEAR!?
IT'S BETTER TO STAY WITH HIM TILL THE END LIKE THIS THAN GO AND RUIN IT BY COMPLICATING THINGS!
YOU KIDS! THIS IS A HOSPITAL!
IF YOU'RE GOING TO KICK UP A FUSS, DO IT OUTSIDE!
SHOO! SHOO!
SORRYYYYY.
...I DIDN'T THINK YOU'D STICK OUT YOUR NECK THIS FAR FOR ME...

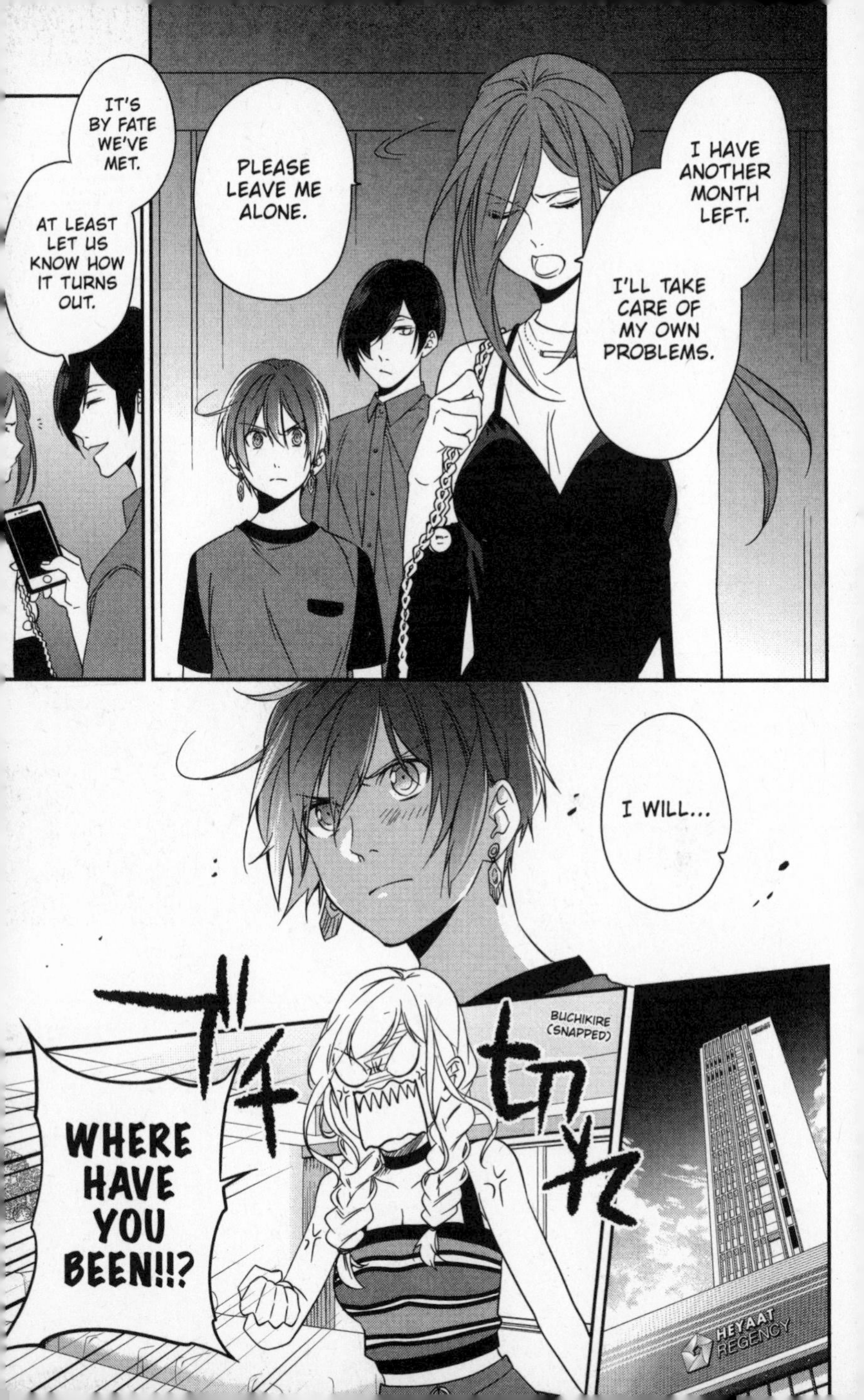
I HAVE ANOTHER MONTH LEFT.
I'LL TAKE CARE OF MY OWN PROBLEMS.
PLEASE LEAVE ME ALONE.
IT'S BY FATE WE'VE MET.
AT LEAST LET US KNOW HOW IT TURNS OUT.
I WILL...
BUCHIKIRE (SNAPPED)
HEYAAT REGENCY
WHERE HAVE YOU BEEN!!?

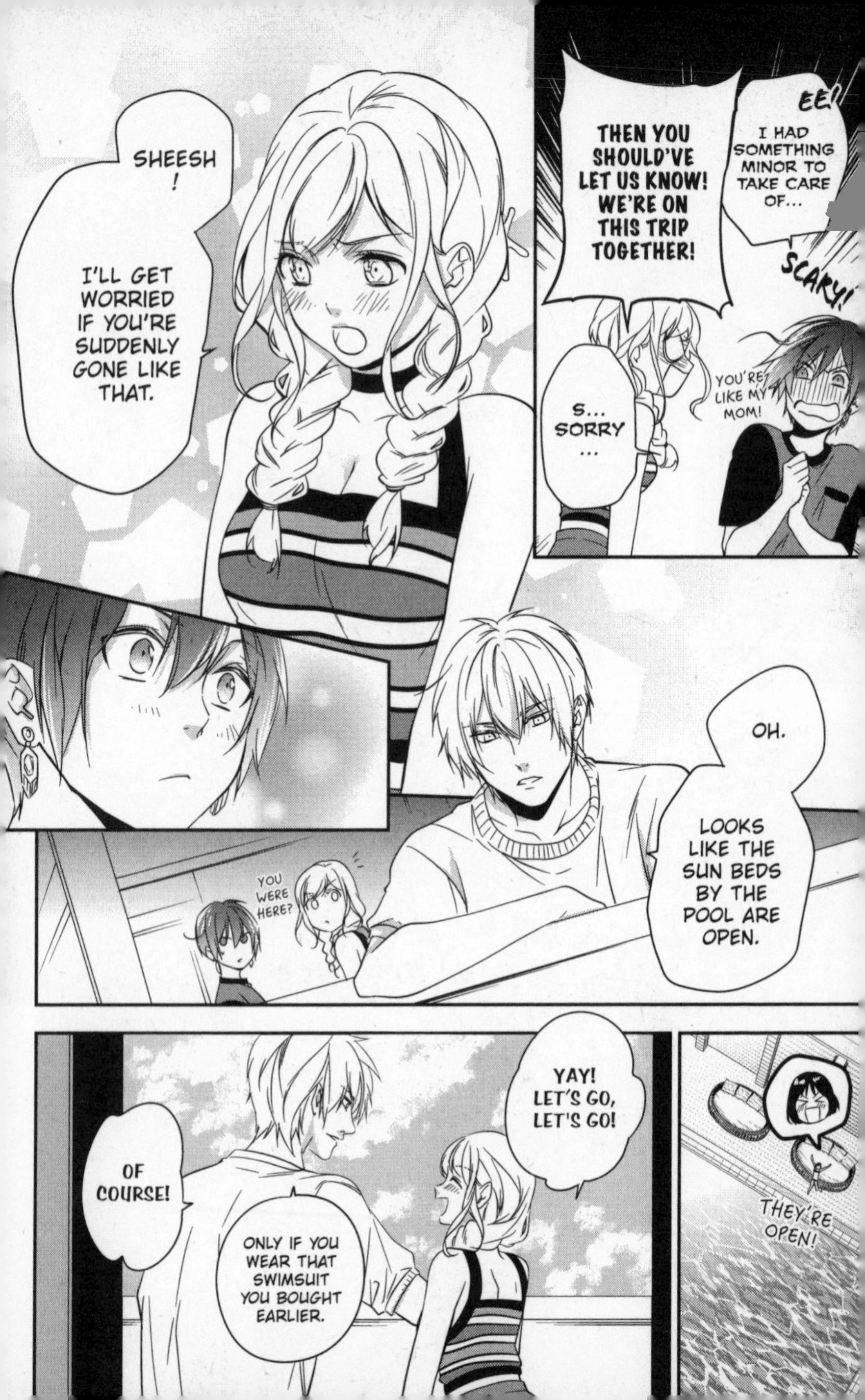
EE!
I HAD SOMETHING MINOR TO TAKE CARE OF...
THEN YOU SHOULD'VE LET US KNOW! WE'RE ON THIS TRIP TOGETHER!
SCARY!
YOU'RE LIKE MY MOM!
S... SORRY...
SHEESH!
I'LL GET WORRIED IF YOU'RE SUDDENLY GONE LIKE THAT.
OH.
LOOKS LIKE THE SUN BEDS BY THE POOL ARE OPEN.
YOU WERE HERE?
THEY'RE OPEN!
YAY! LET'S GO, LET'S GO!
ONLY IF YOU WEAR THAT SWIMSUIT YOU BOUGHT EARLIER.
OF COURSE!

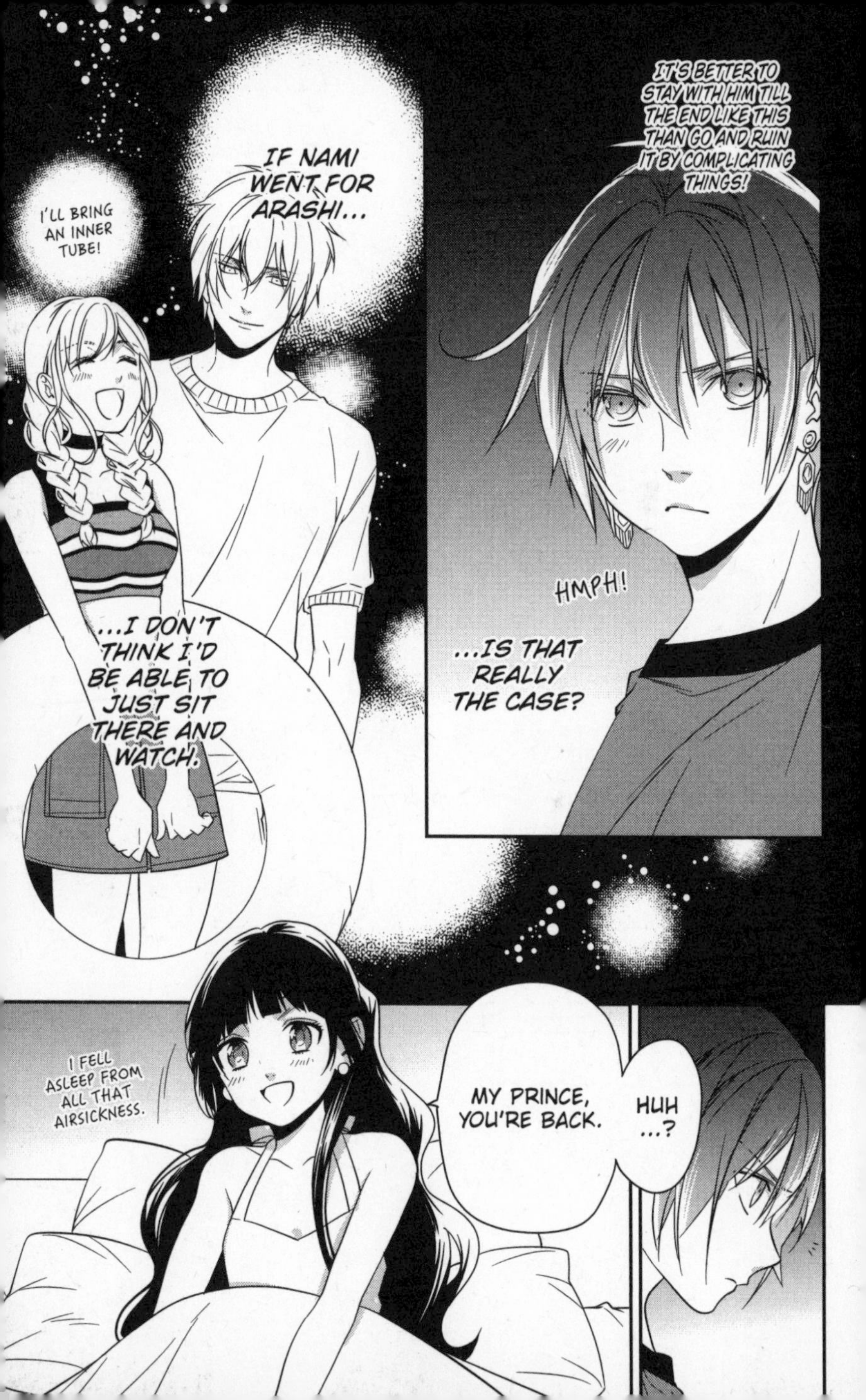
IT'S BETTER TO STAY WITH HIM TILL THE END LIKE THIS THAN GO AND RUIN IT BY COMPLICATING THINGS!
HMPH!
...IS THAT REALLY THE CASE?
IF NAMI WENT FOR ARASHI...
I'LL BRING AN INNER TUBE!
...I DON'T THINK I'D BE ABLE TO JUST SIT THERE AND WATCH.
HUH ...?
MY PRINCE, YOU'RE BACK.
I FELL ASLEEP FROM ALL THAT AIRSICKNESS.

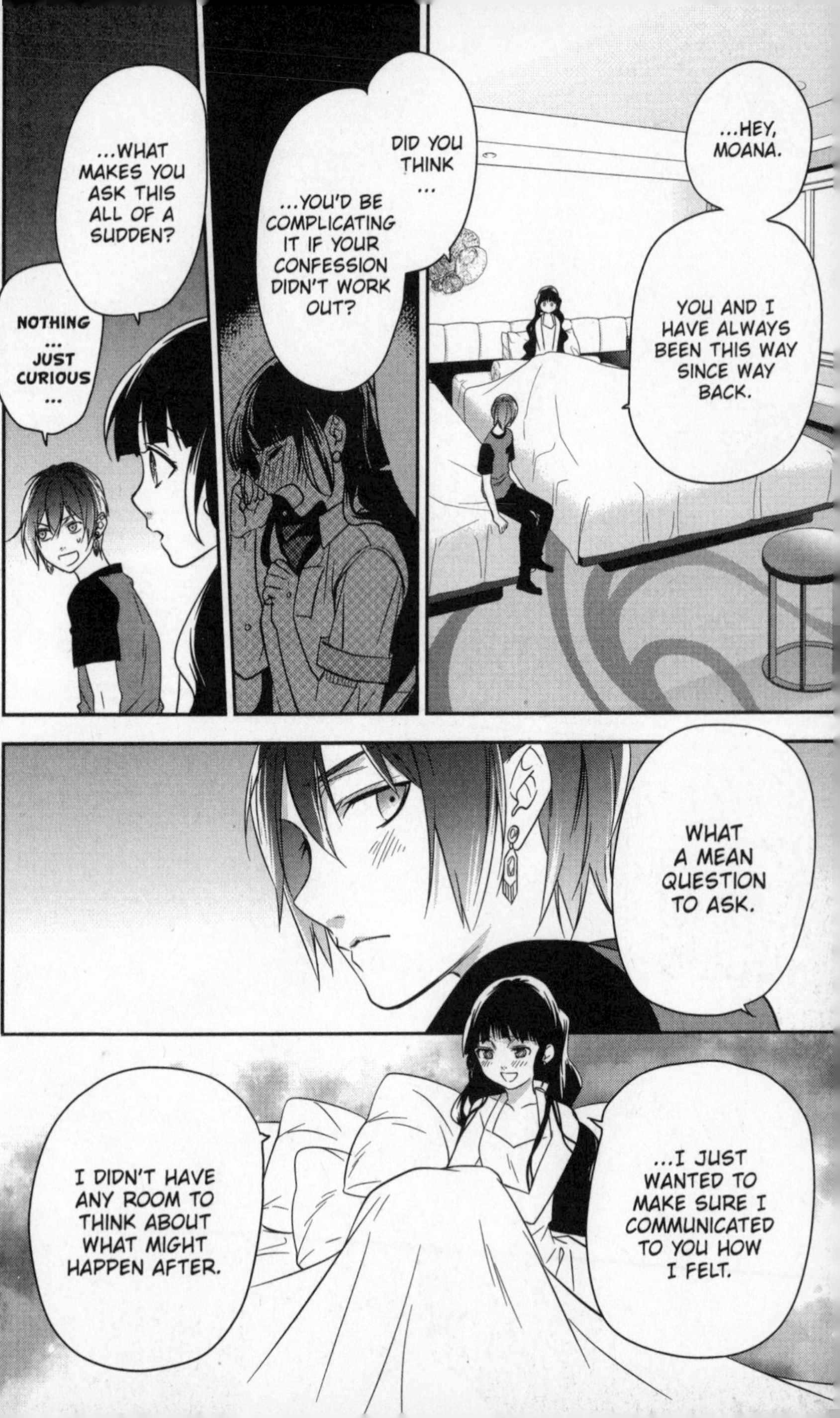
...HEY, MOANA.
YOU AND I HAVE ALWAYS BEEN THIS WAY SINCE WAY BACK.
DID YOU THINK ...
...YOU'D BE COMPLICATING IT IF YOUR CONFESSION DIDN'T WORK OUT?
...WHAT MAKES YOU ASK THIS ALL OF A SUDDEN?
NOTHING ... JUST CURIOUS ...
WHAT A MEAN QUESTION TO ASK.
...I JUST WANTED TO MAKE SURE I COMMUNICATED TO YOU HOW I FELT.
I DIDN'T HAVE ANY ROOM TO THINK ABOUT WHAT MIGHT HAPPEN AFTER.

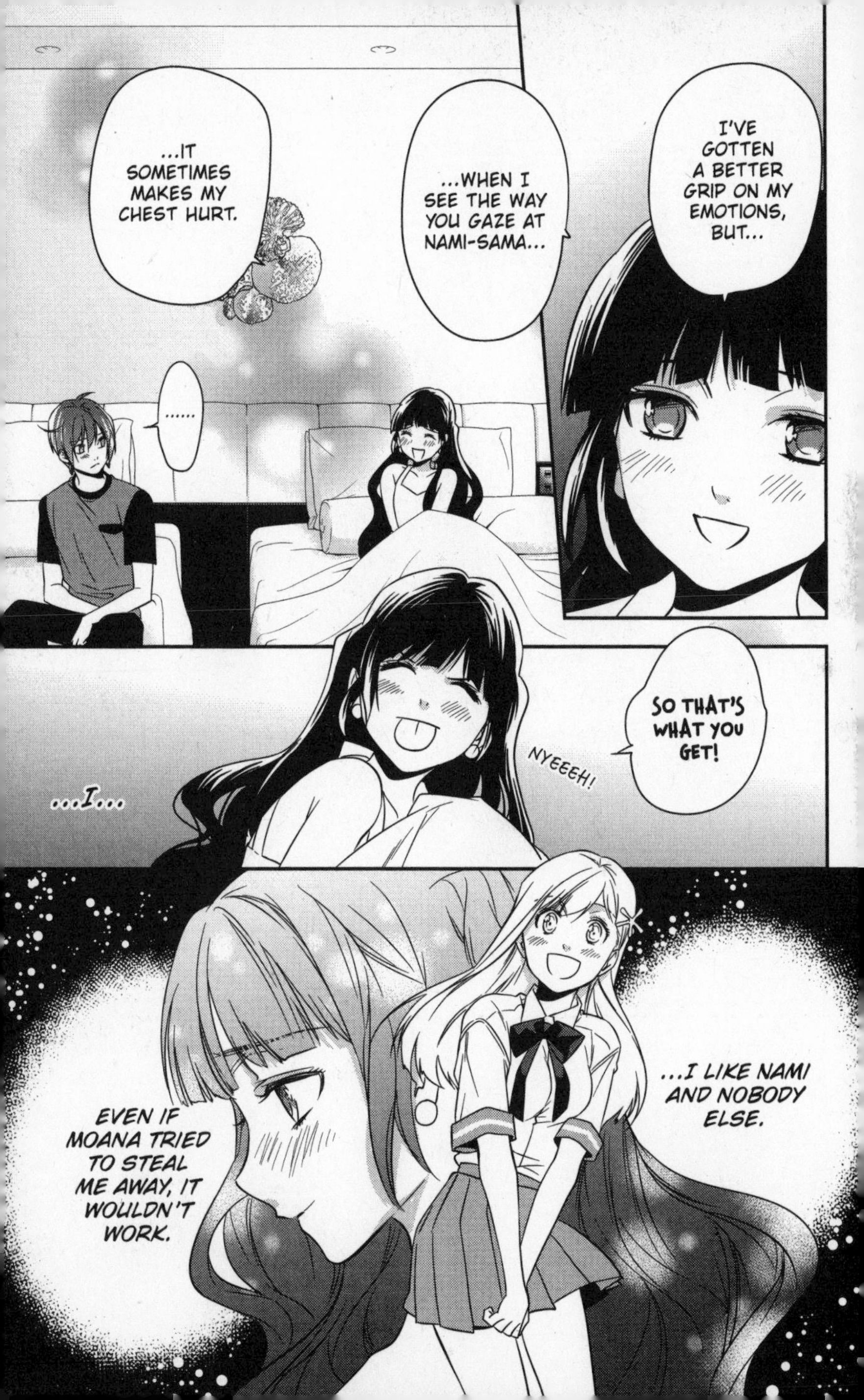
I'VE GOTTEN A BETTER GRIP ON MY EMOTIONS, BUT...
...WHEN I SEE THE WAY YOU GAZE AT NAMI-SAMA...
...IT SOMETIMES MAKES MY CHEST HURT.
......
SO THAT'S WHAT YOU GET!
NYEEEH!
...I...
...I LIKE NAMI AND NOBODY ELSE.
EVEN IF MOANA TRIED TO STEAL ME AWAY, IT WOULDN'T WORK.

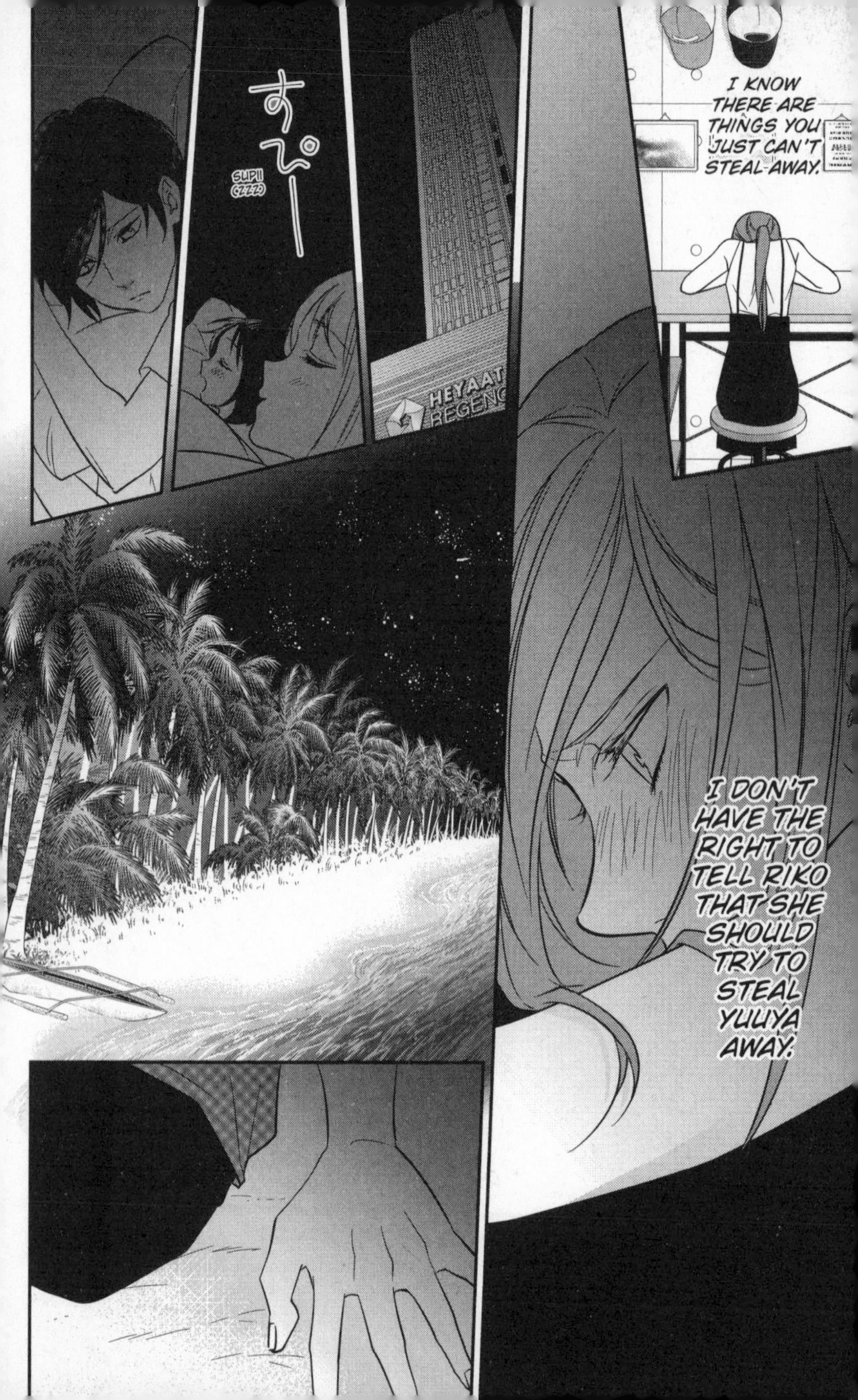
I KNOW THERE ARE THINGS YOU JUST CAN'T STEAL AWAY.
HEYAAT REGENC
すぴー
SUPII (ZZZZ)
I DON'T HAVE THE RIGHT TO TELL RIKO THAT SHE SHOULD TRY TO STEAL YUUYA AWAY.

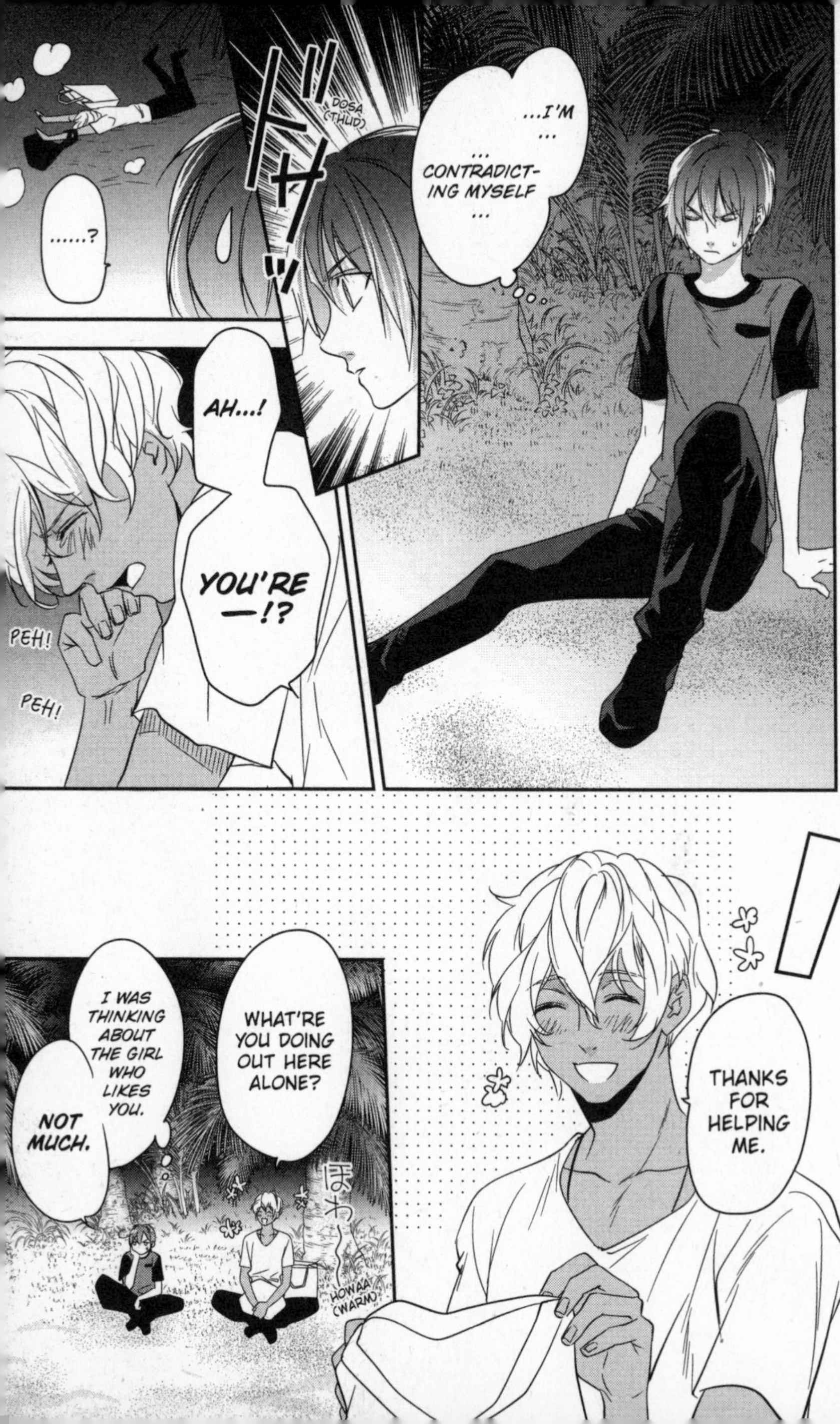
...I'M ... ... CONTRADICT-ING MYSELF ...
DOSA (THUD)
......?
AH...!
YOU'RE—!?
PEH! PEH!
THANKS FOR HELPING ME.
WHAT'RE YOU DOING OUT HERE ALONE?
NOT MUCH.
I WAS THINKING ABOUT THE GIRL WHO LIKES YOU.
ほわ〜
HOWAA (WARM)

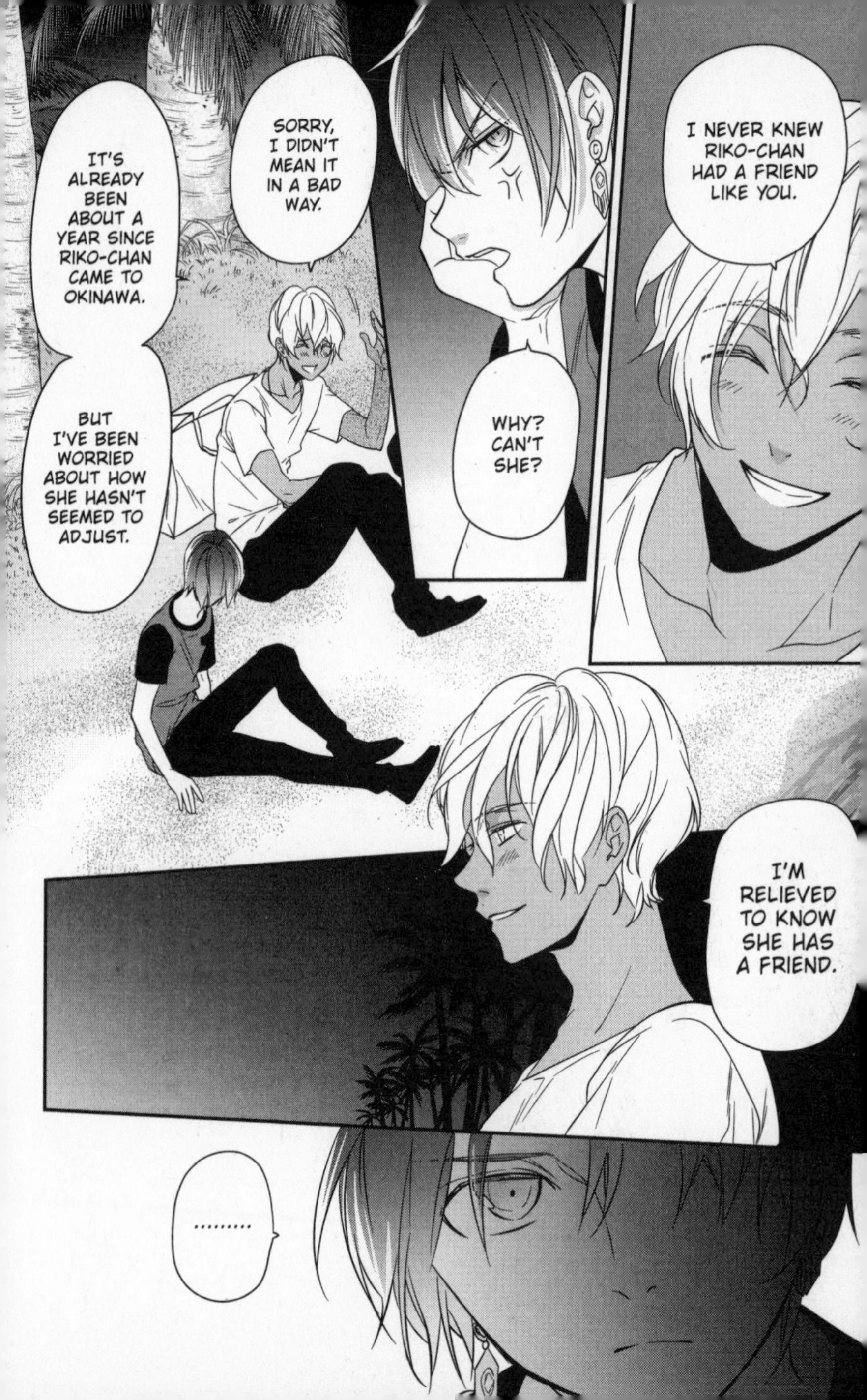
I NEVER KNEW RIKO-CHAN HAD A FRIEND LIKE YOU.
WHY? CAN'T SHE?
SORRY, I DIDN'T MEAN IT IN A BAD WAY.
IT'S ALREADY BEEN ABOUT A YEAR SINCE RIKO-CHAN CAME TO OKINAWA.
BUT I'VE BEEN WORRIED ABOUT HOW SHE HASN'T SEEMED TO ADJUST.
I'M RELIEVED TO KNOW SHE HAS A FRIEND.
....

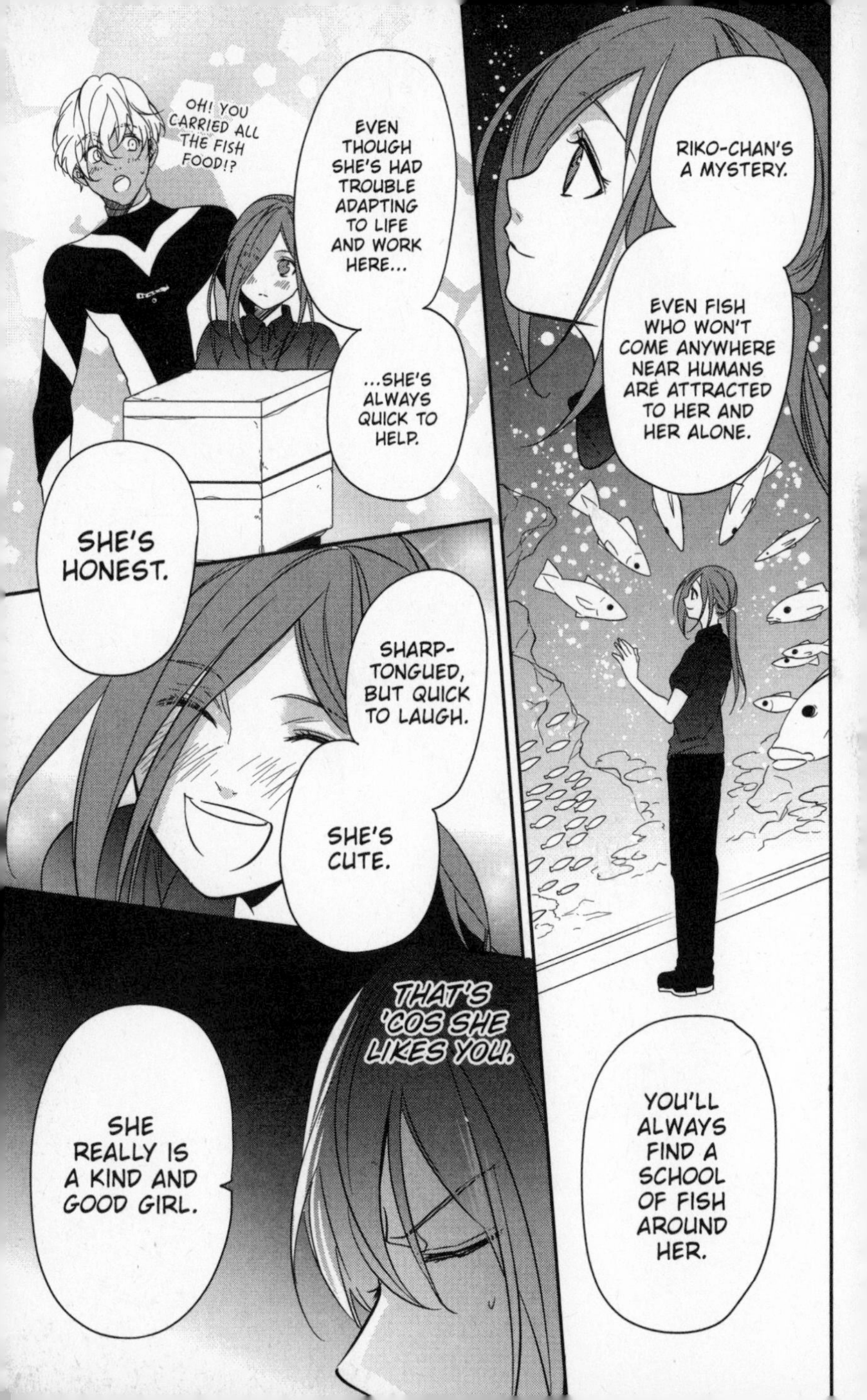
RIKO-CHAN'S A MYSTERY.
EVEN FISH WHO WON'T COME ANYWHERE NEAR HUMANS ARE ATTRACTED TO HER AND HER ALONE.
YOU'LL ALWAYS FIND A SCHOOL OF FISH AROUND HER.
EVEN THOUGH SHE'S HAD TROUBLE ADAPTING TO LIFE AND WORK HERE...
OH! YOU CARRIED ALL THE FISH FOOD!?
...SHE'S ALWAYS QUICK TO HELP.
SHE'S HONEST.
SHARP-TONGUED, BUT QUICK TO LAUGH.
SHE'S CUTE.
THAT'S 'COS SHE LIKES YOU.
SHE REALLY IS A KIND AND GOOD GIRL.

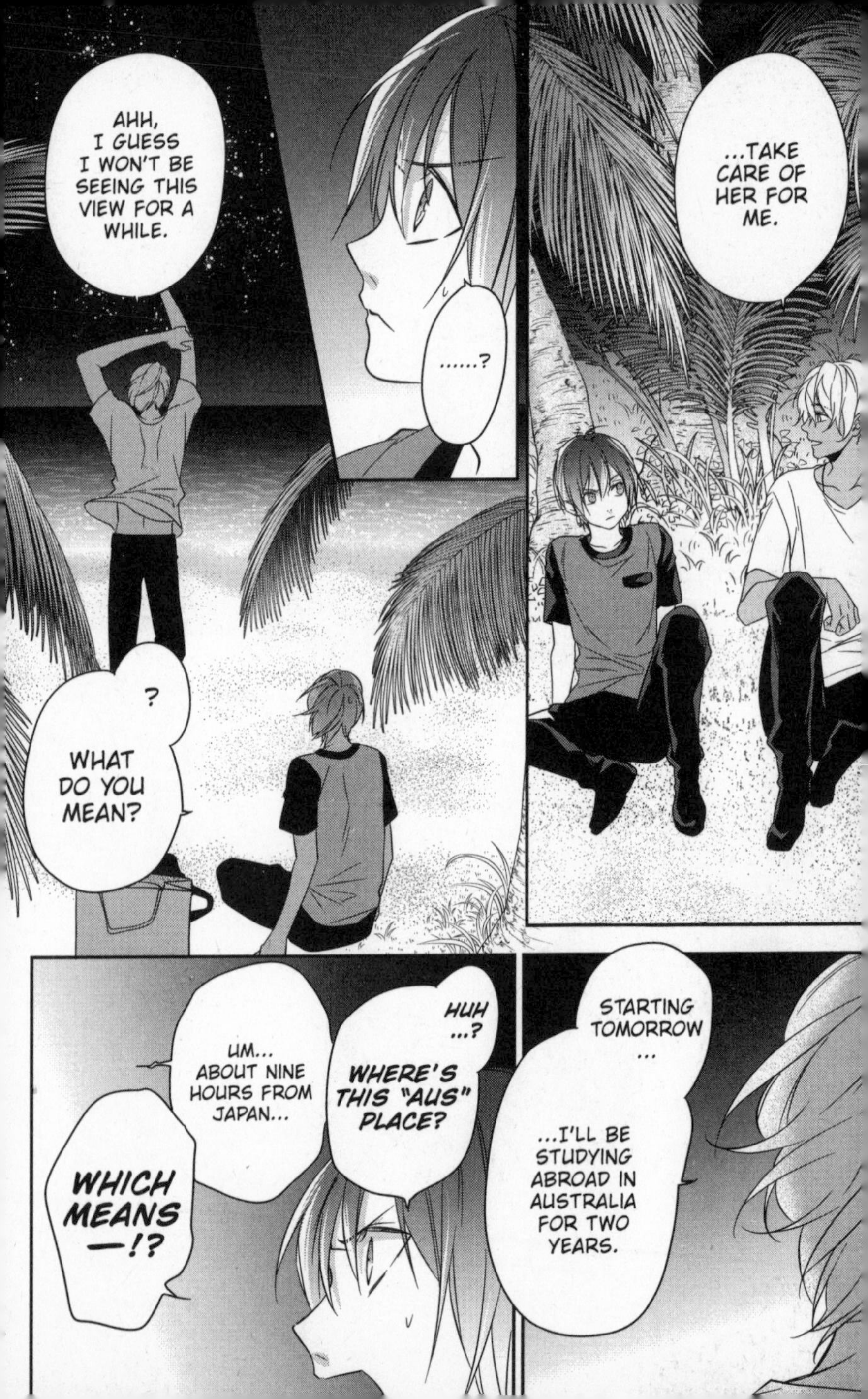
...TAKE CARE OF HER FOR ME.
AHH, I GUESS I WON'T BE SEEING THIS VIEW FOR A WHILE.
......?
? WHAT DO YOU MEAN?
STARTING TOMORROW...
...I'LL BE STUDYING ABROAD IN AUSTRALIA FOR TWO YEARS.
HUH...?
WHERE'S THIS "AUS" PLACE?
UM... ABOUT NINE HOURS FROM JAPAN...
WHICH MEANS—!?

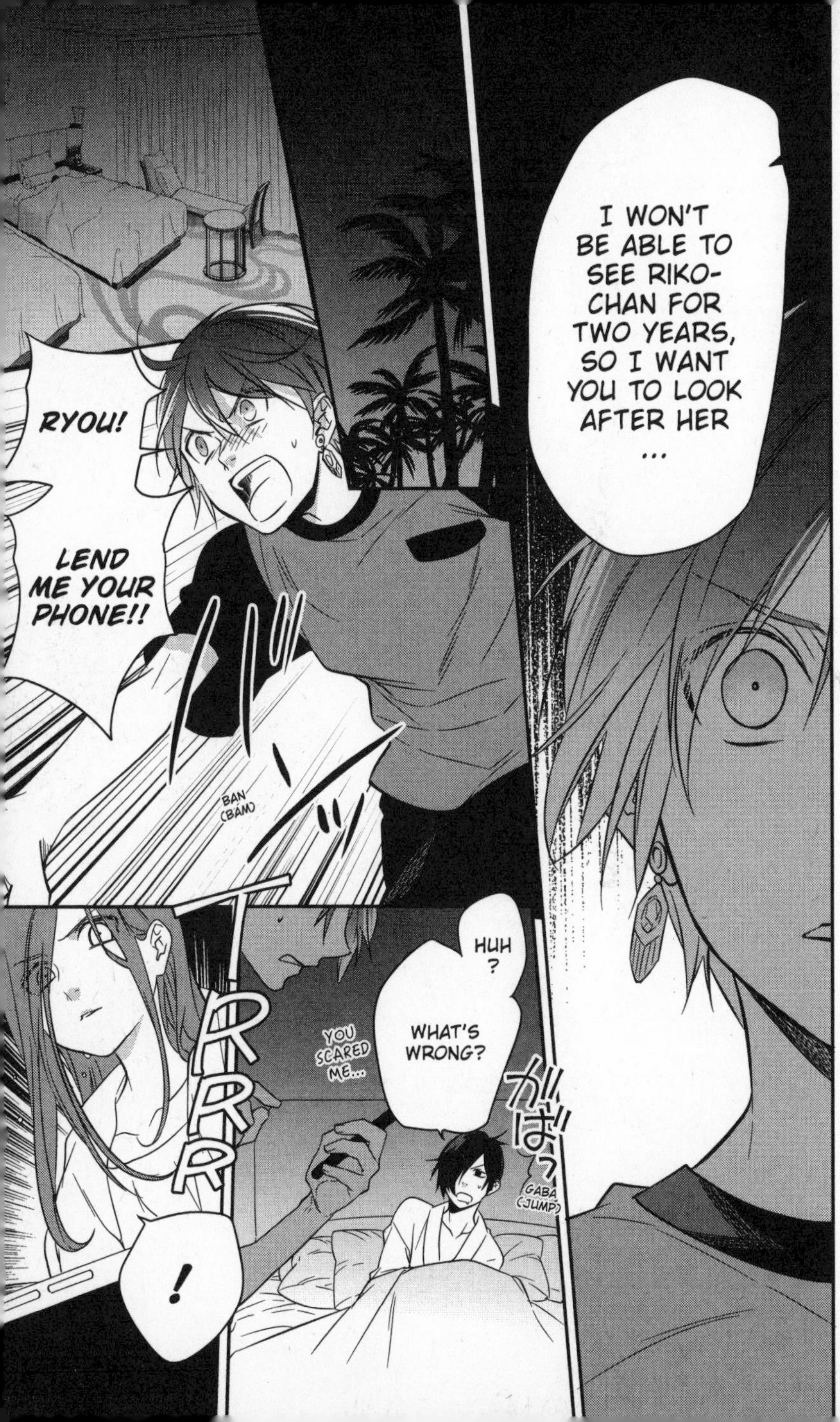
I WON'T BE ABLE TO SEE RIKO-CHAN FOR TWO YEARS, SO I WANT YOU TO LOOK AFTER HER ...
RYOU!
LEND ME YOUR PHONE!!
BAN (BAM)
HUH ?
WHAT'S WRONG?
がばっ
GABA (JUMP)
YOU SCARED ME...
TRRRR
!

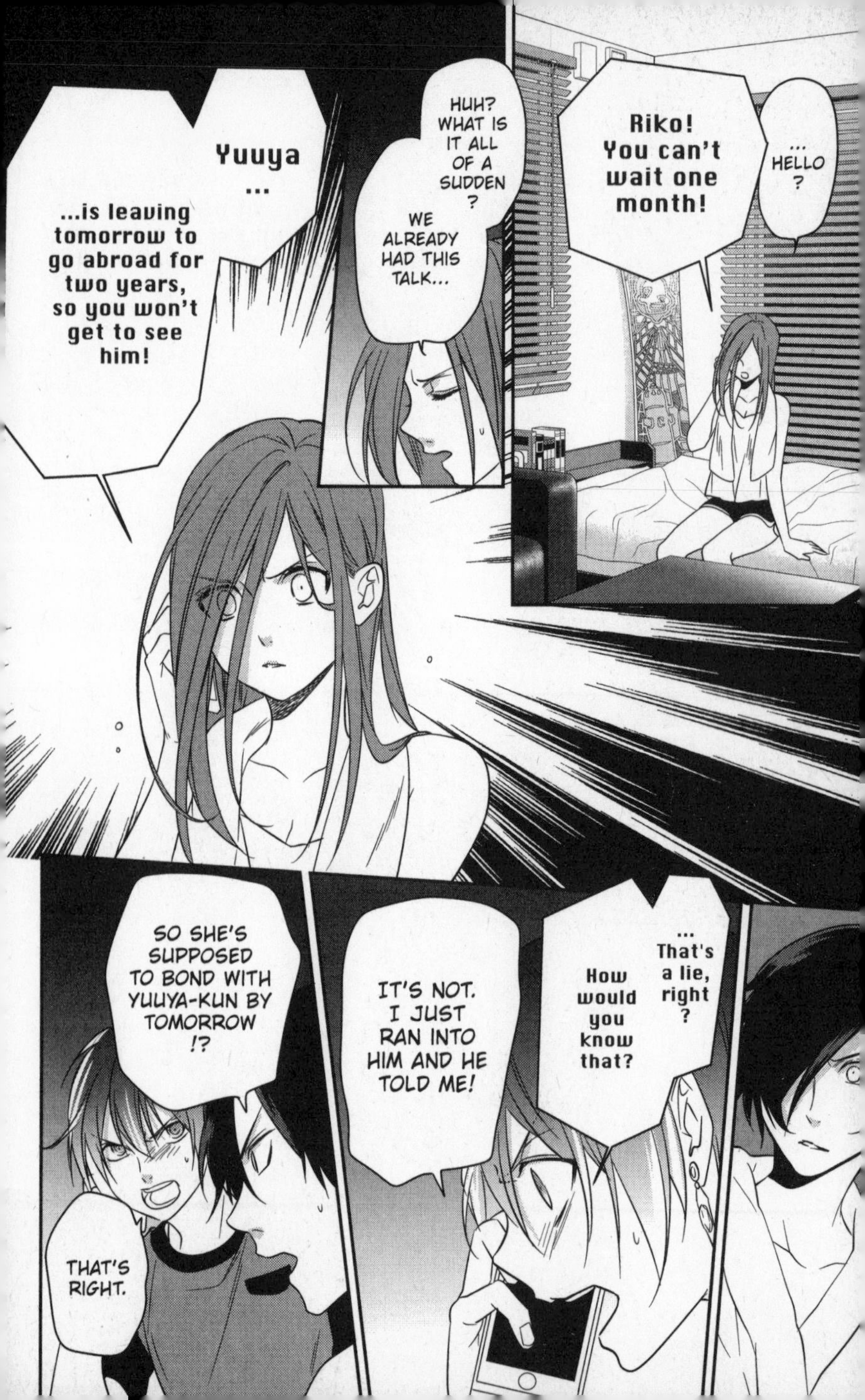
...HELLO?
Riko! You can't wait one month!
HUH? WHAT IS IT ALL OF A SUDDEN?
WE ALREADY HAD THIS TALK...
Yuuya ...
...is leaving tomorrow to go abroad for two years, so you won't get to see him!
...That's a lie, right?
How would you know that?
IT'S NOT. I JUST RAN INTO HIM AND HE TOLD ME!
SO SHE'S SUPPOSED TO BOND WITH YUUYA-KUN BY TOMORROW!?
THAT'S RIGHT.

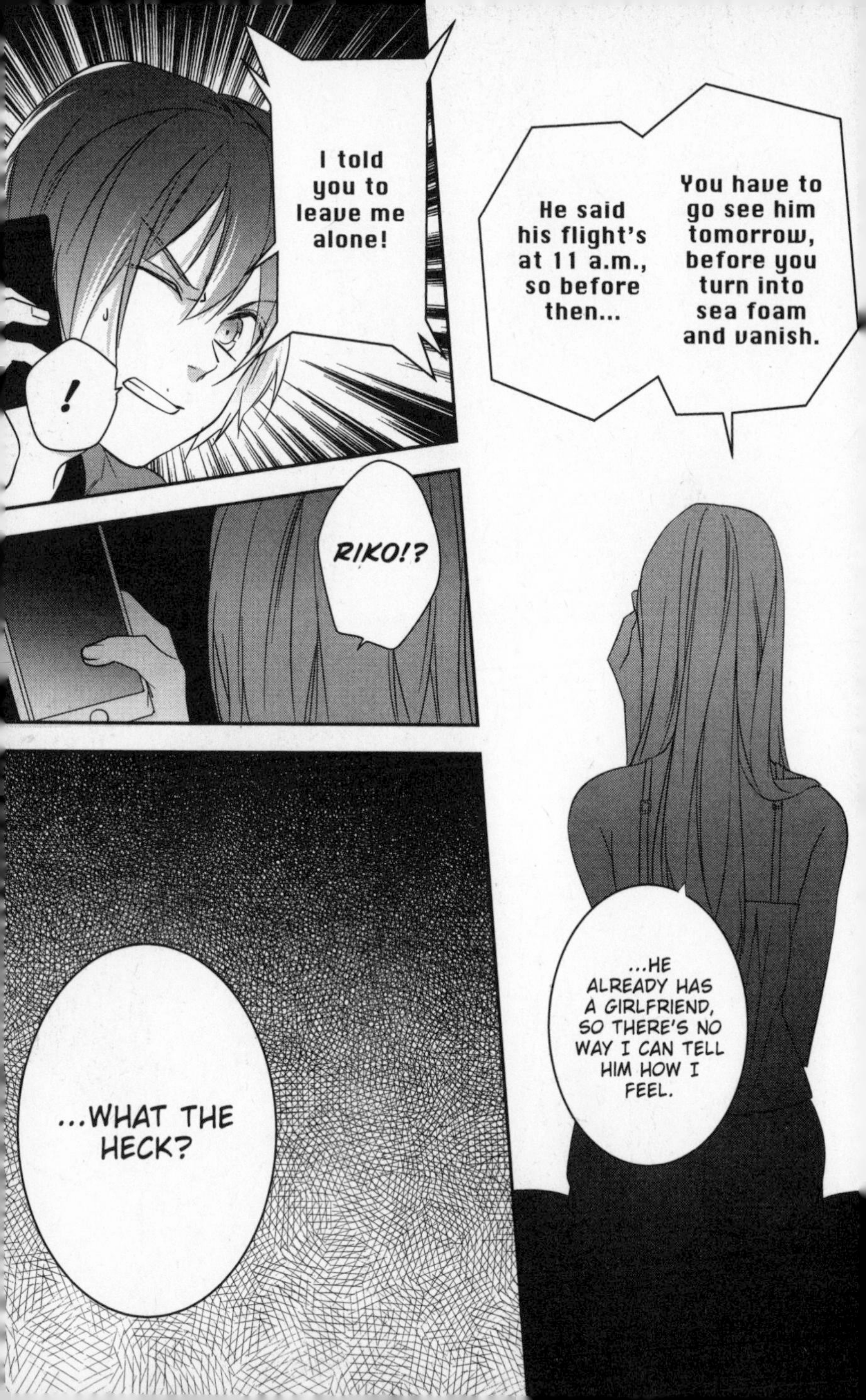
You have to go see him tomorrow, before you turn into sea foam and vanish.
He said his flight's at 11 a.m., so before then...
...HE ALREADY HAS A GIRLFRIEND, SO THERE'S NO WAY I CAN TELL HIM HOW I FEEL.
I told you to leave me alone!
!
RIKO!?
...WHAT THE HECK?

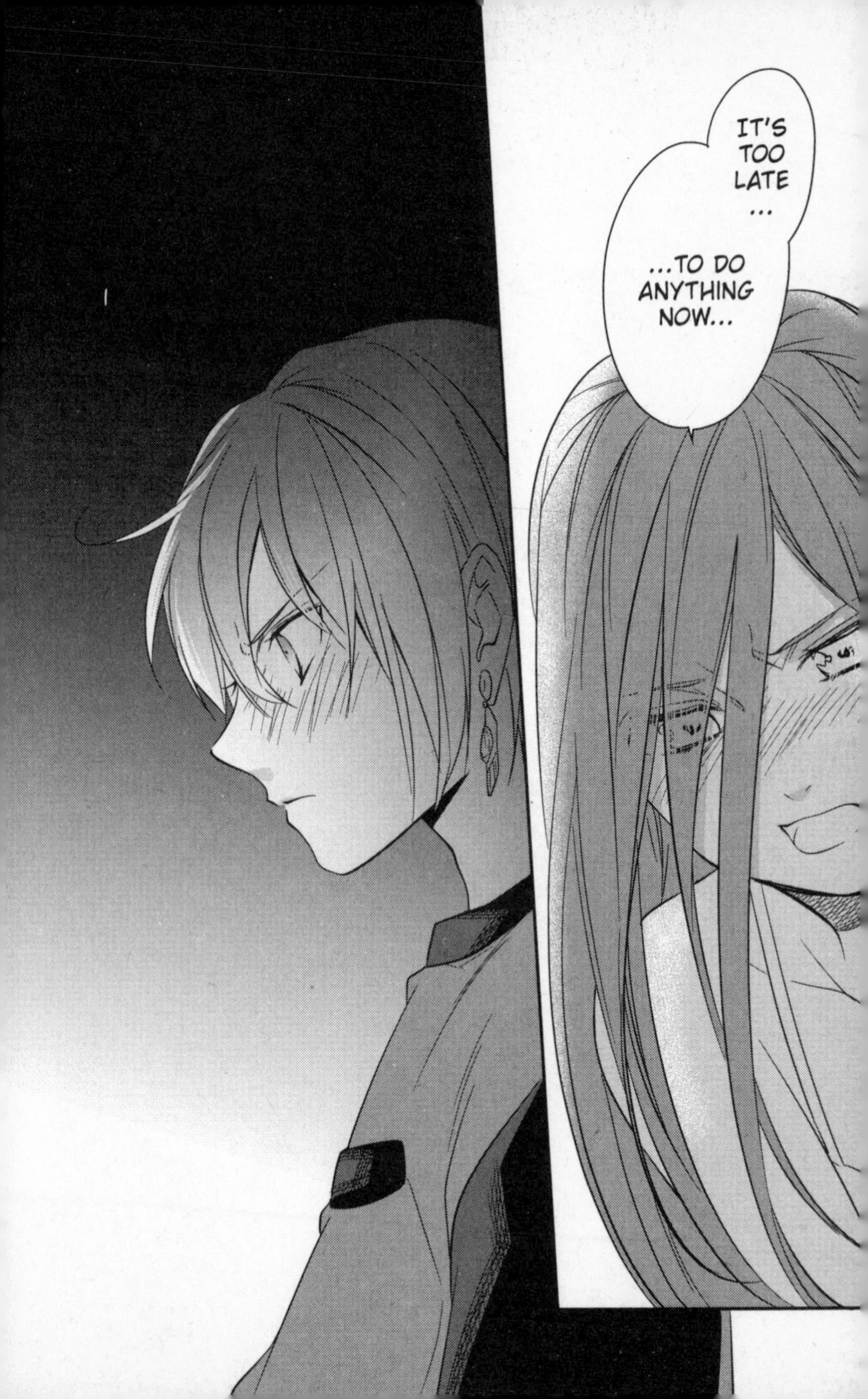
IT'S TOO LATE ...
...TO DO ANYTHING NOW...

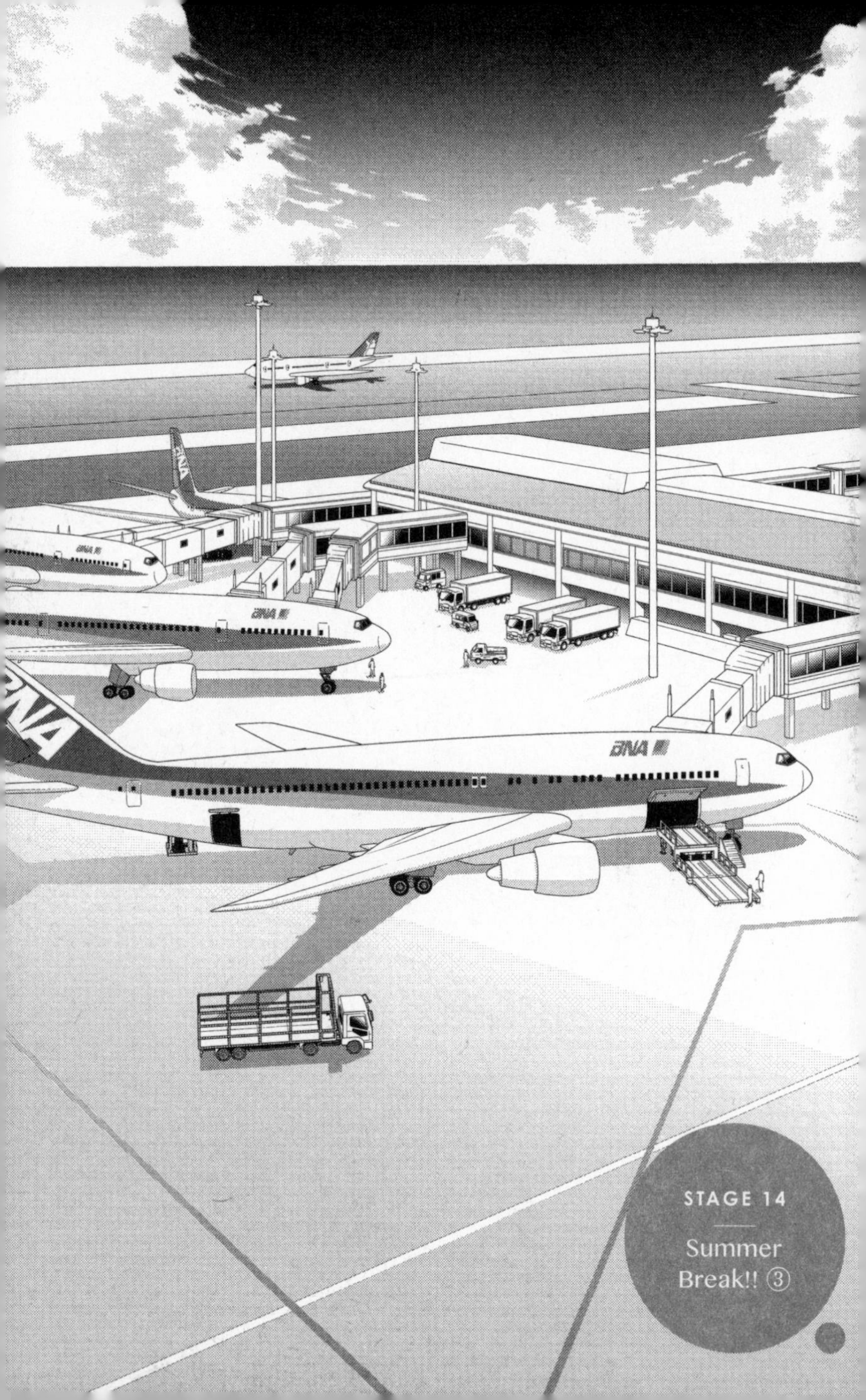
BNA
BNA
BNA
BNA
BNA
STAGE 14
Summer Break!! ③

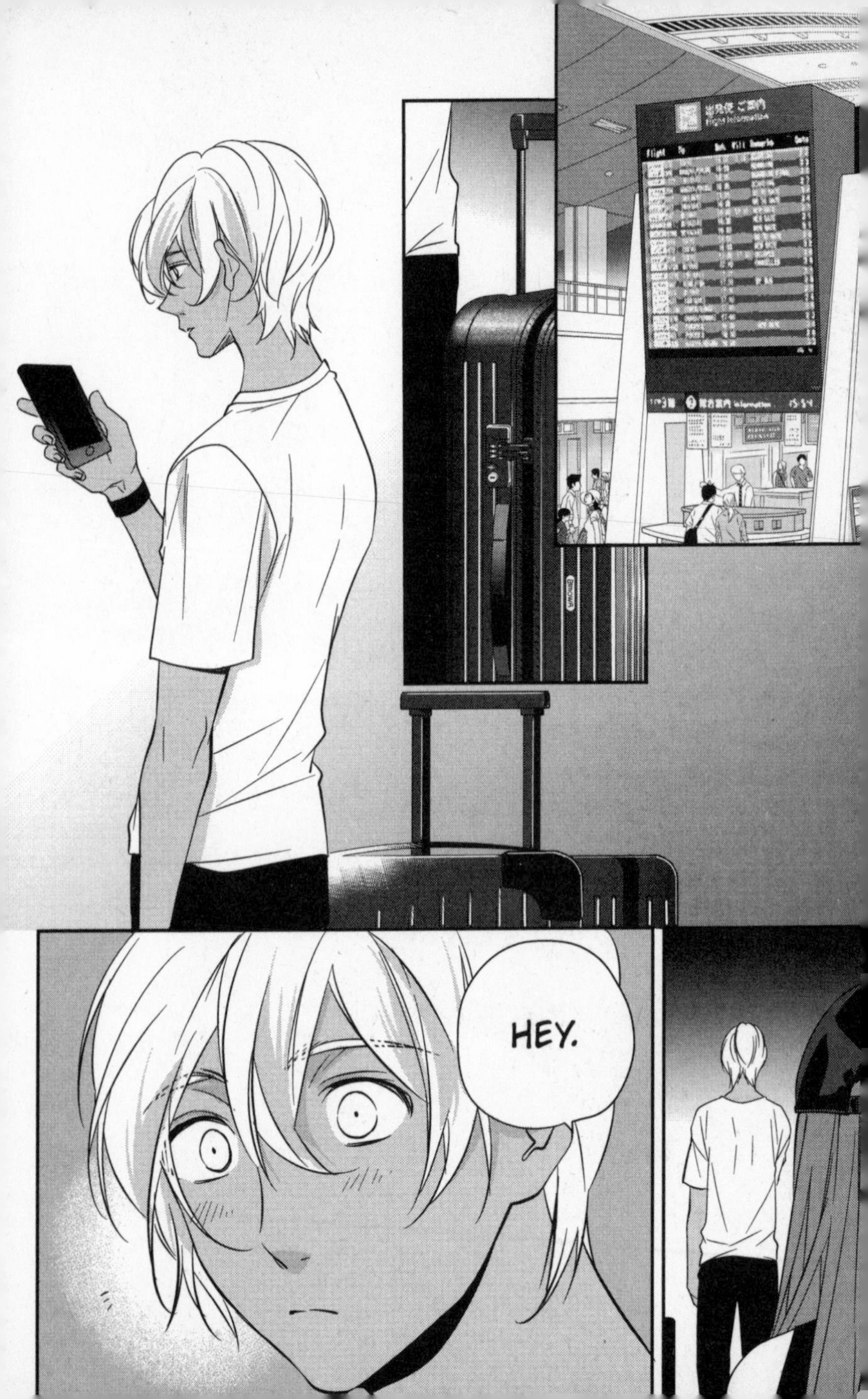
HEY.

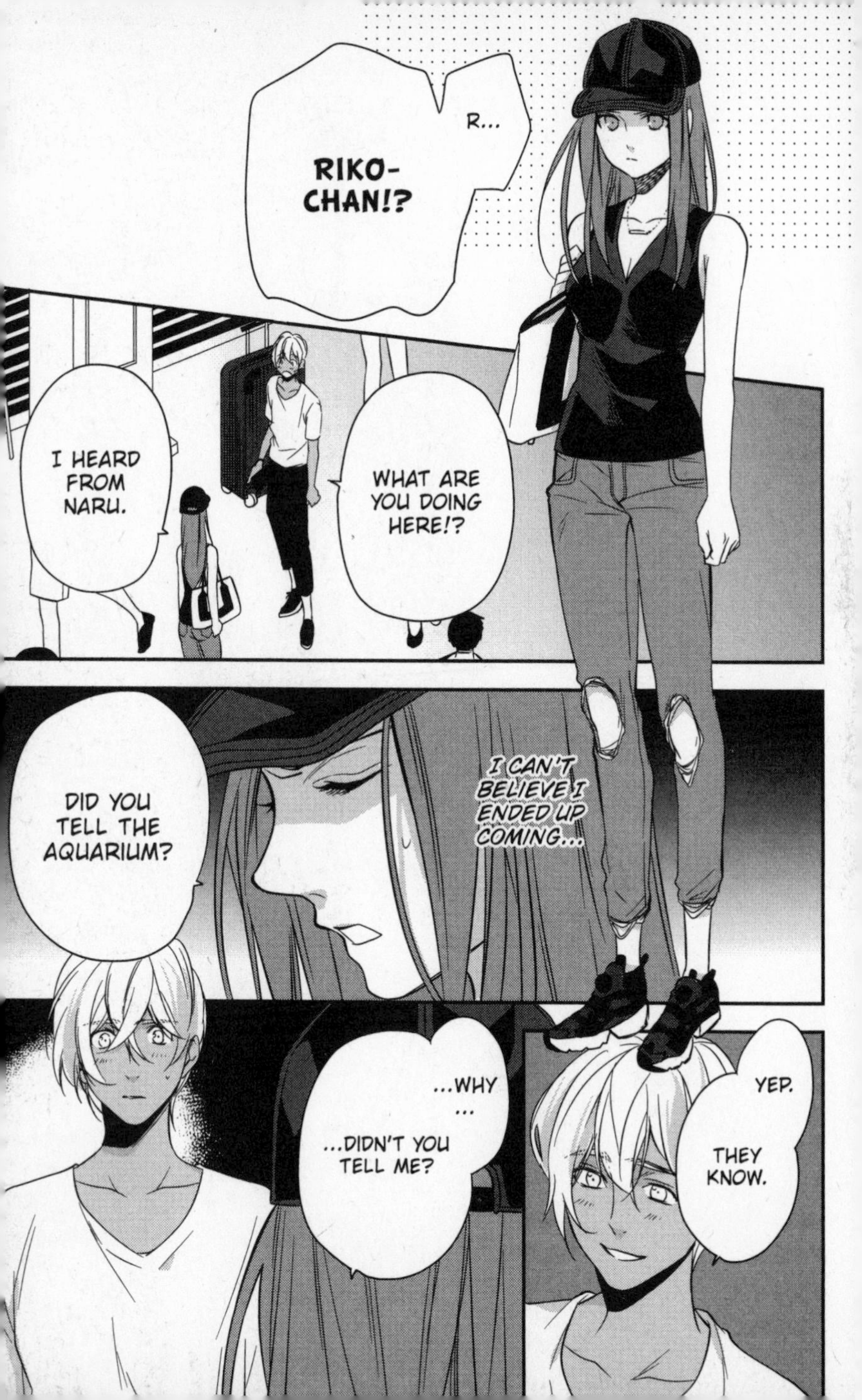
R...
RIKO-CHAN!?
WHAT ARE YOU DOING HERE!?
I HEARD FROM NARU.
I CAN'T BELIEVE I ENDED UP COMING...
DID YOU TELL THE AQUARIUM?
YEP.
THEY KNOW.
...WHY
...
...DIDN'T YOU TELL ME?

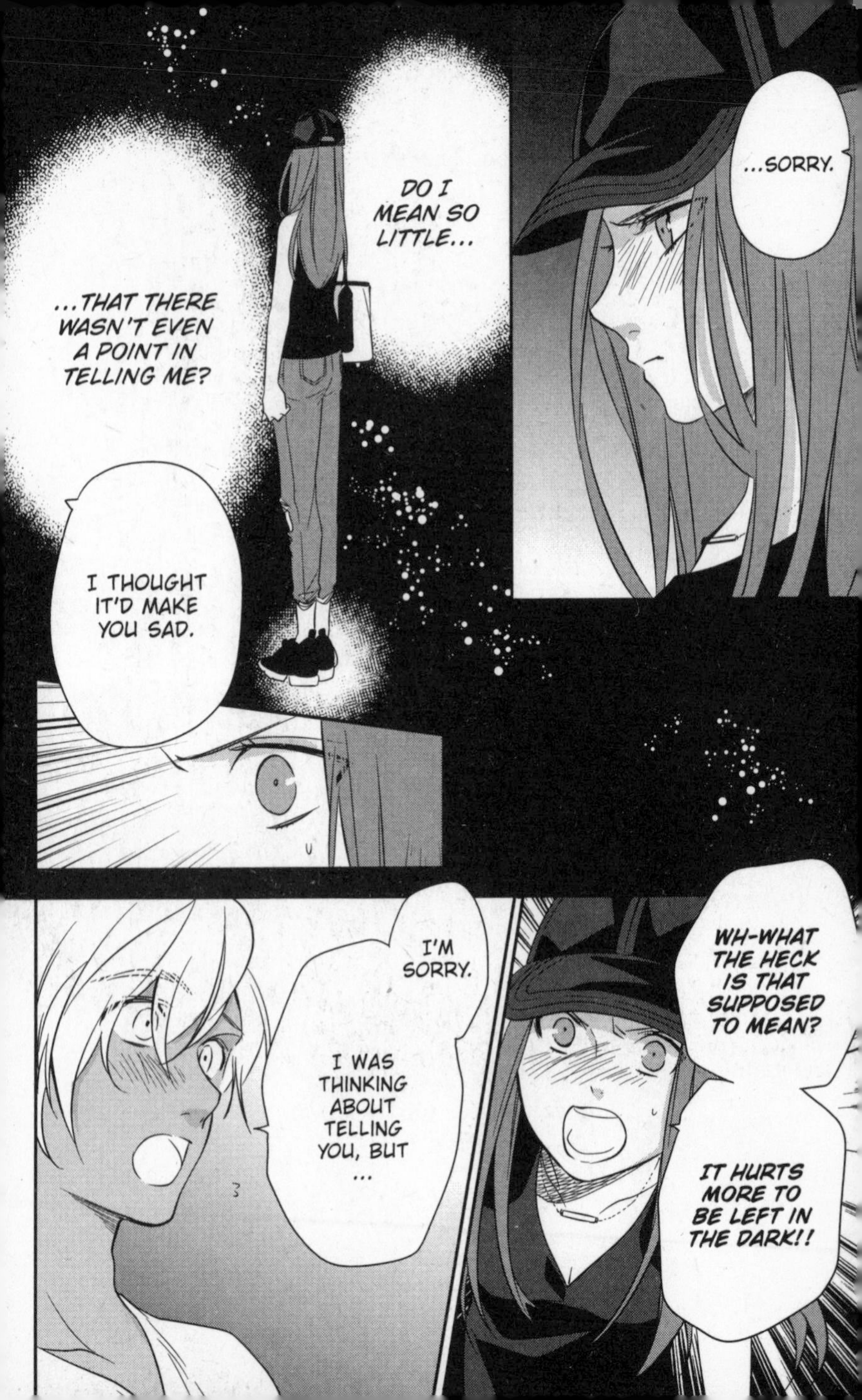
...SORRY.
DO I MEAN SO LITTLE...
...THAT THERE WASN'T EVEN A POINT IN TELLING ME?
I THOUGHT IT'D MAKE YOU SAD.
WH-WHAT THE HECK IS THAT SUPPOSED TO MEAN?
IT HURTS MORE TO BE LEFT IN THE DARK!!
I'M SORRY.
I WAS THINKING ABOUT TELLING YOU, BUT ...

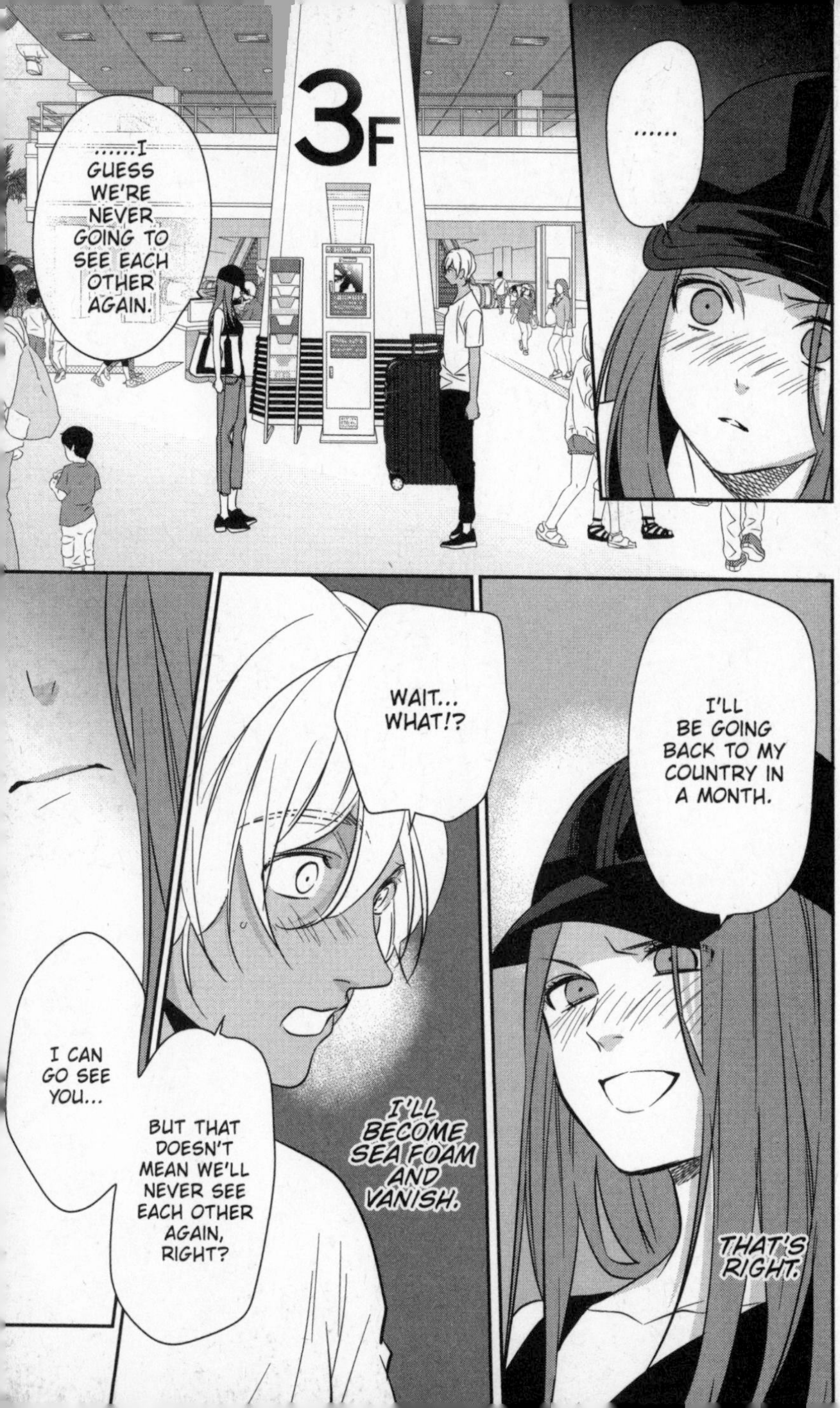
......
......I GUESS WE'RE NEVER GOING TO SEE EACH OTHER AGAIN.
3F
I'LL BE GOING BACK TO MY COUNTRY IN A MONTH.
THAT'S RIGHT.
WAIT... WHAT!?
I'LL BECOME SEA FOAM AND VANISH.
I CAN GO SEE YOU...
BUT THAT DOESN'T MEAN WE'LL NEVER SEE EACH OTHER AGAIN, RIGHT?

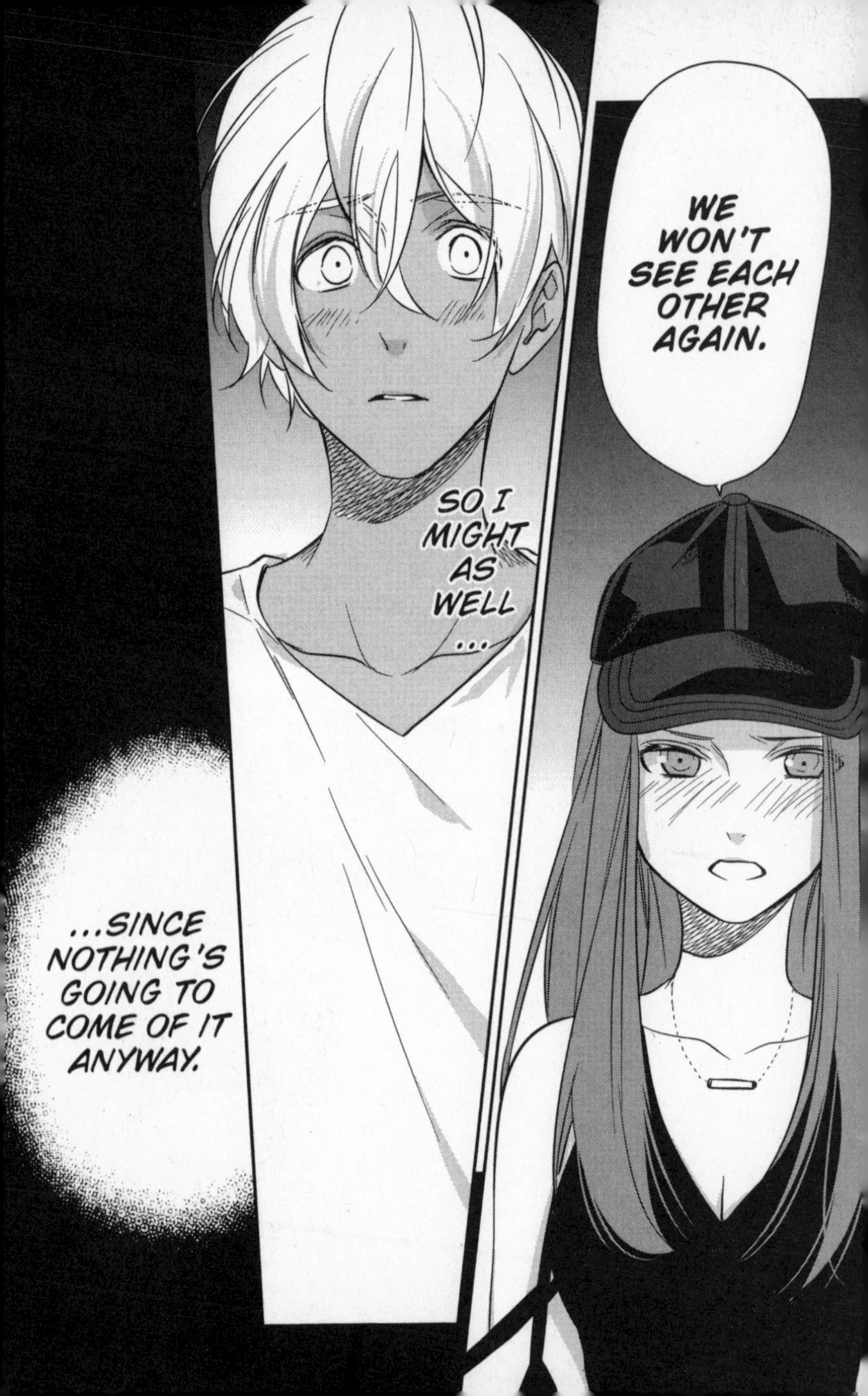
WE WON'T SEE EACH OTHER AGAIN.
SO I MIGHT AS WELL...
...SINCE NOTHING'S GOING TO COME OF IT ANYWAY.

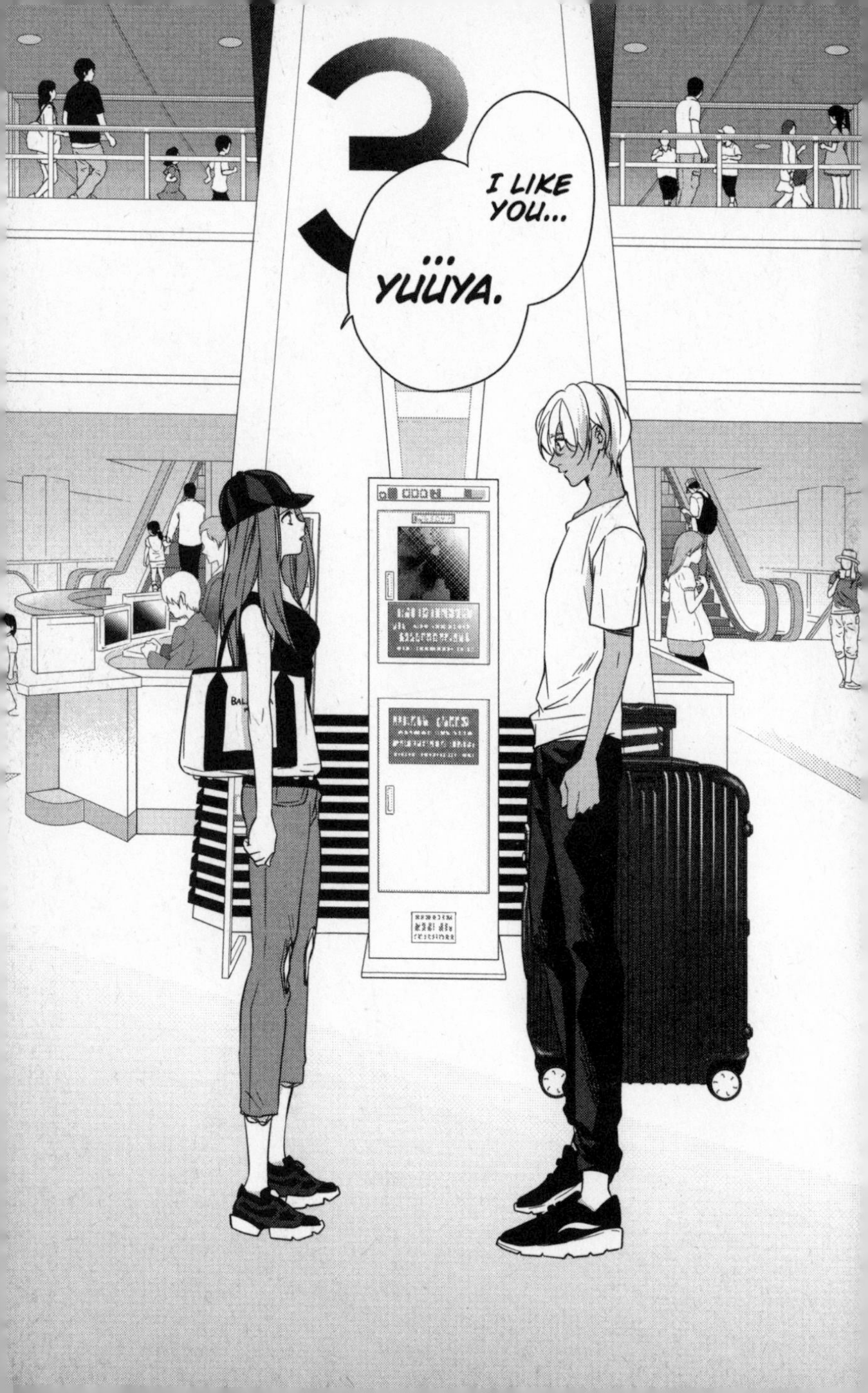
I LIKE YOU...
...YUUYA.

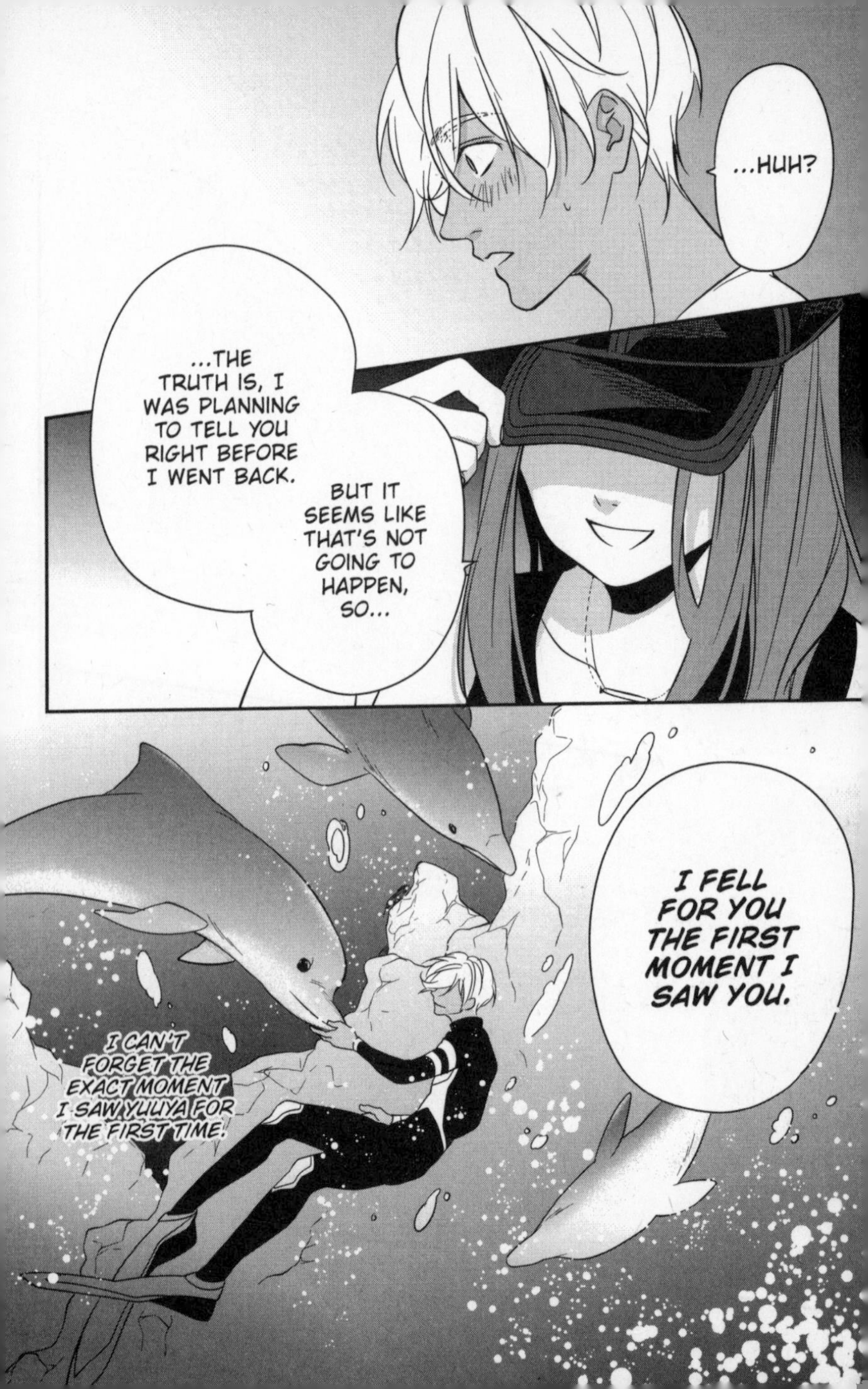
...HUH?
...THE TRUTH IS, I WAS PLANNING TO TELL YOU RIGHT BEFORE I WENT BACK.
BUT IT SEEMS LIKE THAT'S NOT GOING TO HAPPEN, SO...
I FELL FOR YOU THE FIRST MOMENT I SAW YOU.
I CAN'T FORGET THE EXACT MOMENT I SAW YUUYA FOR THE FIRST TIME.

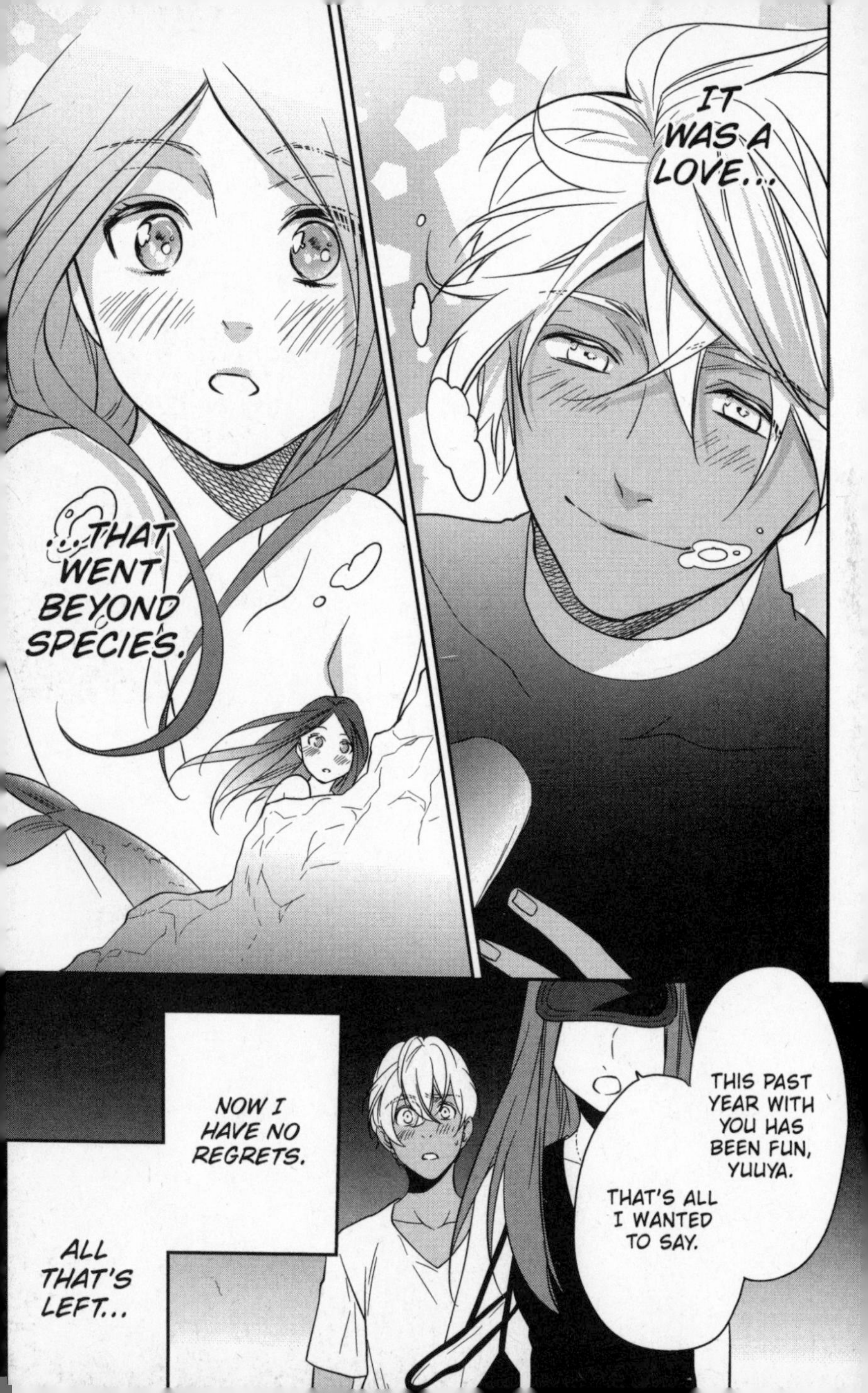
IT WAS A LOVE...
...THAT WENT BEYOND SPECIES.
THIS PAST YEAR WITH YOU HAS BEEN FUN, YUUYA.
THAT'S ALL I WANTED TO SAY.
NOW I HAVE NO REGRETS.
ALL THAT'S LEFT...

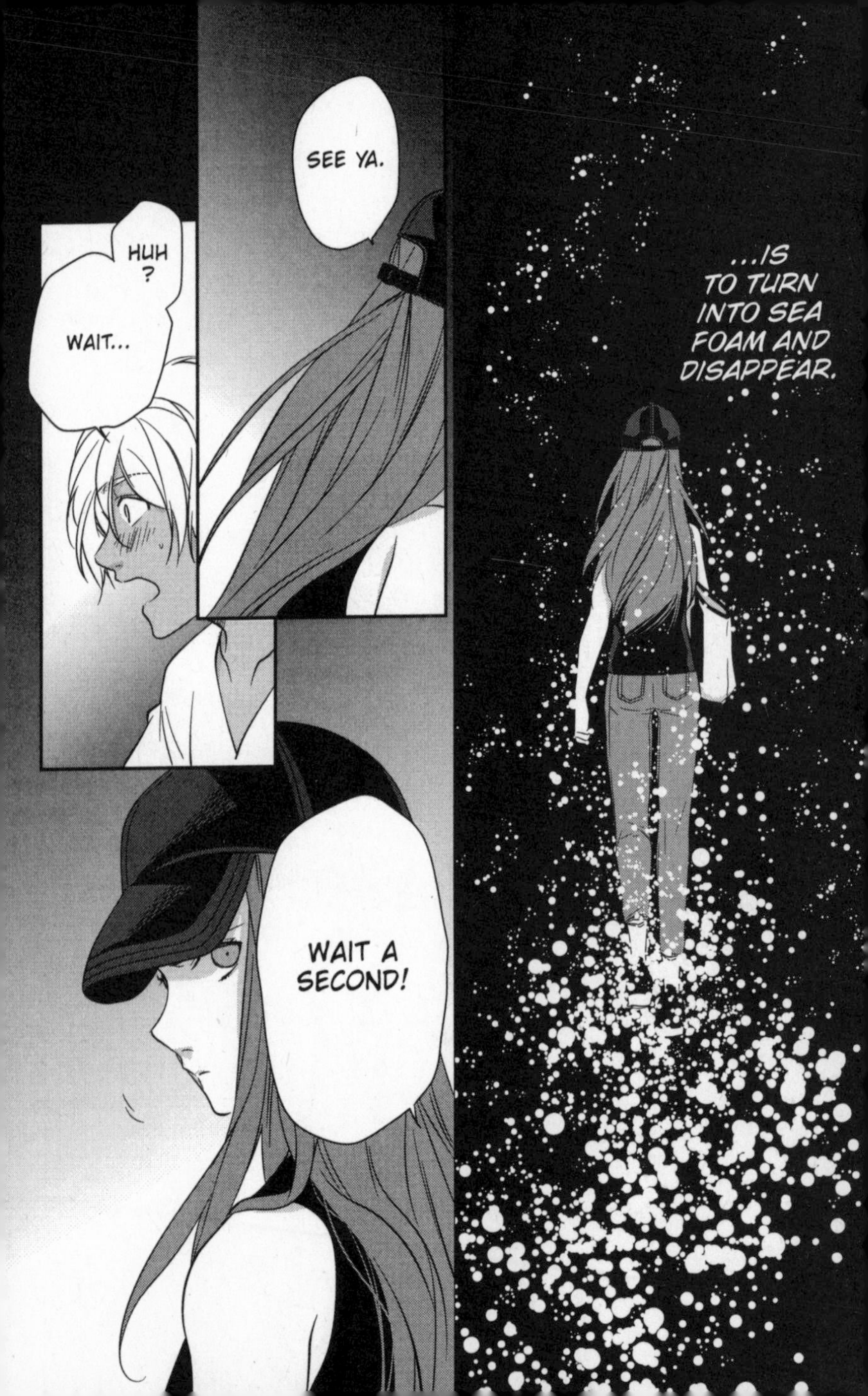
...IS TO TURN INTO SEA FOAM AND DISAPPEAR.
SEE YA.
HUH?
WAIT...
WAIT A SECOND!

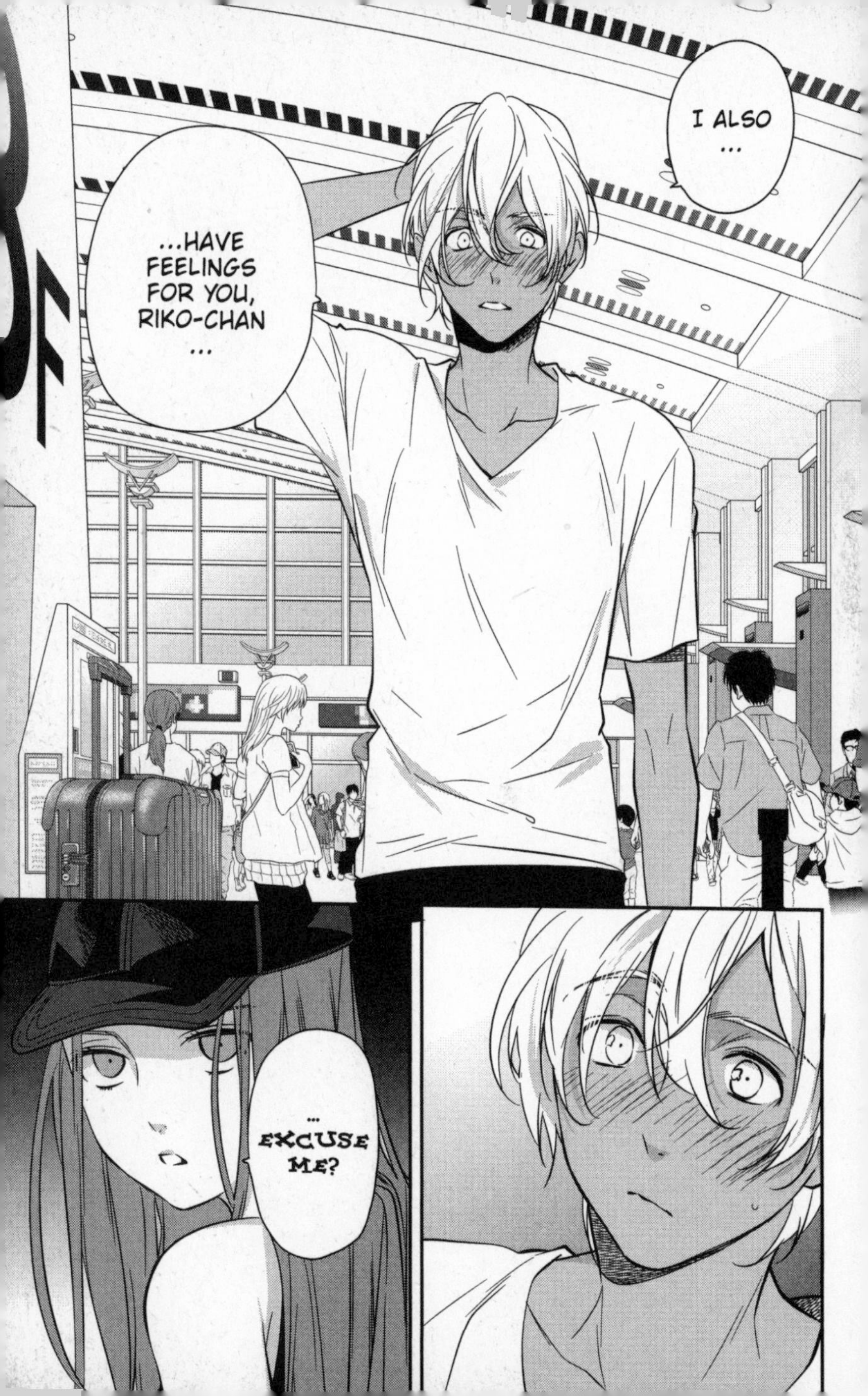
I ALSO ...
...HAVE FEELINGS FOR YOU, RIKO-CHAN ...
... EXCUSE ME?

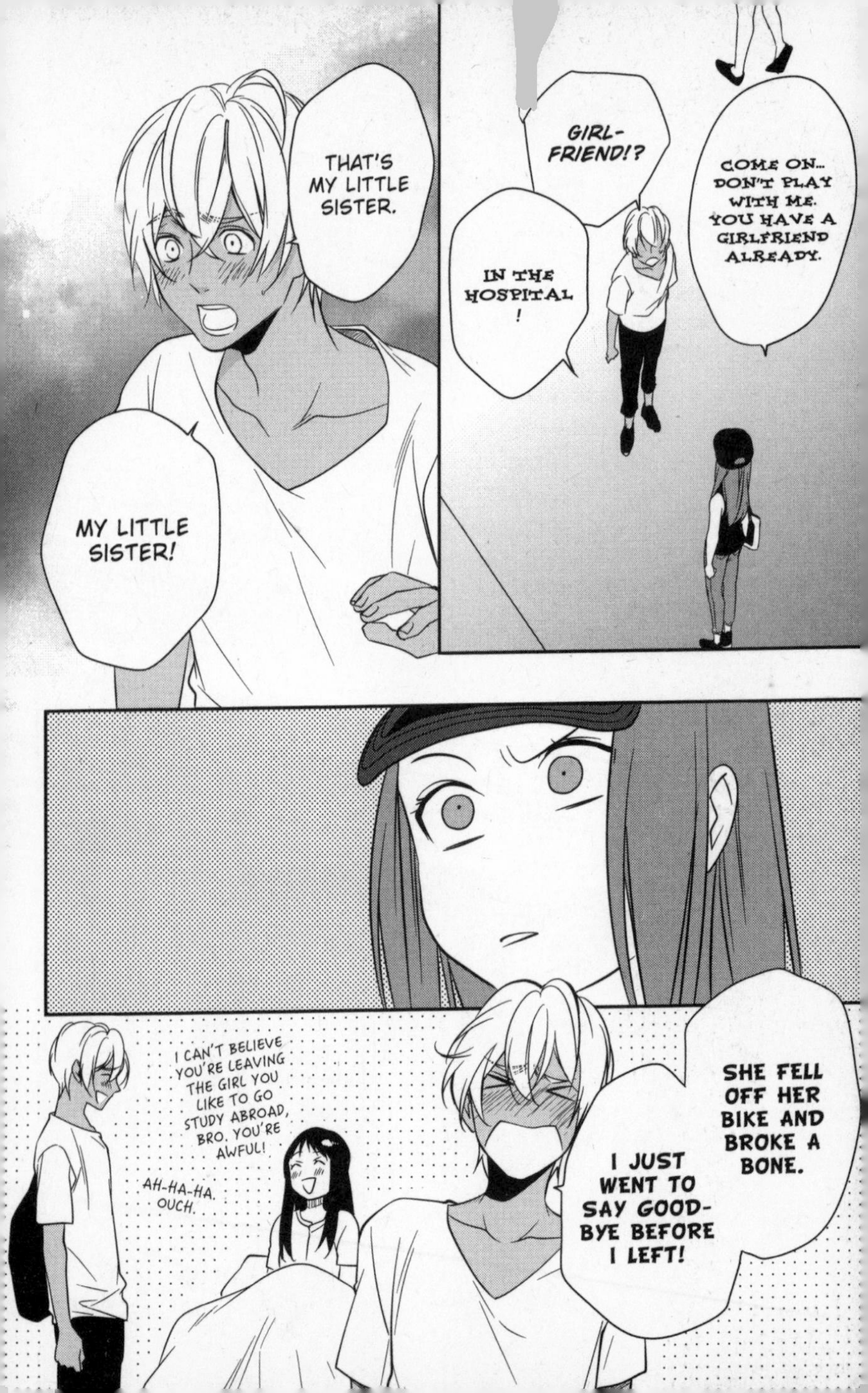

COME ON... DON'T PLAY WITH ME. YOU HAVE A GIRLFRIEND ALREADY.
GIRL-FRIEND!?
IN THE HOSPITAL!
THAT'S MY LITTLE SISTER.
MY LITTLE SISTER!
SHE FELL OFF HER BIKE AND BROKE A BONE.
I JUST WENT TO SAY GOOD-BYE BEFORE I LEFT!
I CAN'T BELIEVE YOU'RE LEAVING THE GIRL YOU LIKE TO GO STUDY ABROAD, BRO. YOU'RE AWFUL!
AH-HA-HA. OUCH.

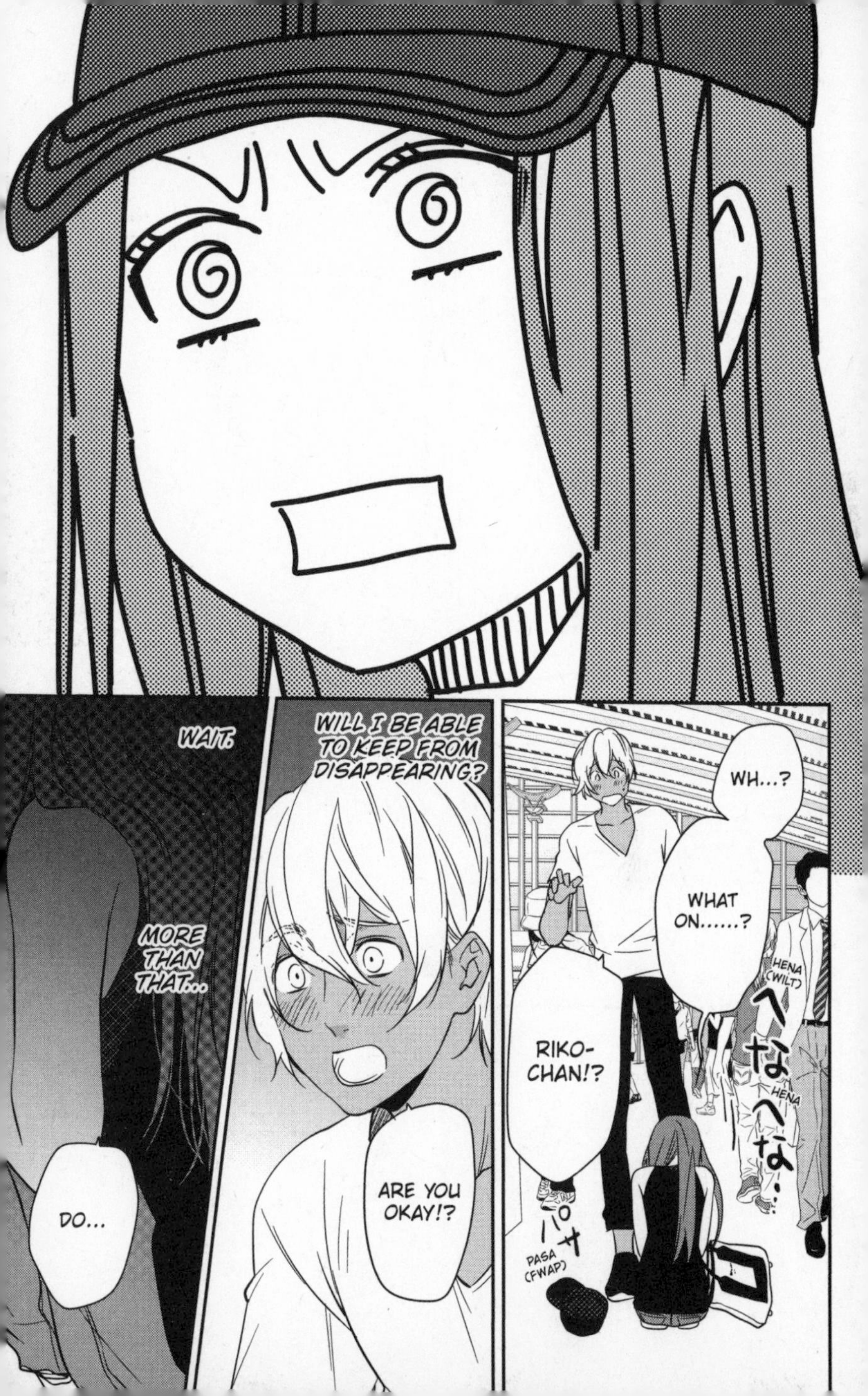
WH...?
WHAT ON......?
へな HENA (WILT)
へな... HENA
RIKO-CHAN!?
パサ PASA (FWAP)
WILL I BE ABLE TO KEEP FROM DISAPPEARING?
ARE YOU OKAY!?
WAIT.
MORE THAN THAT...
DO...

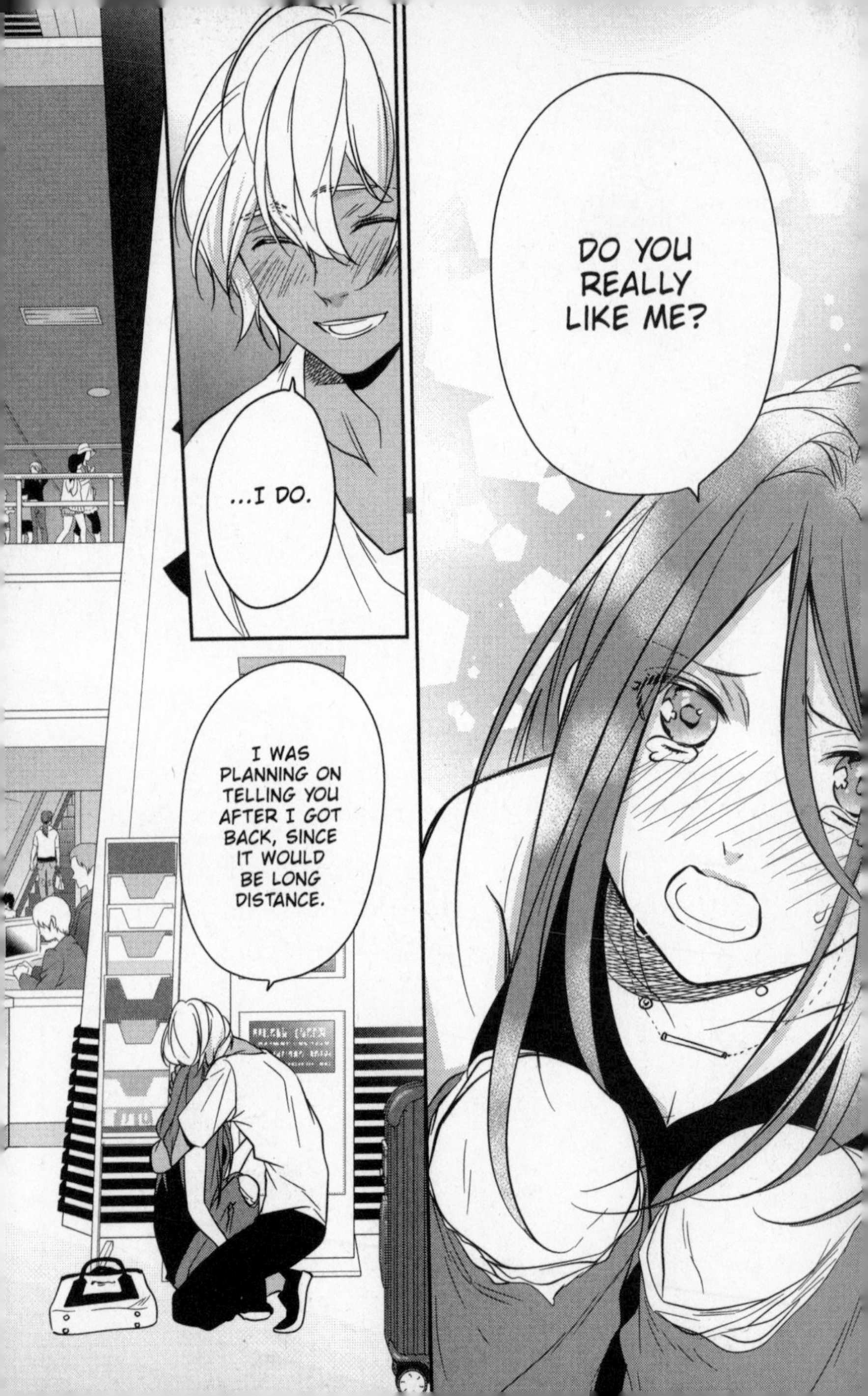
DO YOU REALLY LIKE ME?
...I DO.
I WAS PLANNING ON TELLING YOU AFTER I GOT BACK, SINCE IT WOULD BE LONG DISTANCE.

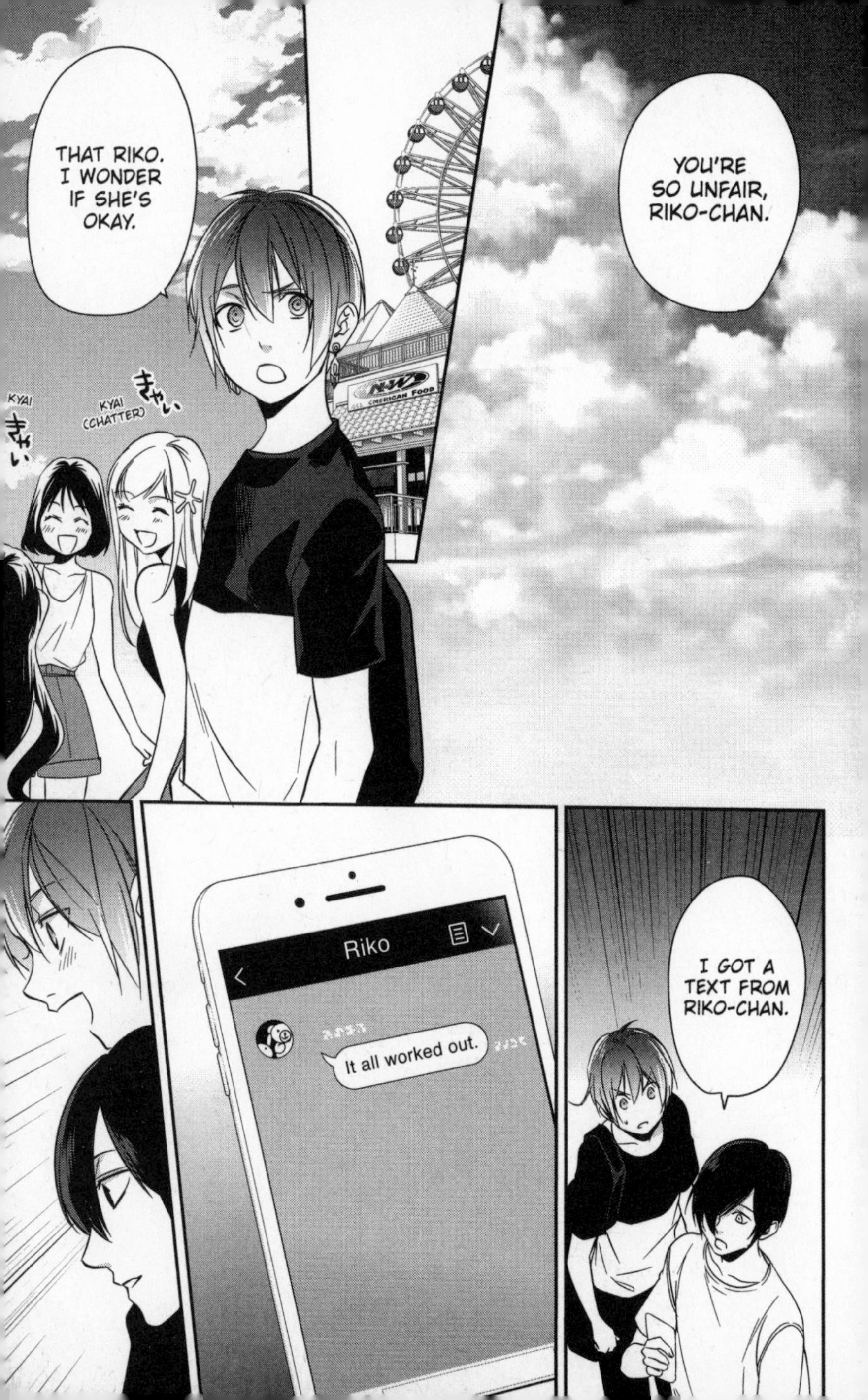
YOU'RE SO UNFAIR, RIKO-CHAN.
THAT RIKO. I WONDER IF SHE'S OKAY.
きゃい
KYAI (CHATTER)
きゃい
KYAI
I GOT A TEXT FROM RIKO-CHAN.
Riko
It all worked out.

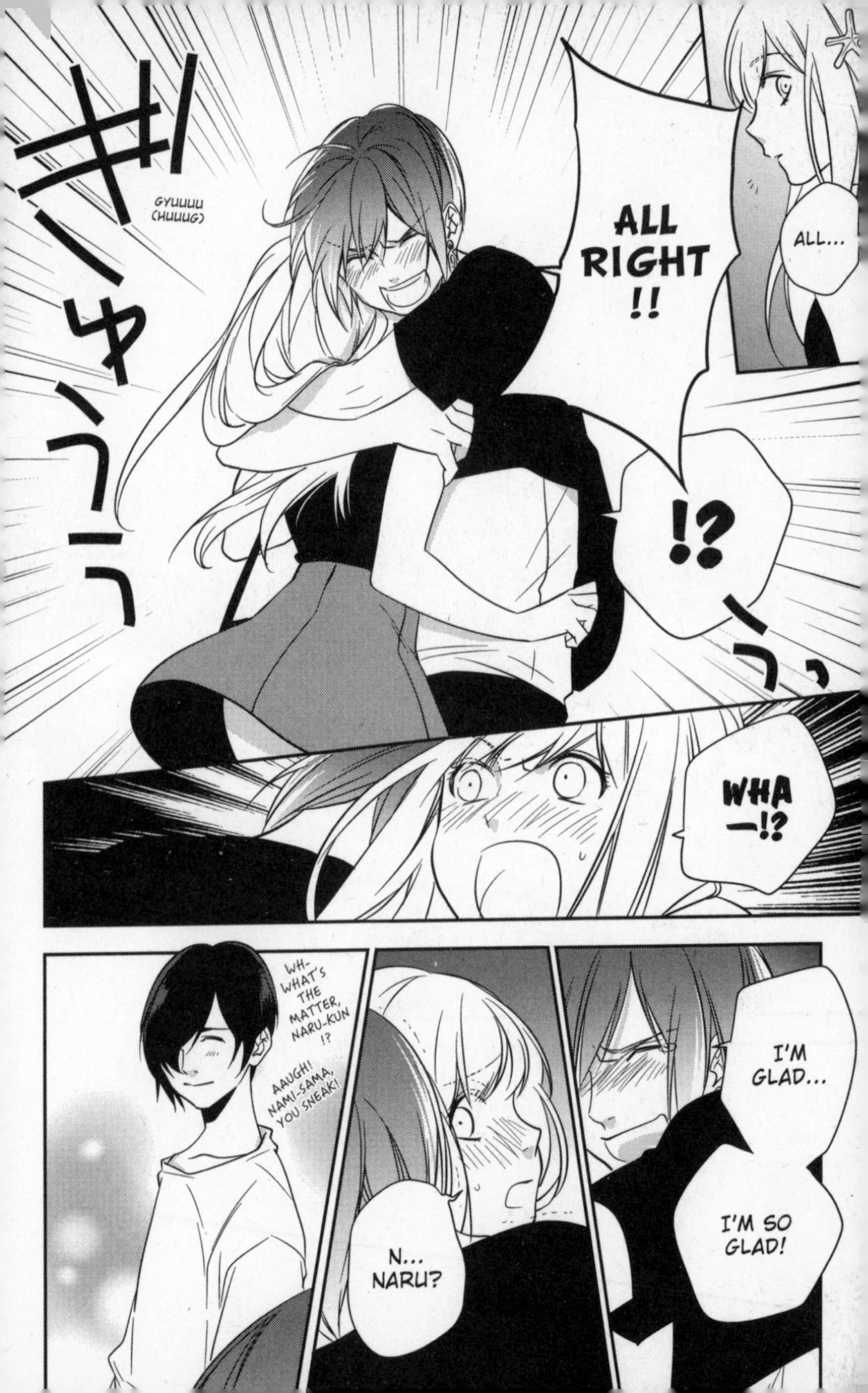
ALL...
ALL RIGHT!!
!?
GYUUUU (HUUUG)
WHA—!?
I'M GLAD...
I'M SO GLAD!
N... NARU?
WH-WHAT'S THE MATTER, NARU-KUN!?
AAUGH! NAMI-SAMA, YOU SNEAK!

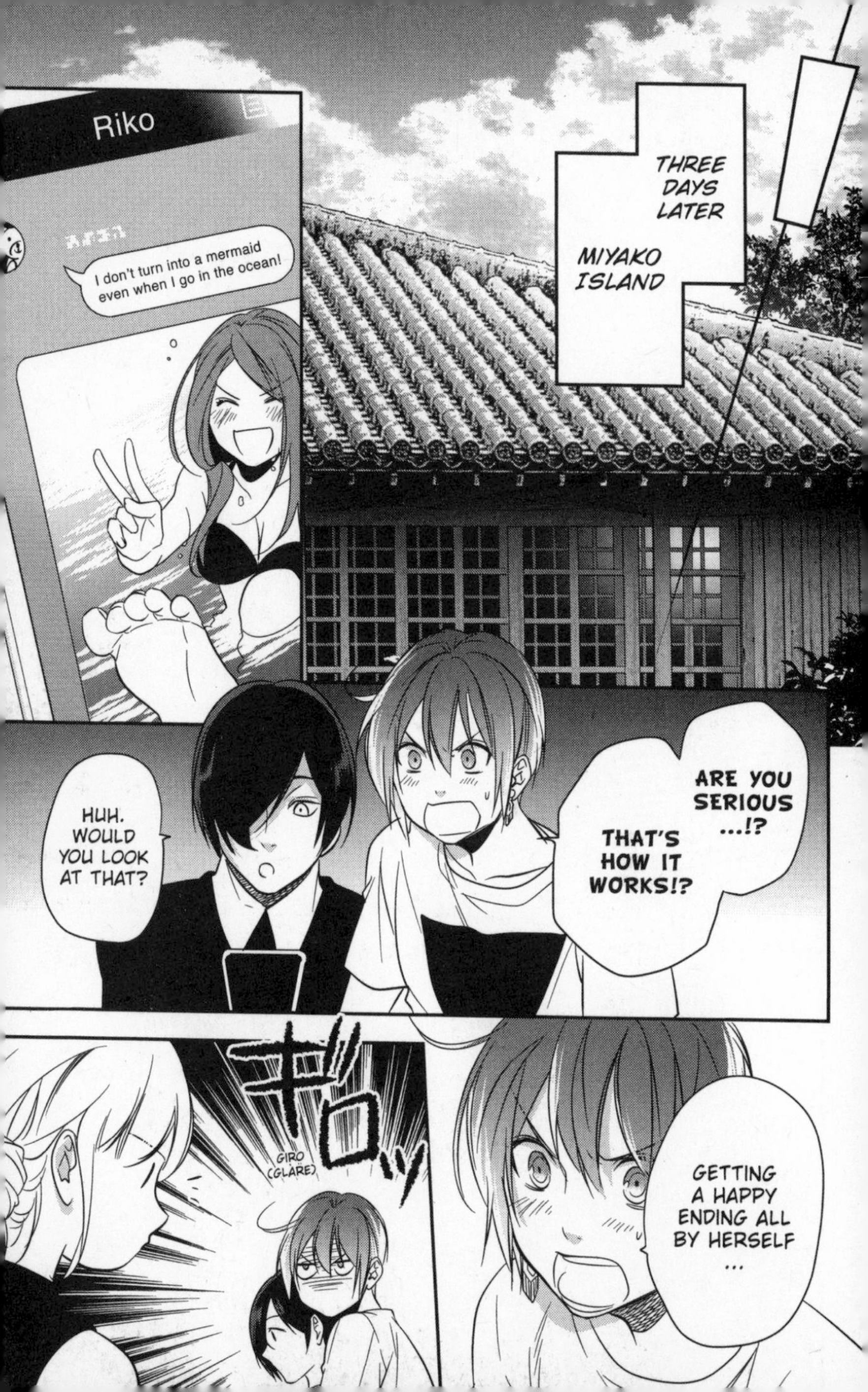
THREE DAYS LATER
MIYAKO ISLAND
Riko
I don't turn into a mermaid even when I go in the ocean!
ARE YOU SERIOUS ...!?
THAT'S HOW IT WORKS!?
HUH. WOULD YOU LOOK AT THAT?
GETTING A HAPPY ENDING ALL BY HERSELF ...
GIRO (GLARE)

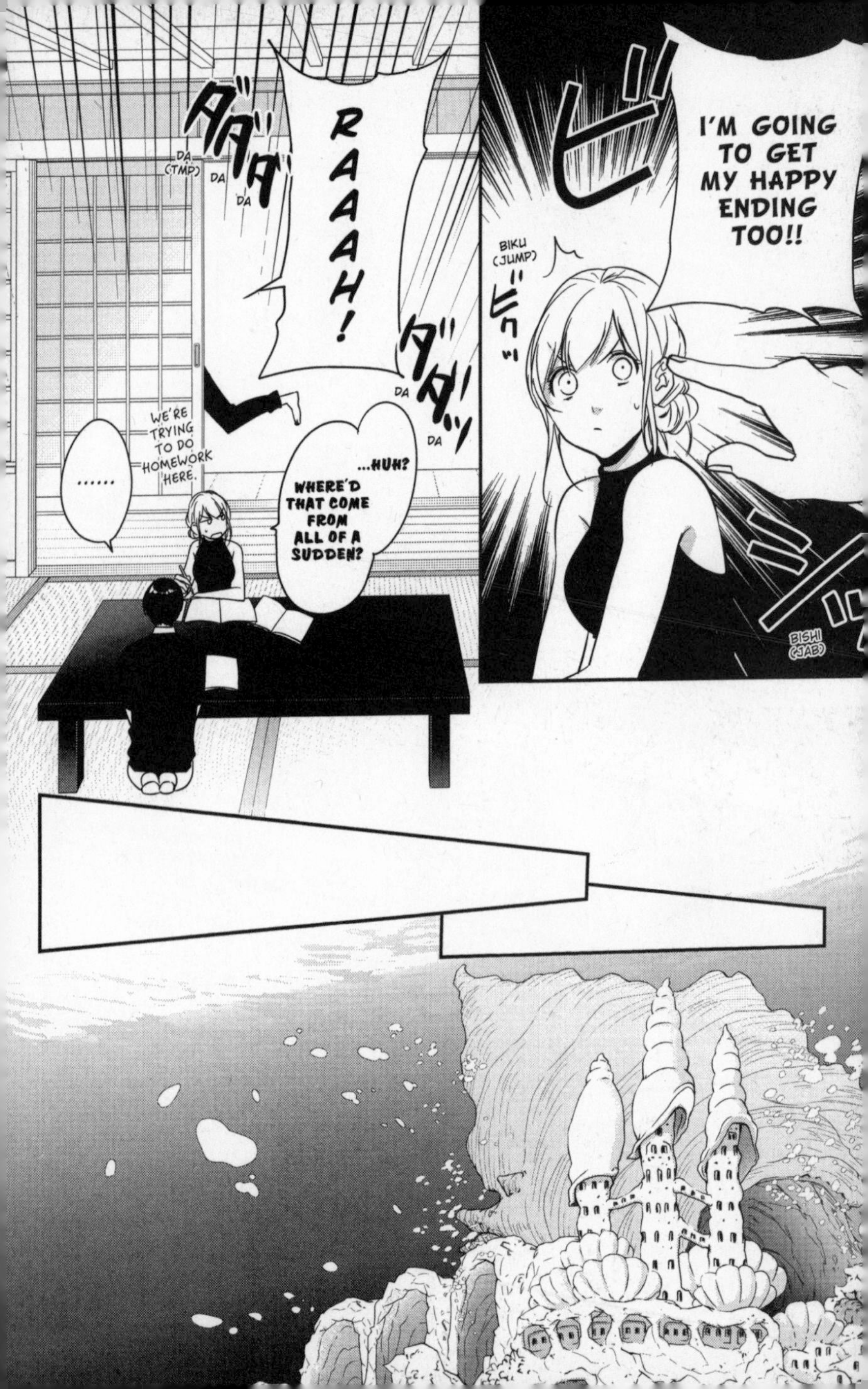
I'M GOING TO GET MY HAPPY ENDING TOO!!
ビクッ
BIKU (JUMP)
BISHI (JAB)
RAAAAH!
ダダダ
DA (TMP) DA DA
ダダッ
DA DA
...HUH? WHERE'D THAT COME FROM ALL OF A SUDDEN?
WE'RE TRYING TO DO HOMEWORK HERE.
......

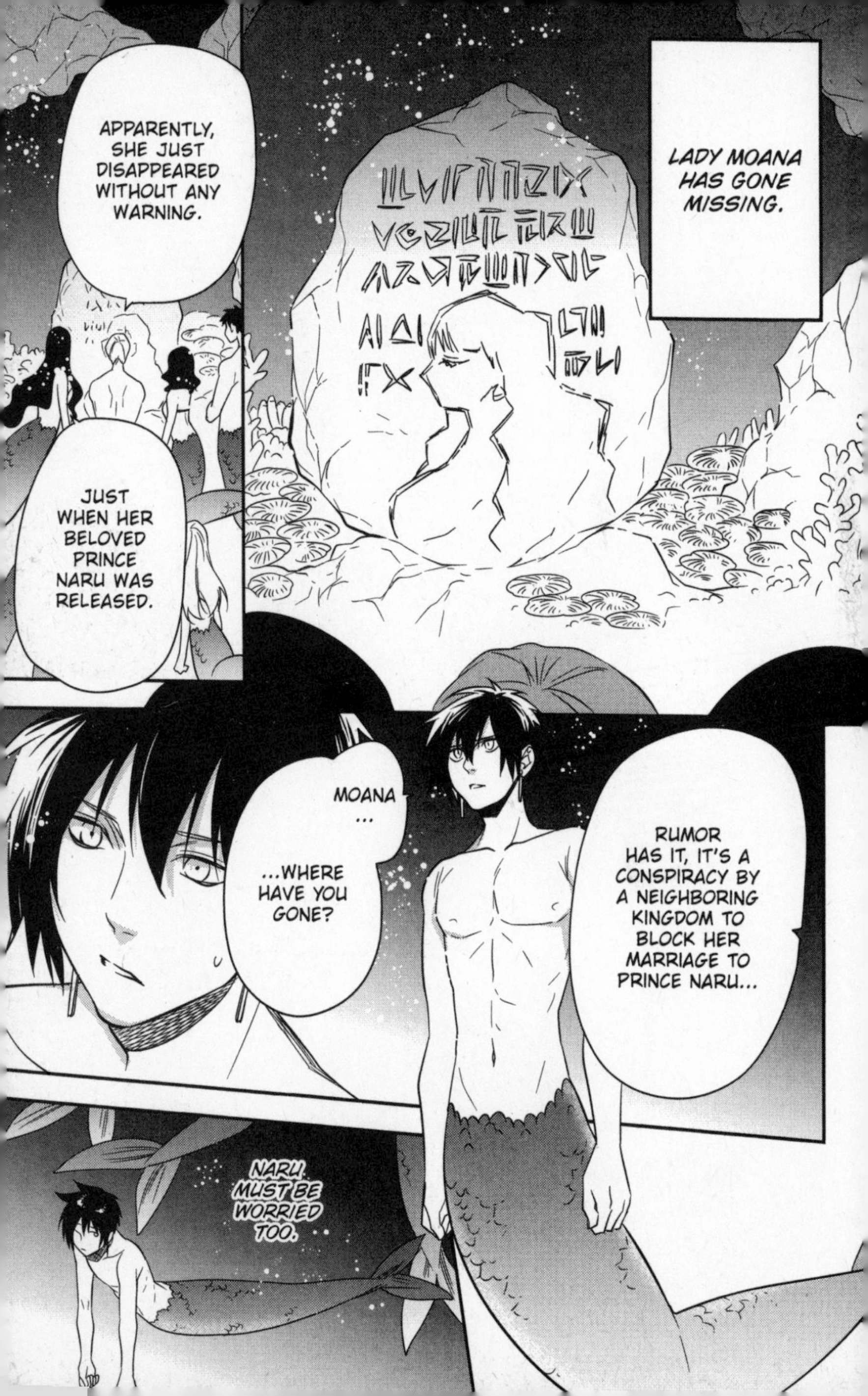
LADY MOANA HAS GONE MISSING.
APPARENTLY, SHE JUST DISAPPEARED WITHOUT ANY WARNING.
JUST WHEN HER BELOVED PRINCE NARU WAS RELEASED.
RUMOR HAS IT, IT'S A CONSPIRACY BY A NEIGHBORING KINGDOM TO BLOCK HER MARRIAGE TO PRINCE NARU...
MOANA...
...WHERE HAVE YOU GONE?
NARU MUST BE WORRIED TOO.

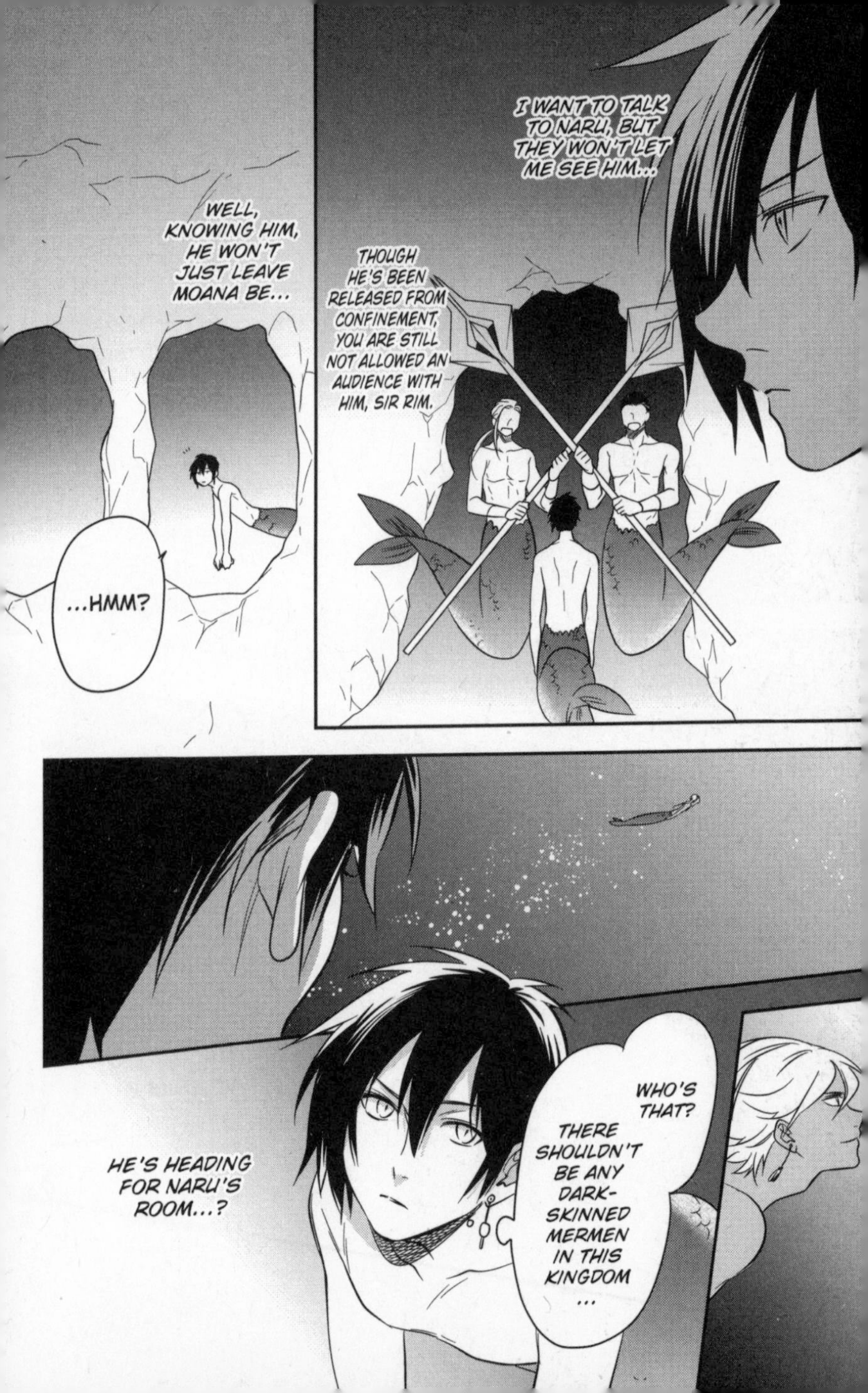
I WANT TO TALK TO NARU, BUT THEY WON'T LET ME SEE HIM...
THOUGH HE'S BEEN RELEASED FROM CONFINEMENT, YOU ARE STILL NOT ALLOWED AN AUDIENCE WITH HIM, SIR RIM.
WELL, KNOWING HIM, HE WON'T JUST LEAVE MOANA BE...
...HMM?
WHO'S THAT?
THERE SHOULDN'T BE ANY DARK-SKINNED MERMEN IN THIS KINGDOM...
HE'S HEADING FOR NARU'S ROOM...?

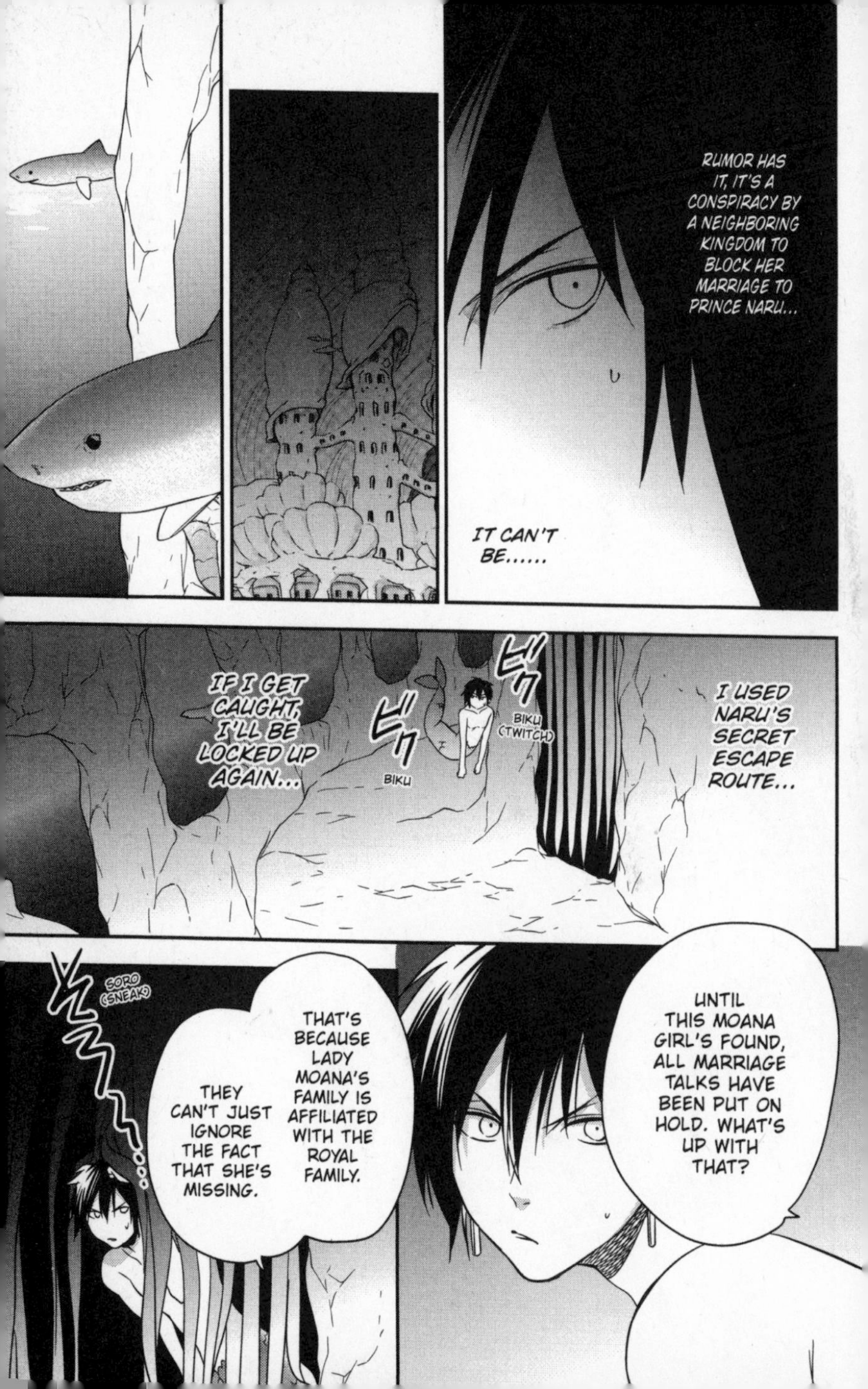
RUMOR HAS IT, IT'S A CONSPIRACY BY A NEIGHBORING KINGDOM TO BLOCK HER MARRIAGE TO PRINCE NARU...
IT CAN'T BE......
I USED NARU'S SECRET ESCAPE ROUTE...
BIKU (TWITCH)
BIKU
IF I GET CAUGHT, I'LL BE LOCKED UP AGAIN...
UNTIL THIS MOANA GIRL'S FOUND, ALL MARRIAGE TALKS HAVE BEEN PUT ON HOLD. WHAT'S UP WITH THAT?
THAT'S BECAUSE LADY MOANA'S FAMILY IS AFFILIATED WITH THE ROYAL FAMILY.
THEY CAN'T JUST IGNORE THE FACT THAT SHE'S MISSING.
SORO (SNEAK)

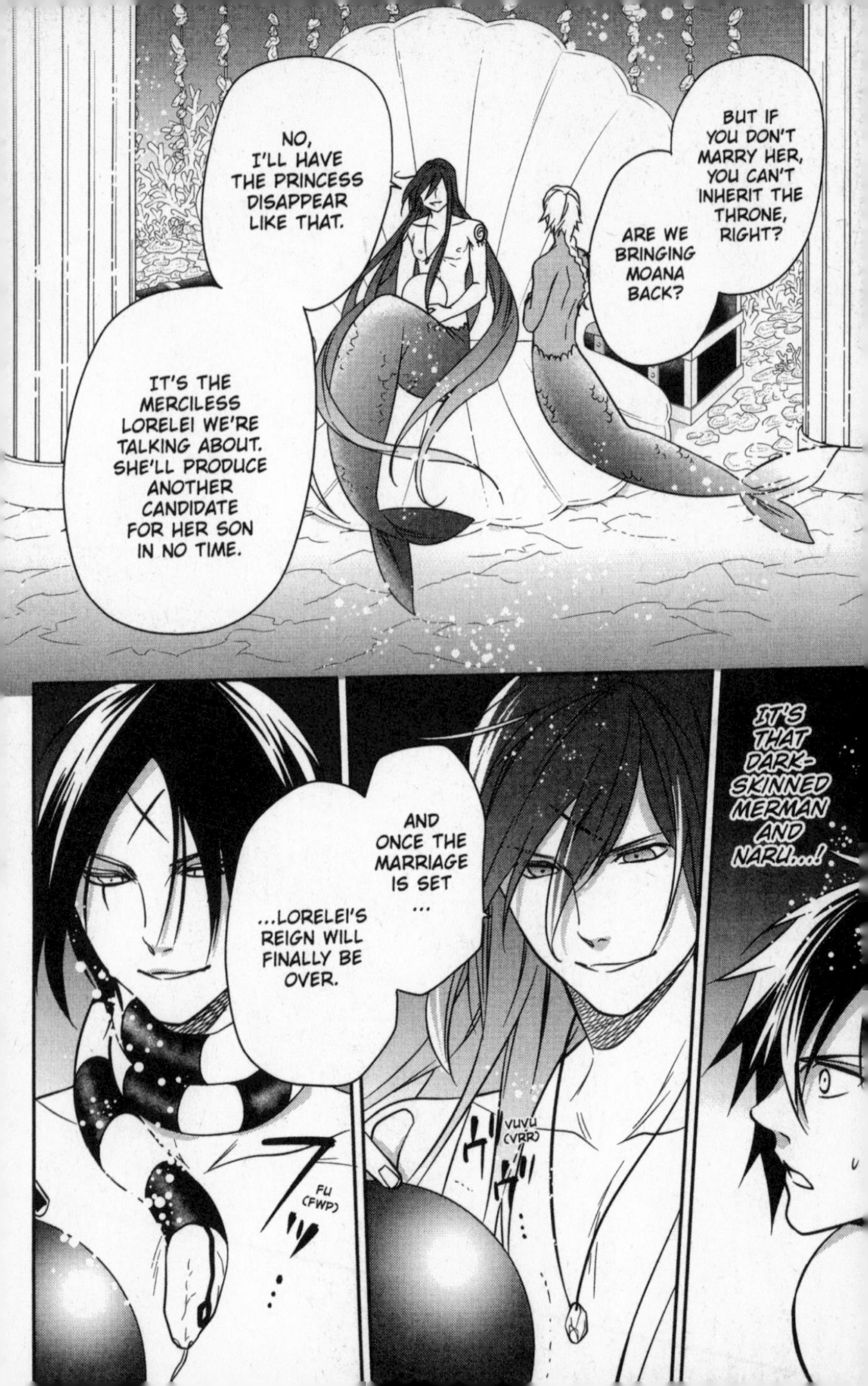
BUT IF YOU DON'T MARRY HER, YOU CAN'T INHERIT THE THRONE, RIGHT?
ARE WE BRINGING MOANA BACK?
NO, I'LL HAVE THE PRINCESS DISAPPEAR LIKE THAT.
IT'S THE MERCILESS LORELEI WE'RE TALKING ABOUT. SHE'LL PRODUCE ANOTHER CANDIDATE FOR HER SON IN NO TIME.
IT'S THAT DARK-SKINNED MERMAN AND NARU...!
AND ONCE THE MARRIAGE IS SET...
VUVU (VRR)
...LORELEI'S REIGN WILL FINALLY BE OVER.
FU (FWP)

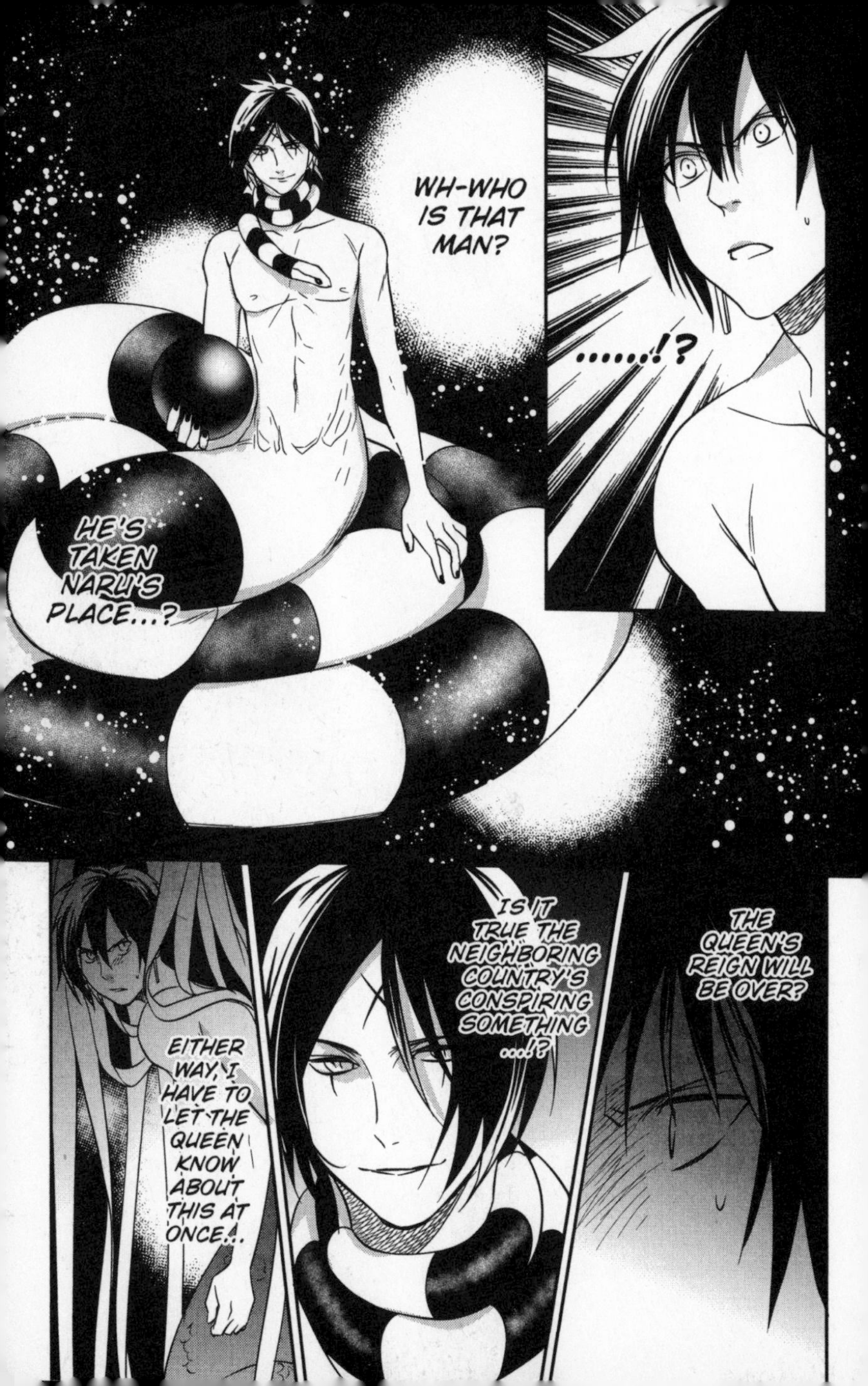
......!?
WH-WHO IS THAT MAN?
HE'S TAKEN NARU'S PLACE...?
THE QUEEN'S REIGN WILL BE OVER?
IS IT TRUE THE NEIGHBORING COUNTRY'S CONSPIRING SOMETHING ...!?
EITHER WAY, I HAVE TO LET THE QUEEN KNOW ABOUT THIS AT ONCE...

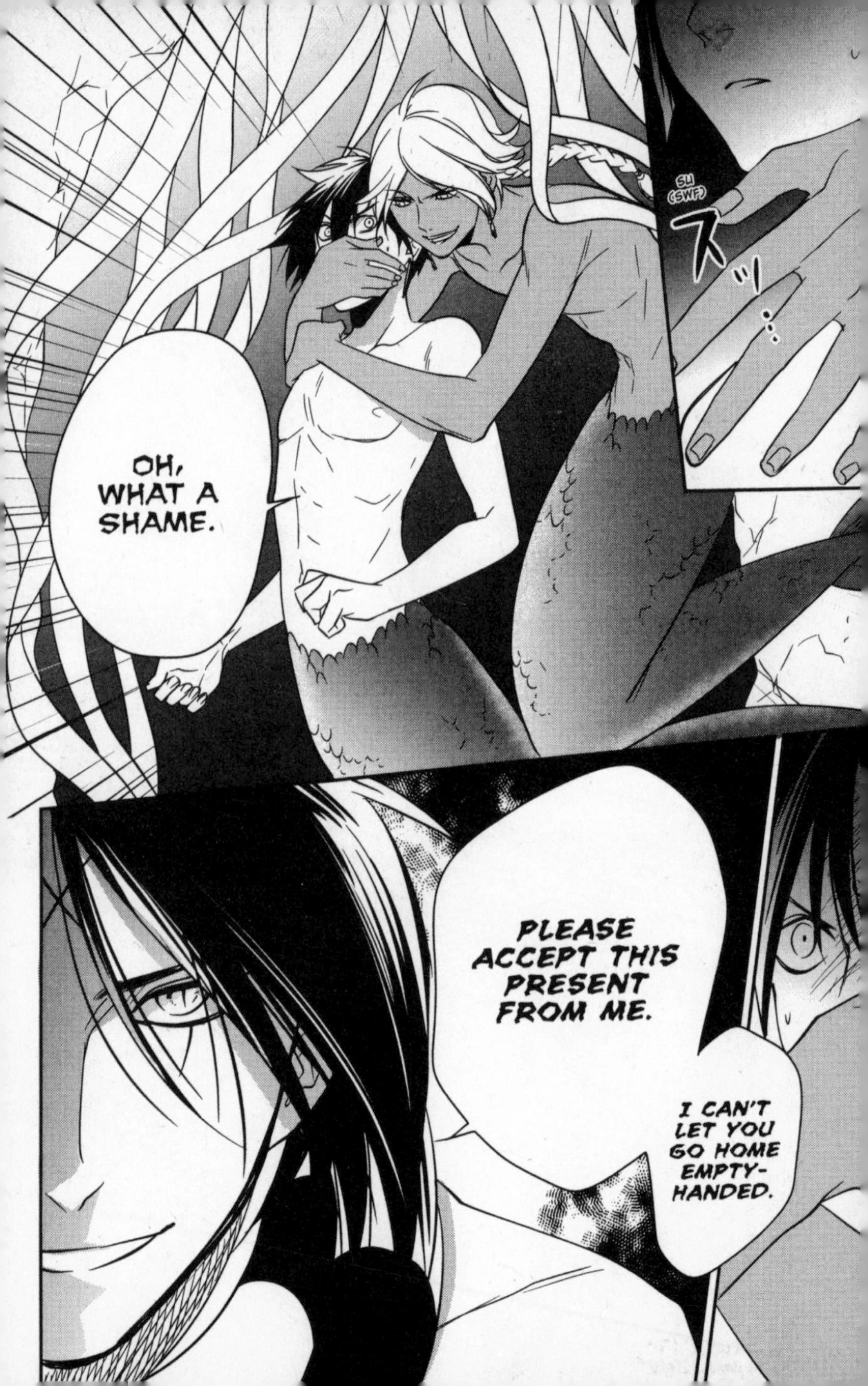
SU (SWF)
スッ…
OH, WHAT A SHAME.
PLEASE ACCEPT THIS PRESENT FROM ME.
I CAN'T LET YOU GO HOME EMPTY-HANDED.

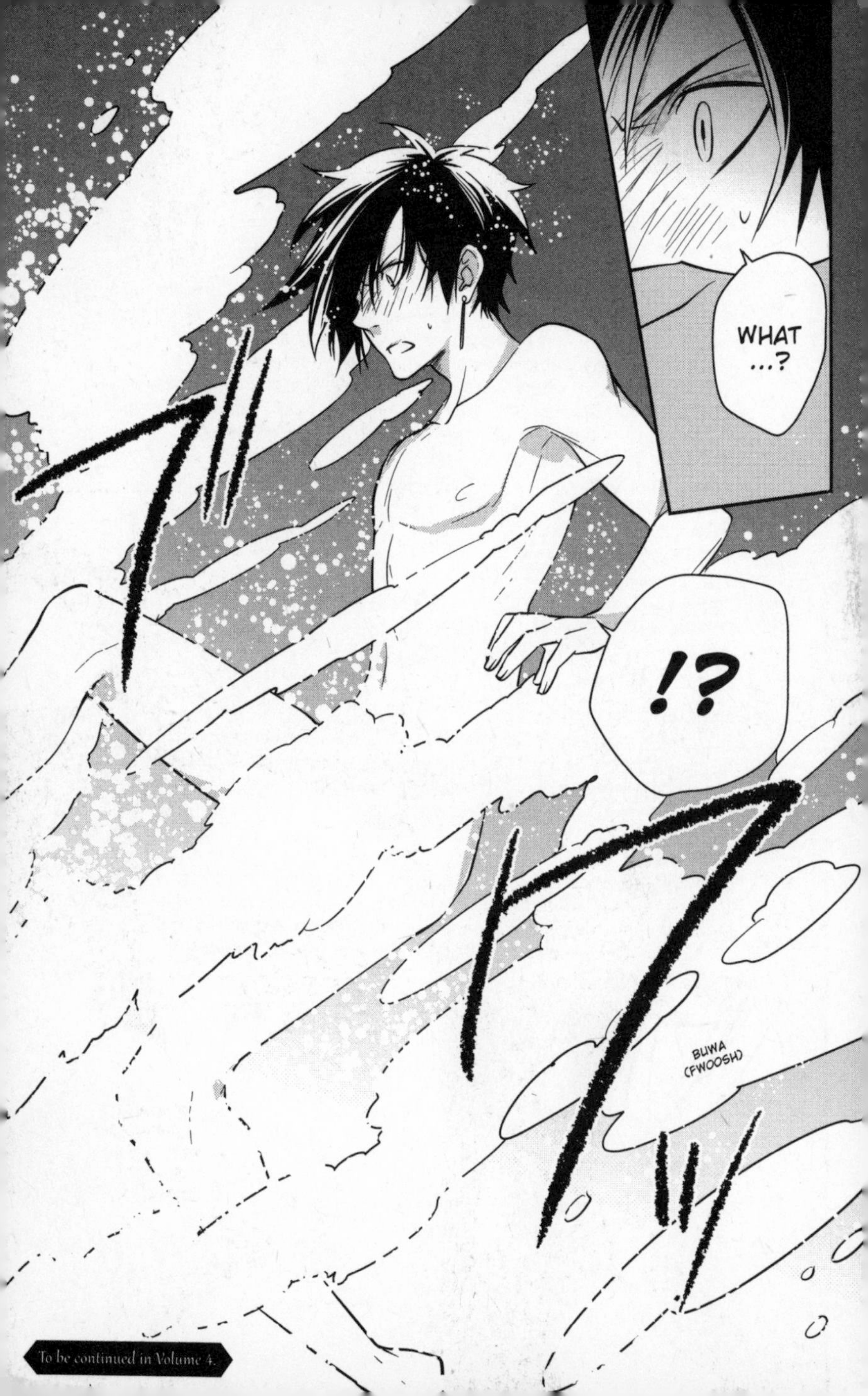
WHAT ...?
!?
BUWA (FWOOSH)
To be continued in Volume 4.

TRANSLATION NOTES

COMMON HONORIFICS

no honorific: Indicates familiarity or closeness; if used without permission or reason, addressing someone in this manner would constitute an insult.

-*san*: The Japanese equivalent of Mr./Mrs./Miss. If a situation calls for politeness, this is the fail-safe honorific.

-*sama*: Conveys great respect; may also indicate that the social status of the speaker is lower than that of the addressee.

-*kun*: Used most often when referring to boys, this indicates affection or familiarity. Occasionally used by older men among their peers, but it may also be used by anyone referring to a person of lower standing.

-*chan*: An affectionate honorific indicating familiarity used mostly in reference to girls; also used in reference to cute persons or animals of either gender.

-*senpai*: A suffix used to address upperclassmen or more experienced coworkers.

-*kouhai*: A suffix used to address underclassmen or less experienced coworkers.

-*sensei*: A respectful term for teachers, artists, or high-level professionals.

PAGE 48

Kana, or Kana Nishino, is a famous Japanese pop singer whose hit song "I Miss You, I Miss You" peaked multiple music charts upon release. Her music can be widely heard in commercials and is extremely popular among teenage girls.

PAGE 89

Churachura here refers to Okinawa Churaumi Aquarium, located in Ocean Expo Park in Okinawa—Japan's most celebrated scenic getaway. The word *chura* is unique to the Okinawan dialect and consists of the character for "beautiful" or "pretty," while *umi* means "ocean."

MERMAID BOYS

'COS IT HAPPENS EVERY YEAR

BONUS FOUR-PANEL

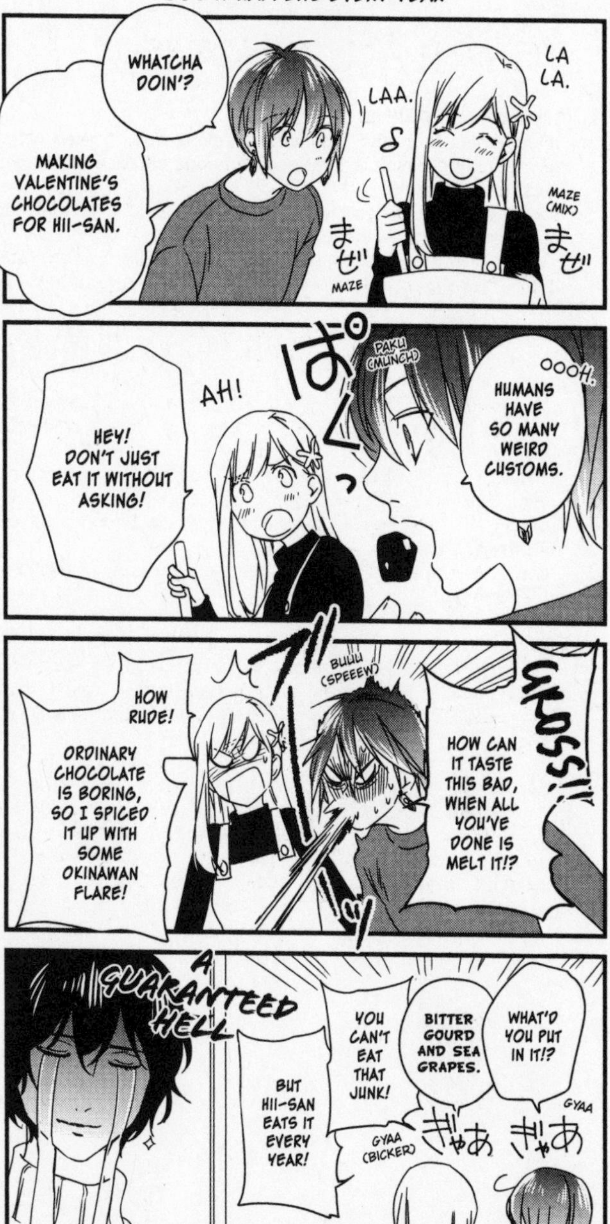
LA LA.
LAA.
WHATCHA DOIN'?
MAZE (MIX)
まぜ
まぜ
MAZE
MAKING VALENTINE'S CHOCOLATES FOR HII-SAN.
OOOH.
HUMANS HAVE SO MANY WEIRD CUSTOMS.
PAKU (MUNCH)
ぱくっ
AH!
HEY! DON'T JUST EAT IT WITHOUT ASKING!
GROSS!!!
HOW CAN IT TASTE THIS BAD, WHEN ALL YOU'VE DONE IS MELT IT!?
BUUU (SPEEEW)
ブーッ
HOW RUDE!
ORDINARY CHOCOLATE IS BORING, SO I SPICED IT UP WITH SOME OKINAWAN FLARE!
WHAT'D YOU PUT IN IT!?
BITTER GOURD AND SEA GRAPES.
GYAA
ぎゃあ
ぎゃあ
GYAA (BICKER)
YOU CAN'T EAT THAT JUNK!
BUT HII-SAN EATS IT EVERY YEAR!
A GUARANTEED HELL

I'LL EAT THEM FOR NAMI-CHAN'S SAKE...

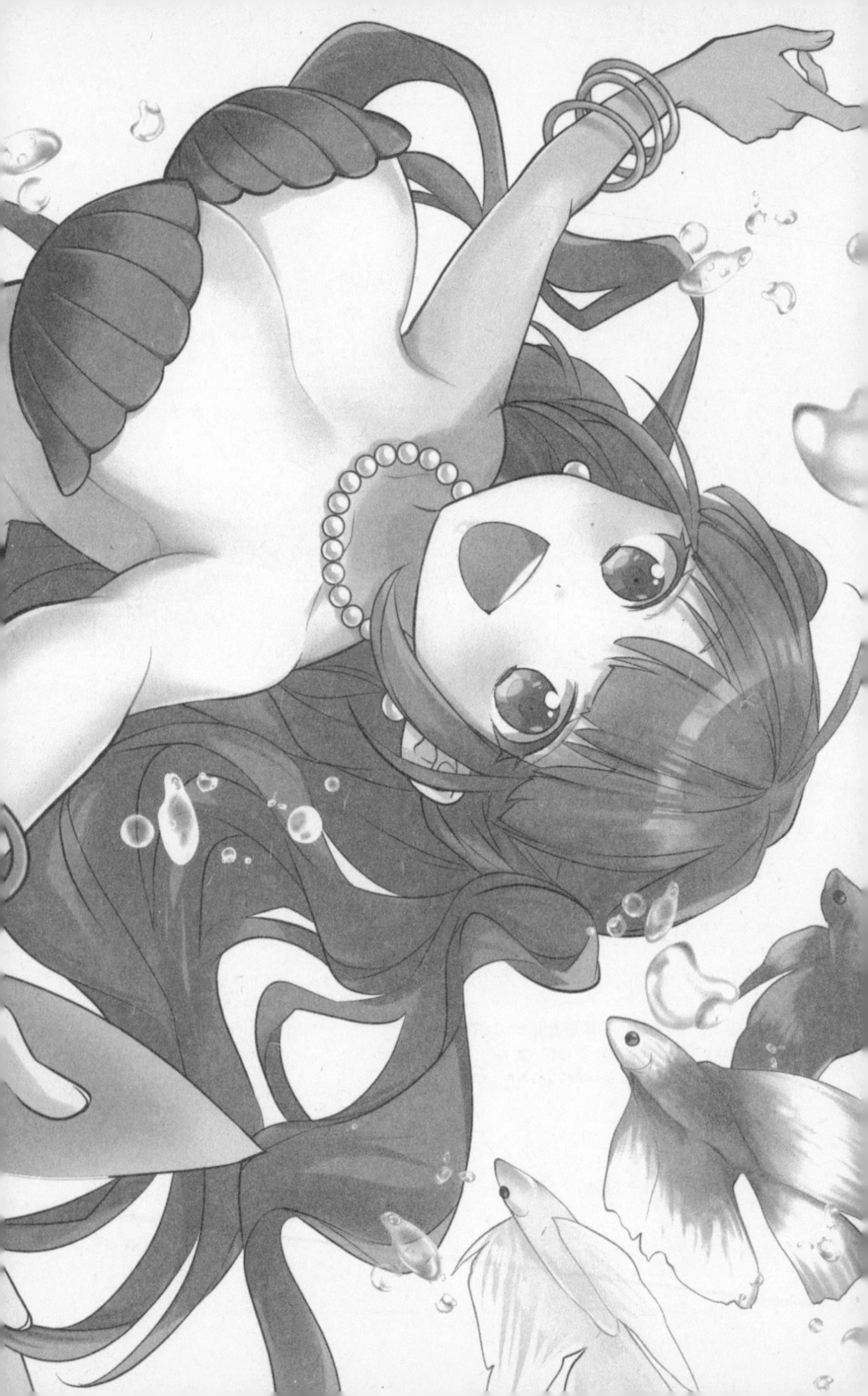

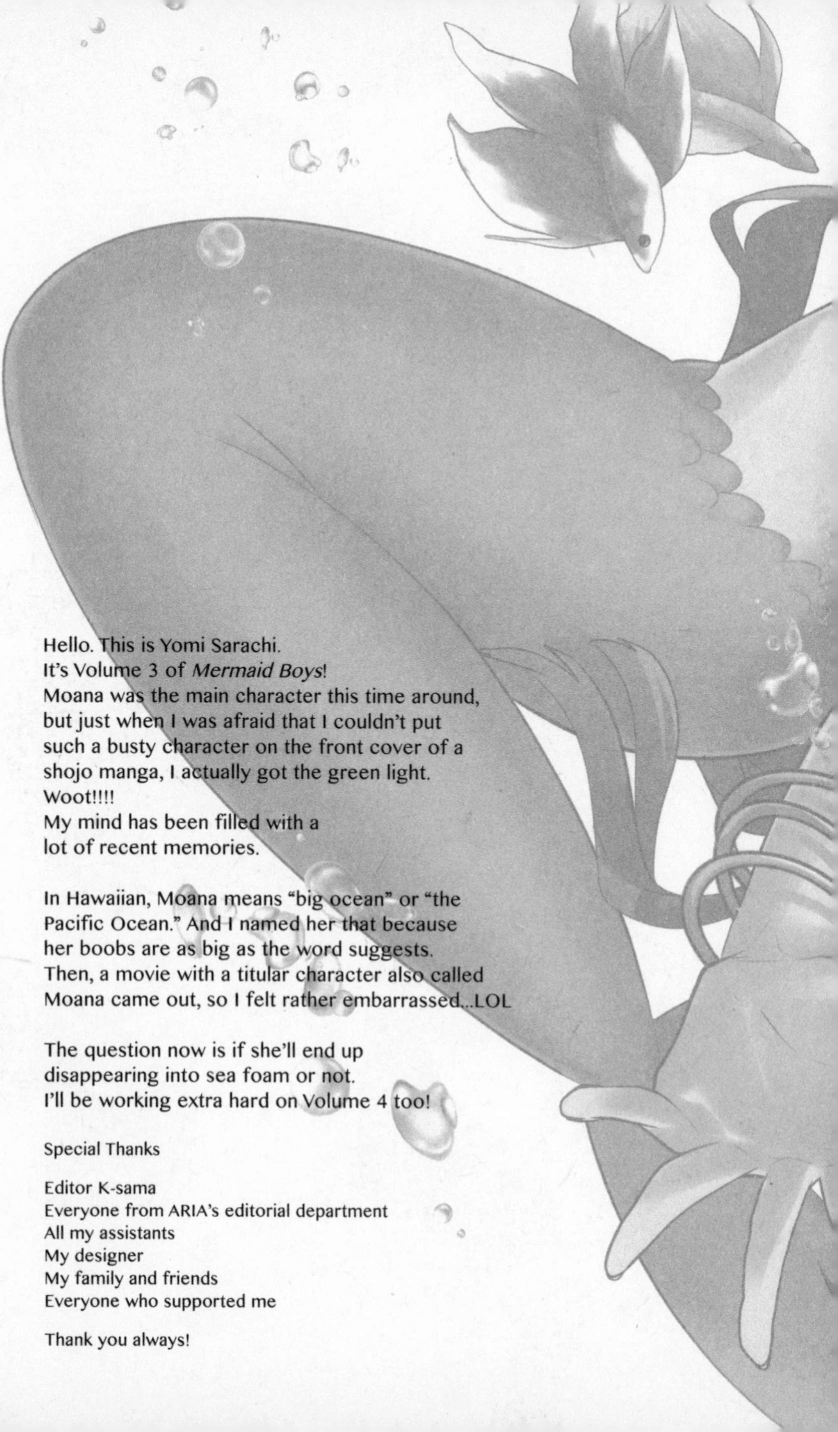

Hello. This is Yomi Sarachi.
It's Volume 3 of *Mermaid Boys*!
Moana was the main character this time around, but just when I was afraid that I couldn't put such a busty character on the front cover of a shojo manga, I actually got the green light. Woot!!!!
My mind has been filled with a lot of recent memories.

In Hawaiian, Moana means "big ocean" or "the Pacific Ocean." And I named her that because her boobs are as big as the word suggests.
Then, a movie with a titular character also called Moana came out, so I felt rather embarrassed...LOL

The question now is if she'll end up disappearing into sea foam or not.
I'll be working extra hard on Volume 4 too!

Special Thanks

Editor K-sama
Everyone from ARIA's editorial department
All my assistants
My designer
My family and friends
Everyone who supported me

Thank you always!

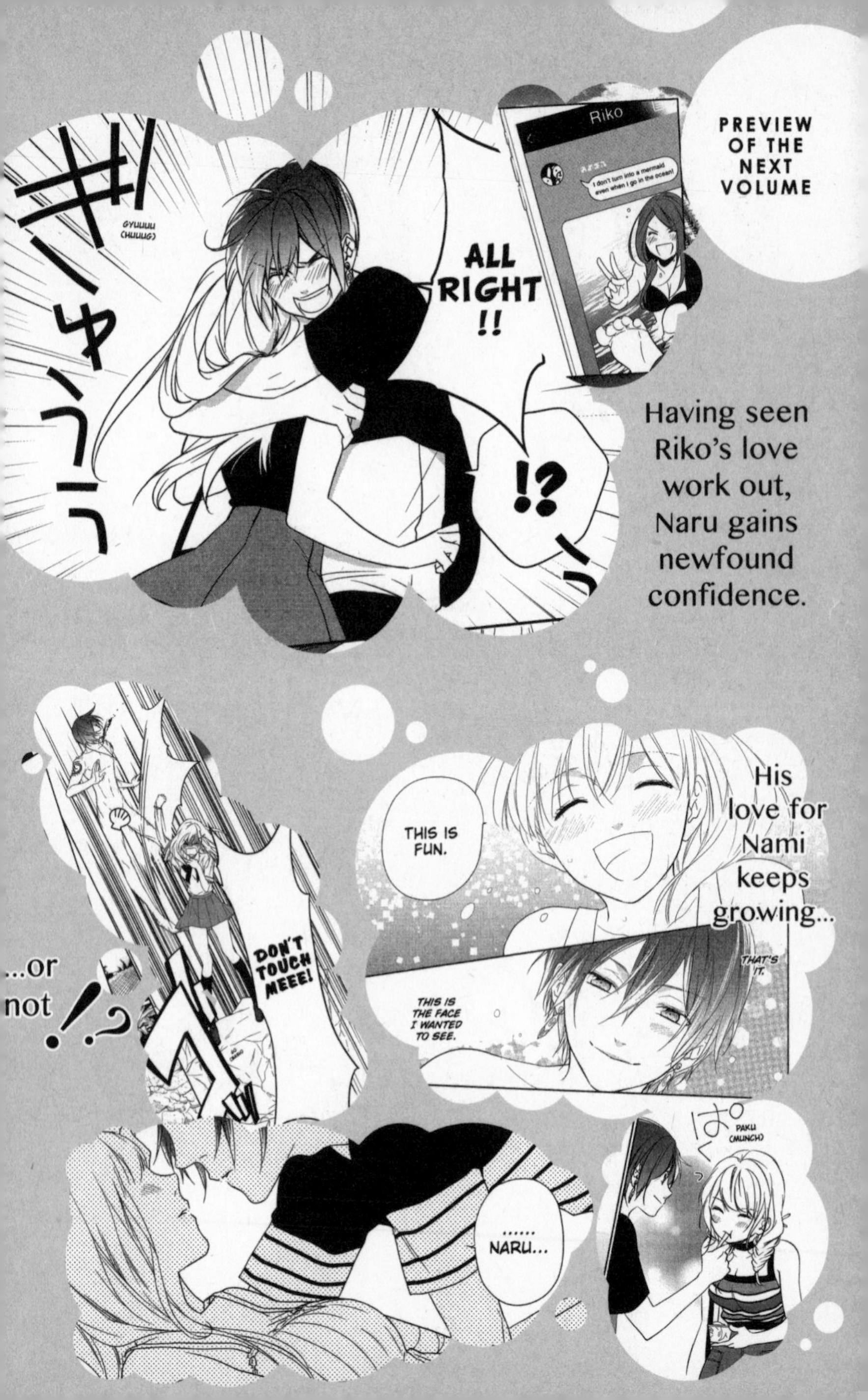
PREVIEW OF THE NEXT VOLUME
Riko
I don't turn into a mermaid even when I go in the ocean!
Having seen Riko's love work out, Naru gains newfound confidence.
ALL RIGHT!!
!?
GYUUUU (HUUUG)
His love for Nami keeps growing...
THIS IS FUN.
THAT'S IT.
THIS IS THE FACE I WANTED TO SEE.
DON'T TOUCH MEEE!
...or not !?
PAKU (MUNCH)
...... NARU...

Meanwhile, in the mer-kingdom of Nirai Kanai, the conspiracy moves forward.

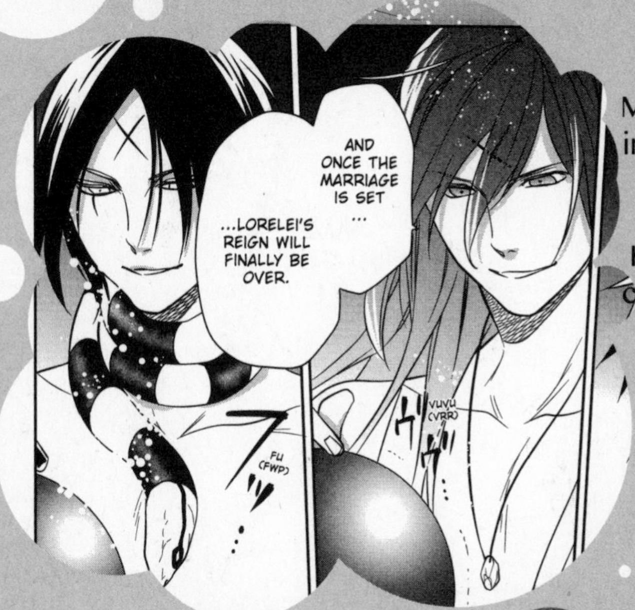

AND ONCE THE MARRIAGE IS SET ...
...LORELEI'S REIGN WILL FINALLY BE OVER.
VUVU (VRR)
FU (FWP)

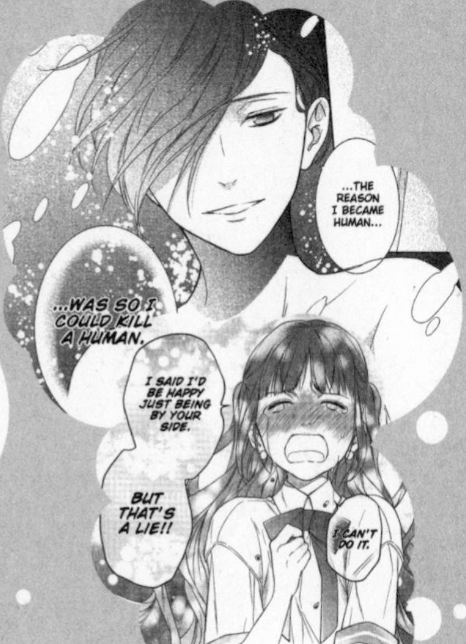

...THE REASON I BECAME HUMAN...
...WAS SO I COULD KILL A HUMAN.
I SAID I'D BE HAPPY JUST BEING BY YOUR SIDE.
BUT THAT'S A LIE!!
I CAN'T DO IT.

What will become of Naru and the other merfolk—!?

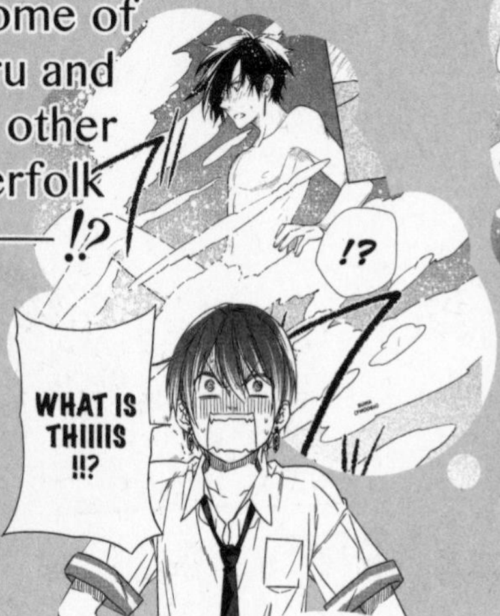

!?
WHAT IS THIIIIS !!?

MERMAID BOYS 4

Coming soon!

Find Your Mermatch

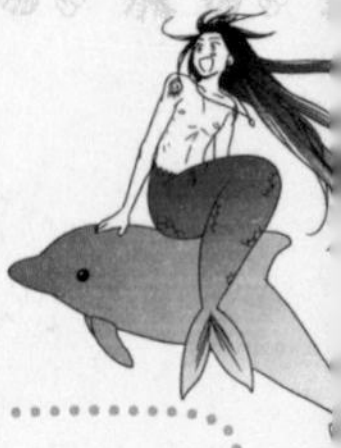

START HERE

What kind of confession do you prefer?

Sweet and gentle with a hand on the waist

Confident and fiery passionate

Why confess? Shouldn't they already know my response?

Clumsy but cute with a few side glances

Short and simple, to the point

You catch your partner lying. You...

Hug, hug, hug. Hugs fix everything. <3

Stay calm

Get mad

Vengeance is mine...

How will you survive a long-distance relationship?

Go see them every weekend, obviously!

I won't survive

Talk whenever we can

Find Your Mermatch

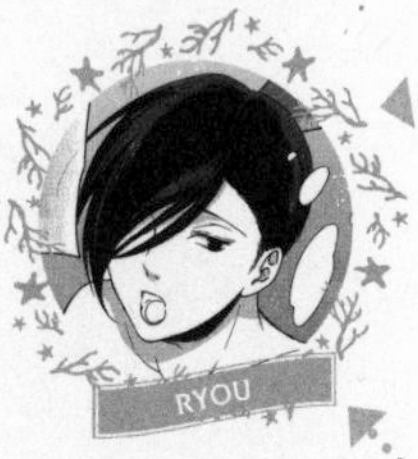
RYOU

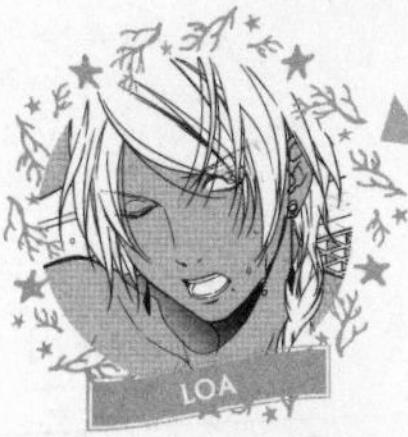
LOA

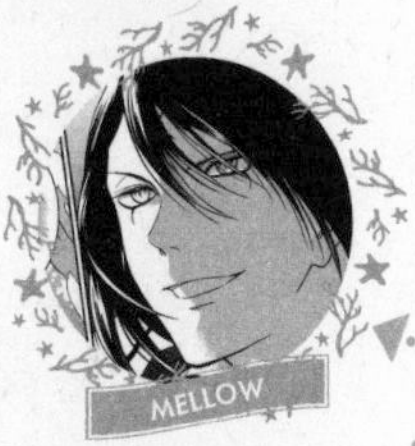
MELLOW

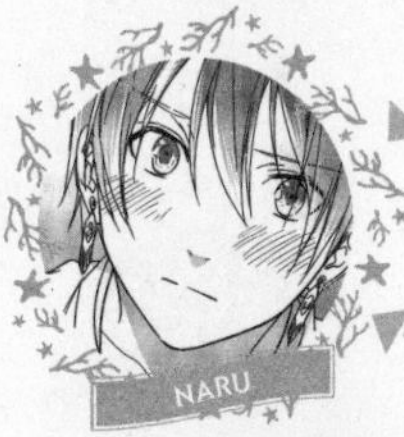
NARU

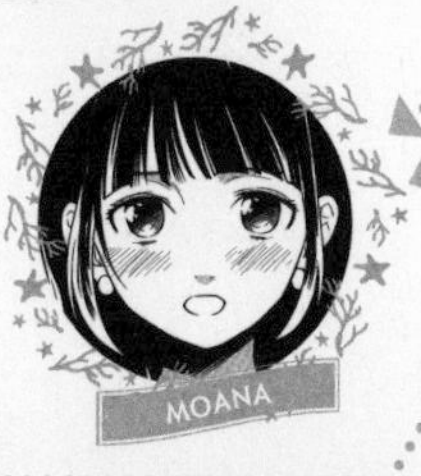
MOANA

What does your first kiss feel like?

- Playful
- Full-on moist smooch
- Who needs that when I'm here in the flesh?

How fast do you reply to their text?

- Take my sweet time
- Right away

Need for touch?
On a scale of 1-10: 1 = don't need it 10 = craving it

- Unless it comes with gold, zero, you imbeciles.
- A 15, damn it!
- We'll see! Tee-hee!

Do you make the first move?

- Yeah, duh!
- Maybe when the time is right...

SINGLE AND READY TO
MERMINGLE!

INTRODUCING...YOUR MERMAIDS!

"BE MY SLAVE."
The most troll-like and mischievous merman of them all. Contrary to his aloof attitude and sharp wit, he has a strong sense of loyalty. Though with that being said, don't be surprised if he pulls a trick or two on you!

RYOU

"YOUR BODY'S PRECIOUS, SO PLEASE BE MORE CAREFUL."
Is somebody in need of attention? The attractive and overly affectionate Loa is at your service. *wink* What's a little PDA? If you're in need of warm hugs, you've come to the right merman.

LOA

"ALL CREATURES WANT WHAT THEY'RE NOT SUPPOSED TO HAVE."
Dangerous and a bit too chummy with his reptilian posse...Go ahead and approach him if you dare...

MELLOW

SINGLE AND READY TO

MERMINGLE!

INTRODUCING...YOUR MERMAIDS!

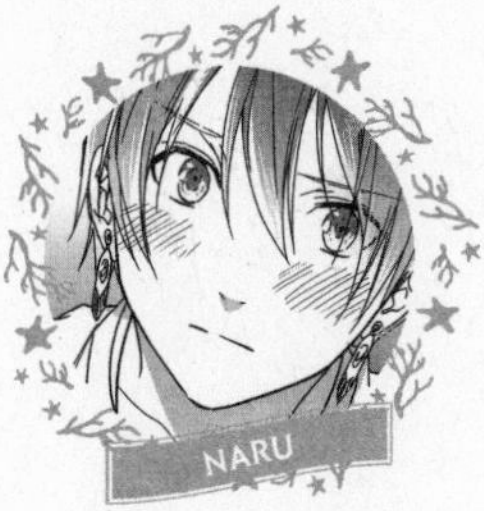
NARU

"I FINALLY GOT TO MEET YOU... MY MERMAID!!"

Nosy and unpredictable, Naru might be better off taking a few chill pills, but when it comes to love, you can always count on him to give a hundred percent.

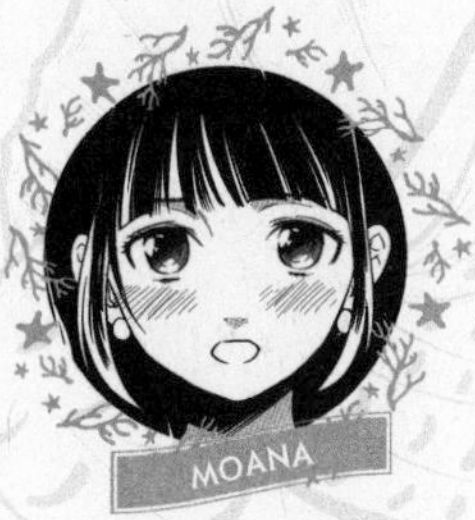
MOANA

"I THREW AWAY EVERYTHING TO COME AFTER YOU."

Love is sacrifice, and no one knows that better than Moana. You wouldn't ever try to hurt her because she's got a heart of gold. Perky and full of energy, she's a real trooper when it comes to love.

WHO DID YOU GET!?

SHARE YOUR RESULTS WITH YOUR FRIENDS!

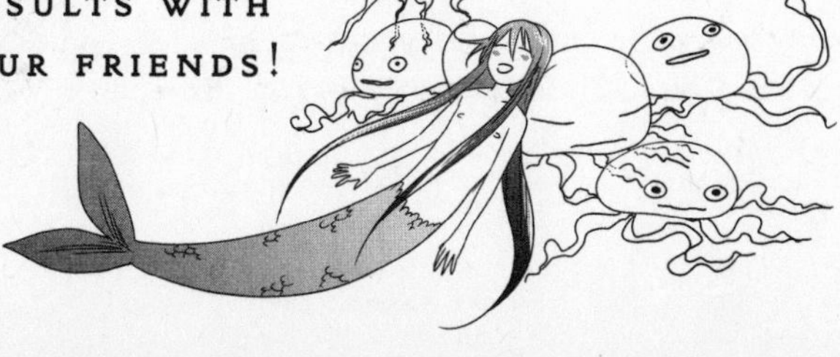

MERMAID BOYS 3

Yomi Sarachi

Translation: CHRISTINE DASHIELL Lettering: ALEXIS ECKERMAN

MERMAID BOYS
© 2017 Yomi Sarachi. All rights reserved.
First published in Japan in 2017 by Kodansha Ltd., Tokyo. Publication rights for this English language edition arranged through Kodansha Ltd., Tokyo.

English translation © 2018 by Yen Press, LLC

Yen Press
1290 Avenue of the Americas
New York, NY 10104

Visit us at yenpress.com
facebook.com/yenpress
twitter.com/yenpress
yenpress.tumblr.com
instagram.com/yenpress

First Yen Press Edition: November 2018

Yen Press is an imprint of Yen Press, LLC.
The Yen Press name and logo are trademarks of Yen Press, LLC.

The publisher is not responsible for websites (or their content) that are not owned by the publisher.

Library of Congress Control Number: 2017963580

ISBN: 978-1-9753-0231-3

10 9 8 7 6 5 4 3 2 1

WOR

Printed in the United States of America